FOUR PLAYS

OF

GIL VICENTE

CAMBRIDGE
UNIVERSITY PRESS

University Printing House, Cambridge CB2 8BS, United Kingdom

Published in the United States of America by Cambridge University Press, New York

Cambridge University Press is part of the University of Cambridge.

It furthers the University's mission by disseminating knowledge in the pursuit of
education, learning and research at the highest international levels of excellence.

www.cambridge.org
Information on this title: www.cambridge.org/9781107684409

© Cambridge University Press 1920

First published 1920
First paperback edition 2014

A catalogue record for this publication is available from the British Library

ISBN 978-1-107-68440-9 Paperback

COPILAÇAM DE

TODALAS OBRAS DE GIL VICENTE, A Q VAL SE
REPARTE EM CINCO LIVROS O PRIMEYRO HE DE TODAS
suas cousas de deuaçam O segundo as comedias. O terceyro as
tragicomedias. No quarto as farsas. No quinto as
obras meudas.

¶Empremiose em a muy nobre & sempre leal cidade de Lixboa
em casa de Ioam Aluarez impressor delRey nosso senhor
Anno de M D LXII
¶Por visto polos deputados da sancta Inquisiçam.

COM PRIVILEGIO REAL.

¶Vendemse a cruzado em papel em casa de Francisco fernandez na rua noua

TITLE-PAGE OF THE FIRST (1562) EDITION OF GIL VICENTE'S WORKS

FOUR PLAYS

OF

GIL VICENTE

Edited from the *editio princeps* (1562), with
Translation and Notes, by

AUBREY F. G. BELL

Θαρρεῖν χρὴ τὸν καὶ σμικρόν τι δυνάμενον
εἰς τὸ πρόσθεν ἀεὶ προϊέναι.

PLATO, *Sophistes.*

CAMBRIDGE
AT THE UNIVERSITY PRESS
1920

TO ALL THOSE WHO HAVE LABOURED IN
THE VICENTIAN VINEYARD

PREFACE

GIL VICENTE, that sovereign genius[1], is too popular and indigenous for translation and this may account for the fact that he has not been presented to English readers. It is hoped, however, that a fairly accurate version, with the text in view[2], may give some idea of his genius. The religious, the patriotic-imperial, the satirical and the pastoral sides of his drama are represented respectively by the *Auto da Alma*, the *Exhortação*, the *Almocreves* and the *Serra da Estrella*, while his lyrical vein is seen in the *Auto da Alma* and in two delightful songs: the *serranilha* of the *Almocreves* and the *cossante* of the *Serra da Estrella*. Many of his plays, including some of the most charming of his lyrics, were written in Spanish and this limited the choice from the point of view of Portuguese literature, but there are others of the Portuguese plays fully as well worth reading as the four here given.

The text is that of the exceedingly rare first edition (1562). Apart from accents and punctuation, it is reproduced without alteration, unless a passage is marked by an asterisk, when the text of the *editio princeps* will be found in the foot-notes, in which variants of other editions are also given.

In these notes A represents the *editio princeps* (1562): *Copilaçam de todalas obras de Gil Vicente, a qval se reparte em cinco livros. O primeyro he de todas suas cousas de deuaçam. O segundo as comedias. O terceyro as tragicomedias. No quarto as farsas. No quinto as obras meudas. Empremiose em a muy nobre & sempre leal cidade de Lixboa em casa de Ioam Aluarez impressor del Rey nosso senhor. Anno de* MDLXII. The second (1586) edition (B) is the *Copilaçam de todalas obras de Gil Vicente...Lixboa, por Andres Lobato, Anno de* MDLXXXVJ. A third edition in three volumes appeared in 1834 (C): *Obras de Gil Vicente, correctas e emendadas pelo cuidado e diligencia de J. V. Barreto Feio e J. G. Monteiro.* Hamburgo, 1834. This was based, although not always with scrupulous accuracy, on the *editio princeps*, and subsequent editions have faithfully adhered to that of 1834: *Obras*, 3 vol. Lisboa, 1852 (D), and *Obras*, ed. Mendes dos Remedios, 3 vol. Coimbra,

---

[1] *Este soberano ingenio.* Marcelino Menéndez y Pelayo, *Antología*, tom. 7, p. clxiii.

[2] Although the text has been given without alteration it has not been thought necessary to provide a precise rendering of the coarser passages.

1907, 12, 14 [*Subsidios*, vol. 11, 15, 17][1] (E). Although there has been a tendency of late to multiply editions of Gil Vicente, no attempt has been made to produce a critical edition. It is generally felt that that must be left to the master hand of Dona Carolina Michaëlis de Vasconcellos[2]. Since the plays of Vicente number over forty the present volume is only a tentative step in this direction, but it may serve to show the need of referring to, and occasionally emending, the *editio princeps* in any future edition of the most national poet of Portugal[3].

AUBREY F. G. BELL.

8 *April* 1920.

[1] The Paris 1843 edition is the Hamburg 1834 edition with a different title-page. The *Auto da Alma* was published separately at Lisbon in 1902 and again (in part) in *Autos de Gil Vicente. Compilação e prefacio de Affonso Lopes Vieira*, Porto, 1916; while extracts appeared in *Portugal. An Anthology, edited with English versions, by George Young.* Oxford, 1916. The present text and translation are reprinted, by permission of the Editor, from *The Modern Language Review.*

[2] I understand that the eminent philologist Dr José Leite de Vasconcellos is also preparing an edition.

[3] Facsimiles of the title-pages of the two early editions of Vicente's works are reproduced here through the courtesy of Senhor Anselmo Braamcamp Freire.

CONTENTS

INTRODUCTION

I. LIFE AND PLAYS OF GIL VICENTE

THOSE who read the voluminous song-book edited by jolly Garcia de Resende in 1516 are astonished at its narrowness and aridity. There is scarcely a breath of poetry or of Nature in these Court verses. In the pages of Gil Vicente[1], who had begun to write fourteen years before the *Cancioneiro Geral* was published, the Court is still present, yet the atmosphere is totally different. There are many passages in his plays which correspond to the conventional love-poems of the courtiers and he maintains the personal satire to be found both in the *Cancioneiro da Vaticana* and the *Cancioneiro de Resende*. But he is also a child of Nature, with a marvellous lyrical gift and the insight to revive and renew the genuine poetry which had existed in Galicia and the north of Portugal before the advent of the Provençal love-poetry, had sprung into a splendid harvest in rivalry with that poetry and died down under the Spanish influence of the fourteenth and fifteenth centuries. He was moreover a national and imperial poet, embracing the whole of Portuguese life and the whole rapidly growing Portuguese empire. We can only account for the difference by saying that Gil Vicente was a genius, the only great genius of that day in Portugal, and the most gifted poet of his time. It is therefore all the more tantalizing that we should know so little about him. A few documents recently unearthed, one or two scanty references by contemporary or later authors, are all the information we have apart from that which may be gleaned from the rubrics and colophons of his plays and from the plays themselves. The labours of Dona Carolina Michaëlis de Vasconcellos, Dr José Leite de Vasconcellos[2] and Snr Anselmo Braamcamp Freire are likely to provide us before long with the first critical edition of his plays. The ingenious suppositions of Dr Theophilo Braga[3] have, as usual, led to much discussion and research. He is the Mofina Mendes of critics, putting forward a hypothesis, translating it a few pages further on into a certainty and building rapidly on

---

[1] *Falamos do nosso Shakespeare, de Gil Vicente* (A. Herculano, *Historia da Inquisição em Portugal*, ed. 1906, vol. I. p. 223). The references throughout are to the Hamburg 3 vol. 1834 edition.

[2] See infra *Bibliography*, p. 86, Nos. 42, 62, 79.

[3] *Bibliography*, Nos. 21, 24, 25, 26, 30, 51, 52, 59, 89.

these foundations till an argument adduced or a document discovered by another critic brings the whole edifice toppling to the ground. The documents brought to light by General Brito Rebello[1] and Senhor Anselmo Braamcamp Freire[2] enable us to construct a sketch of Gil Vicente's life, while D. Carolina Michaëlis has shed a flood of light upon certain points[3]. The chronological table at the end of this volume is founded mainly, as to the order of the plays, on the documents and arguments recently set forth by one of the most distinguished of modern historical critics, Senhor Anselmo Braamcamp Freire. The plays, read in this order, throw a certain amount of new light on Gil Vicente's life and give it a new cohesion. Whether we consider it from the point of view of his own country or of the world, or of literature, art and science, his life coincides with one of the most wonderful periods in the world's history. At his birth Portugal was a sturdy mediaeval country, proud of her traditions and heroic past. Her heroes were so national as scarcely to be known beyond her own borders. Nun' Alvarez (1360–1431), one of the greatest men of all time, is even now unknown to Europe. And Portugal herself as yet hardly appraised at its true worth the life and work of Prince Henry the Navigator (1394–1460), at whose incentive she was still groping persistently along the western coast of Africa. His nephew Afonso V, the amiable grandson of Nun' Alvarez' friend, the Master of Avis, and the English princess Philippa of Lancaster, daughter of John of Gaunt, was on the throne, to be succeeded by his stern and resolute son João II in 1481. In his boyhood, spent in the country, somewhere in the green hills of Minho or the rugged grandeur and bare, flowered steeps of the Serra da Estrella, all *ossos e burel*[4], Gil Vicente might hear dramatic stories of the doings at the capital and Court, of the beginning of the new reign, of the beheadal of the Duke of Braganza in the Rocio of Evora, of the stabbing by the King's own hand of his cousin and brother-in-law, the young Duke of Viseu, of the baptism and death at Lisbon of a native prince from Guinea.

The place of his birth is not certain. Biographers have hesitated between Lisbon, Guimarães and Barcellos: perhaps he was not born in any of these towns but in some small village of the north of Portugal. We can at least say that he was not brought up at Lisbon. The proof is his knowledge and love of Nature and his intimate acquaintance with the ways of villagers, their character, customs, amusements, dances, songs and language. It is legitimate to draw certain inferences—provided

---

[1] *Bibliography*, Nos. 29, 48, 57, 66, 83, 95.
[2] *Bibliography*, Nos. 53, 73, 82, 88, 97.
[3] *Bibliography*, Nos. 44, 84, 90, 101, 102.
[4] Guerra Junqueiro, *Os Simples*.

we do not attach too great importance to them—from his plays, especially since we know that he himself staged them and acted in them[1]. His earliest compositions are especially personal and we may be quite sure that the parts of the herdsman in the *Visitaçam* (1502) and of the mystically inclined shepherd, Gil Terron, in the *Auto Pastoril Castelhano* (1502) and the *rustico pastor* in the *Auto dos Reis Magos* (1503) were played by Vicente himself. It is therefore well to note the passage in which Silvestre and Bras express surprise at Gil's learning:

> *S.* Mudando vas la pelleja,
> Sabes de achaque de igreja!
> *G.* Ahora lo deprendi....
> *B.* Quien te viese no dirá
> Que naciste en serranía.
> *G.* Dios hace estas maravillas.

It is possible that Gil Vicente, like Gil Terron, had been born *en serrania*. Dr Leite de Vasconcellos was the first to call attention to his special knowledge of the province of Beira, and the reference to the Serra da Estrella dragged into the *Comedia do Viuvo* is of even more significance than the conventional *beirão* talk of his peasants. Nor is the learning in his plays such as to give a moment's support to the theory that he had, like Enzina, received a university education, or, as some, relying on an unreliable *nobiliario*, have held, was tutor (*mestre de rhetorica*) to Prince, afterwards King, Manuel. The King, according to Damião de Goes, 'knew enough Latin to judge of its style.' Probably he did not know much more of it than Gil Vicente himself. His first productions are without the least pretension to learning: they are close imitations of Enzina's eclogues. Later his outlook widened; he read voraciously[2] and seems to have pounced on any new publication that came to the palace, among them the works of two slightly later Spanish playwrights, Lucas Fernández and Bartolomé de Torres Naharro. With the quickness of genius and spurred forward by the malicious criticism of his audience, their love of new things and the growing opposition of the introducers of the new style from Italy, he picked up a little French and Italian, while Church Latin and law Latin early began to creep into his plays. The parade of erudition (which is also a satire on pedants) at the beginning of the *Auto da Mofina Mendes* is, however, that of a comparatively uneducated man in a library, of rustic Gil Vicente in the palace. Rather we would believe that he spent his early life in peasant surroundings, perhaps actually

---

[1] Cf. André de Resende, *Gillo auctor et actor.* (For the accurate text of this passage see C. Michaëlis de Vasconcellos, *Notas Vicentinas*, I. p. 17.)

[2] *Os livros das obras que escritas vi* (Letter of G. V. to King João III).

keeping goats in the scented hills like his Prince of Wales, Dom Duardos: *De mozo guardé ganado*, and then becoming an apprentice in the gold-smith's art, perhaps to his father or uncle, Martim Vicente, at Guimarães. It is extremely probable that he was drawn to the Court, then at Evora, for the first time in 1490 by the unprecedented festivities in honour of the wedding of the Crown Prince and Isabel, daughter of the Catholic Kings, and was one of the many goldsmiths who came thither on that occasion[1]. If that was so, his work may have at once attracted the attention of King João II, who, as Garcia de Resende tells us, keenly encouraged the talents of the young men in his service, and the protec-tion of his wife, Queen Lianor. He may have been about 25 years old at the time. The date of his birth has become a fascinating problem, over which many critics have argued and disagreed. As to the exact year it is best frankly to confess our ignorance. The information is so flimsy and conflicting as to make the acutest critics waver. While a perfectly un-warranted importance has been given to a passage in Vicente's last *comedia*, the *Floresta de Enganos* (1536), in which a judge declares that he is 66 (therefore Gil Vicente was born in 1470), sufficient stress has perhaps not been laid on the lines in the play from the Conde de Sabu-gosa's library, the *Auto da Festa*, in which Gil Vicente is declared to be 'very stout and over 60.' This cannot be dismissed like the former passage, for it is evidently a personal reference to Gil Vicente. It was the comedian's ambition to raise a laugh in his audience and this might be effected by saying the exact opposite of what the audience knew to be true: e.g. to speak of Gil Vicente as very stout and over 60 if he was very young and spectre-thin. But Vicente was certainly not very young when this play was written and we may doubt whether the victim of *calentura* and hater of heat (he treats summer scurvily in his *Auto dos Quatro Tempos*) was thin. We have to accept the fact that he was over 60 when the *Auto da Festa* was written. But when was it written? Its editor, the Conde de Sabugosa, to whom all Vicente lovers owe so deep a debt of gratitude[2], assigned it to 1535, while Senhor Braamcamp Freire, who uses Vicente's age as a double-edged weapon[3], places it

---

[1] 'E assi mandou de Castella e outras partes vir muitos ourives para fazerem arreos e outras cousas esmaltadas.' (Garcia de Resende, *Cronica del Rei D. João II*, cap. 117.)

[2] *Bibliography*, Nos. 70, 71.

[3] He argues that Vicente was not old enough to be King Manuel's tutor, but in other passages he is clearly in favour of the date 1460 or 1452. He is born 'considerably before' 1470 (*Revista de Historia*, t. 21, p. 11), in 1460? (*ib.* p. 27), in 1452? (*ib.* pp. 28, 31, and t. 22, p. 155), 'about 1460' (t. 22, p. 150), he is from two to seven years younger than King Manuel, born in 1469 (t. 21, p. 35). He is nearly 80 in 1531 (*ib.* p. 30). His marriage is placed between 1484 and 1492, preferably in the years 1484–6 (*ib.* p. 35).

twenty years earlier, in 1515. This was indeed necessary if the year 1452 was to be maintained as the date of his birth. The theory of the exact date 1452 was due to another passage of the plays: the old man in *O Velho da Horta*, formerly assigned to 1512, is 60 (III. 75). Yet there is something slightly comical in stout old Gil Vicente beginning his actor's career at the age of 50 and keeping it up till he was 86. Other facts that may throw light on his age are as follows: in 1502 he almost certainly acted the boisterous part of *vaqueiro* in the *Visitaçam*[1]. In 1512 he is over 40 and married (inference from his appointment as one of the 24 representatives of Lisbon guilds in that year). In 1512 a 'son of Gil Vicente' is in India. His son Belchior is a small boy in 1518. In 1515 he received a sum of money to enable his sister Felipa Borges to marry. In 1531 he declares himself to be 'near death[2],' although evidently not ill at the time. He died very probably at the end of 1536 or beginning of 1537[3]. Accepting the fact that the *Auto da Festa* was written before the *Templo de Apolo* (1526) I would place it as late as possible, i.e. in the year 1525, and subtracting 60 believe that the date *c.* 1465 for Gil Vicente's birth will be found to agree best with the various facts given above.

The wedding of the Crown Prince of Portugal and the Infanta Isabel was celebrated most gorgeously at Evora. The Court gleamed with plate and jewellery[4]. There were banquets and tournaments, *ricos momos* and *singulares antremeses*, pantomimes or interludes produced with great splendour—e.g. a sailing ship moved on the stage over what appeared to be waves of the sea, a band of twenty pilgrims advanced with gilt staffs, etc., etc.—all the luxurious show which had made the *entremeses* of Portugal famous and from which Vicente must have taken many an idea for the staging of his plays. Next year the tragic death of the young prince, still in his teens, owing to a fall from his horse at Santarem, turned all the joy to ashes. Gil Vicente was certainly not less impressed than Luis Anriquez, who laments the death of Prince Afonso in the *Cancioneiro Geral*, or Juan del Enzina, who made it the subject of his version or paraphrase of Virgil's 5th eclogue. Vicente's acquaintance with Enzina's works may date from this period, although we need not press Enzina's words *yo vi* too literally to mean that he was actually present at the Portuguese Court. Vicente may have accompanied the King and Queen to Lisbon in October of this year, but for the next ten years we know as much of his life as for the preceding twenty, that is

---

[1] Gil Terron in the same year is *alegre y bien asombrado* (I. 12).

[2] Cf. *Nao de Amores* (1527), *Viejo, vuestro mundo es ido,* and II. 478 (1529).

[3] See A. Braamcamp Freire in *Revista de Historia*, t. 26, p. 123.

[4] *Grandes baxillas y pedraria* (*Canc. Geral*, vol. III. (1913), p. 57).

to say, we know nothing at all. The only reference to his sojourn at the Court of King João II occurs in the mouth of Gil Terron (I, 9):

¿Conociste a Juan domado
Que era pastor de pastores?
Yo lo vi entre estas flores
Con gran hato de ganado
Con su cayado real.

A note in the *editio princeps* declares the reference to be to King João II. If we read *domado* it can only be applied to the indomitable João II in the sense of having yielded to the will of Queen Lianor in acknowledging as heir her brother Manuel in preference to his illegitimate son Jorge. Perhaps however it is best to read *damado*, which recurs in the same play. Perhaps we may even see in the passage an allusion merely to an incident occurring in the time of João II and not to the King himself[1]. We may surmise that about this time, perhaps as early as 1490, Vicente became goldsmith to Queen Lianor. The events of this wonderful decade must have moved him profoundly, events sufficient to stir even a dullard's imagination as new world after new world swept into his ken: the conquest of Granada from the Moors in 1492, the arrival of Columbus at Lisbon from America in 1493, the similar return of Vasco da Gama six years later from India, the discovery of Brazil in 1500. Two years later Vicente emerges into the light of day. King Manuel had succeeded to the throne on the death of King João (25 Oct. 1495) and had married the princess Maria, daughter of the Catholic Kings. Their eldest son, João, who was to rule Portugal as King João III from 1521 to 1557, was born on June 6, 1502, on which day a great storm swept over Lisbon. On the following evening[2] or on the evening of June 8 Gil Vicente, dressed as a herdsman, broke into the Queen's chamber in the presence of the Queen, King Manuel, his mother Dona Beatriz, his sister Queen Lianor, who was one of the prince's godmothers, and others, and recited in Spanish a brief monologue of 114 lines. Having expressed rustic wonder at the splendour of the palace and the universal joy at the birth of an heir to the throne he calls in some thirty companions to offer their humble gifts of eggs, milk, curds, cheese and honey. Queen Lianor was so pleased with this ' new thing '

---

[1] Cf. *Canc. Geral*, vol. I. (1910), p. 259:

Vejam huns autos Damado,
Huũ judeu que foi queimado
No rressyo por seu mal.

[2] There is a slight confusion. The 'second night of the birth' of the rubric may mean the night following that of the birth (June 6–7), i.e. the evening of June 7, or the second night *after* the birth, i.e. the evening of June 8; but the former is the more probable.

—for hitherto there had been no literary entertainments to vary either the profane *seraos de dansas e bailos* or the religious solemnities of the Court—that she wished Vicente to repeat the performance at Christmas. He preferred, however, to compose a new *auto* more suitable to the occasion and duly produced the *Auto Pastoril Castelhano*. King Manuel had just returned to Lisbon from a pilgrimage to Santiago de Compostela in Galicia in thanksgiving for the discovery of the sea-route to India. He found the Queen in the palace of Santos o Velho and was received *com muita alegria*. But no allusion to great contemporary events troubles the rustic peace of this *auto*, which is some four times as long as the *Visitaçam*, and which introduces several simple shepherds to whom the Angel announces the birth of the Redeemer. Queen Lianor was delighted (*muito satisfeita*) and a few days later, on the Day of Kings (6 Jan. 1503), a third pastoral play, the *Auto dos Reis Magos*, was acted, the introduction of a knight and a hermit giving it a greater variety. The *Auto da Sibila Cassandra* has been assigned to the same year, and the *Auto dos Quatro Tempos* and *Quem tem farelos?* to 1505, but there are good reasons for giving them a later date. The only play that can be confidently asserted to have been produced by Vicente between January 1503 and the end of 1508 is the brief dialogue between the beggar and St Martin: the *Auto de S. Martinho*, in ten Spanish verses *de rima cuadrada*, recited before Queen Lianor in the Caldas church during the Corpus Christi procession of 1504. The reasons for this silence are not far to seek. In September 1503, Dom Vasco da Gama returned from his second voyage to India with the first tribute of gold: 'The lords and nobles who were then at Court went to visit him on his ship and accompanied him to the palace. A page went before him bearing in a bason the 2000 *miticaes* of gold of the tribute of the King of Quiloa and the agreement made with him and the Kings of Cananor and Cochin. Of this gold King Manuel ordered a monstrance to be wrought for the service of the altar, adorned with precious stones, and commanded that it should be presented to the Convent of Bethlehem[1].' At this monstrance, still the pride of Portuguese art, Gil Vicente worked during three years (1503–6). He was perhaps already living in the Lisbon house in the *Rua de Jerusalem* assigned to him by his patroness, Queen Lianor[2]. There were other reasons for his silence. The death of Queen Isabella of Spain in 1504 and again the death of King Manuel's mother, Dona Beatriz, in

---

[1] Damião de Goes, *Chronica do felicissimo Rey Dom Emanvel*, Pt i. cap. 69.
[2] See A. Braamcamp Freire in *Revista de Historia*, vol. XXII. (1917), p. 124 and *Critica e Historia*, vol. I. (1910), p. 325; Brito Rebello, *Gil Vicente* (1902), p. 106–8.

1506, threw the Portuguese Court into mourning. Plague and famine raged at Lisbon from 1505 to 1507, while, after the awful massacre of Jews at Easter 1506, during which some thousands were stabbed or burnt to death, the city of Lisbon was placed under an interdict which was not raised till 1508.

Let us take advantage of Vicente's long silence to explain why it can be asserted so confidently that he was now at work on the Belem *custodia*. The burden of producing some definite document to show that Gil Vicente the poet and Gil Vicente the goldsmith were two different persons rests on the opponents of identity. The late Marcelino Menéndez y Pelayo, whose death in 1912 was a great blow to Portuguese as well as to Spanish literature, would certainly have changed his view if he had lived. In his brilliant study of Gil Vicente, a 'sovereign genius,' 'the most national playwright before Lope de Vega[1],' 'the greatest figure of our primitive theatre[2],' he remarked that if Vicente had been a goldsmith and one of such skill he must infallibly have left some trace of it in his dramatic works and that the contemporaries who mention him would not have preserved a profound silence as to his artistic talent[3]; yet Menéndez y Pelayo himself speaks of Vicente's *alma de artista*[4] and of the plastic character which the most fantastic allegorical figures receive at his hands[5]. If we were assured that the dreamy Bernardim Ribeiro had fashioned the Belem monstrance we might well remain sceptical, but Vicente stands out from among the vaguer poets of Portugal in having, like Garcia de Resende, an extremely definite style, and his imagination, as in his dream of fair women in the *Templo de Apolo*, coins concrete figures, not intellectual abstractions. Resende, we know, was a skilled draughtsman as well as poet, chronicler and musician, and it is curious that the very phrase applied by Vicente to Resende, *de tudo entende* (II, 406), is used of Vicente himself in an anecdote quoted by Senhor Braamcamp Freire. As to his own silence and that of his contemporaries, their silence[6] concerning the presence of two Gil Vicentes at Court would be quite as astonishing, especially as they distinguish between other homonyms of the time, and the silent satellite dogged the poet Vicente's steps with the strangest persistence. According to the discoveries or inventions of the Visconde

[1] *Antología de poetas líricos castellanos*, t. 7, p. clxiii.
[2] *Orígenes de la Novela*, t. 3, p. cxlv.
[3] *Antol.* t. 7, p. clxvi.
[4] *Ib.* p. clxxvi.
[5] *Ib.* p. clxiv.
[6] Especially that of Garcia de Resende, who in one verse (185) of his *Miscellanea* mentions the goldsmiths and in the next verse the plays of Gil Vicente.

Sanches de Baena[1] he was the poet's uncle; according to Dr Theophilo Braga they were cousins[2]. The poet, as many passages in his plays show, was interested in the goldsmith's art[3]; the goldsmith wrote verses[4]. The poet made his first appearance in 1502, the artist in 1503. Splendid as was the Portuguese Court and although its members had almost doubled in number in less than a century[5], the King did not keep men there merely on the chance of their producing 'a new thing.' The sovereign of a great and growing empire had something better to do than to indulge in forecasts as to the potential talents of his subjects. When Gil Vicente in 1502 produced a new thing in Portugal his presence in the palace can only be explained by his having an employment there, and since we know that Queen Lianor had a goldsmith called Gil Vicente who wrote verses and since the poet wrote all his earlier plays for Queen Lianor[6], it is rational to suppose that this employment was that of goldsmith to the Queen-Dowager. His presence at Court was certainly not by right of birth: Vicente was not a 'gentleman of good family,' as Ticknor and others·have supposed, but the noble art of the goldsmith (its practice was forbidden in the following century to slaves and negroes) would enable him to associate familiarly with the courtiers. In 1509 or

---

[1] *Bibliography*, No. 45.

[2] Cf. his earlier studies, in favour of identity, with his later works, maintaining cousinhood.

[3] Cf. *Obras*, i. 154 (Jupiter is the god of precious stones), i. 93, 286; ii. 38, 46, 47, 210, 216, 367, 384, 405; iii. 67, 70, 86, 296, etc. Cf. passages in the *Auto da Alma* and especially the *Farsa dos Almocreves*. Vicente evidently sympathizes with the goldsmith to whom the *fidalgo* is in debt, and if the poet took the part of *Diabo* in the *Auto da Feira* (1528) the following passage gains in point if we see in it an allusion to the debts of courtiers to him as goldsmith:

> Eu não tenho nem ceitil
> E bem honrados te digo
> E homens de muita renda
> Que tem divedo comigo (i. 158).

[4] The MS. note by a sixteenth century official written above the document appointing Gil Vicente to the post of *Mestre da Balança* should be conclusive as to the identity of poet and goldsmith: *Gil Vte trouador mestre da balança* (*Registos da Cancellaria de D. Manuel*, vol. XLII. f. 20 v. in the *Torre do Tombo*, Lisbon).

[5] Garcia de Resende († 1536) was of opinion that it had no rival in Europe:

> nam ha outra igual
> na Christamdade no meu ver.

(*Miscellanea*, v. 281, ed. Mendes dos Remedios (1917), p. 97.)

It contained 5000 *moradores* (*ibid.*). In the days of King Duarte (1433–8) the number was 3000.

[6] Cf. the dedication of *Dom Duardos* (*folha volante* of the Bib. Municipal of Oporto, N. 8. 74) to Prince João: 'Como quiera Excelente Principe y Rey mui poderoso que las Comedias, Farças y Moralidades que he compuesto en servicio de la Reyna vuestra tia....'

later[1] the poet joined, at the request of Queen Lianor, in a poetical contest concerning a gold chain, in which another poet, addressing Vicente, refers especially to necklaces and jewels. In the same year Gil Vicente is appointed overseer of works of gold and silver at the Convent of the Order of Christ, Thomar, the Hospital of All Saints, Lisbon, and the Convent of Belem. At the Hospital of All Saints the poet staged one of his plays. To Thomar and its fevers he refers more than once and presented the *Farsa de Ines Pereira* there in 1523. In 1513 he is appointed *Mestre da Balança*, in 1517 he resigns and in 1521 the poet alludes to the goldsmith's former colleagues: *os da Moeda*, while his production as playwright increases after the resignation and his complaints of poverty become more frequent[2]. In 1520 Gil Vicente the goldsmith is entrusted by King Manuel with the preparations for the royal entry into Lisbon, an *auto* figuring in the programme. If there was nothing new in a goldsmith writing verses the drama of Vicente was an innovation and João de Barros would quite naturally refer (as André de Resende before him) to the poet-goldsmith as *Gil Vicente comico*. On the other hand there is an almost brutal egoism in the silence concerning his unfortunate uncle (or cousin) maintained by Gil Vicente, who refers to himself as poet more than once, with evident pride in his *autos*. Recently General Brito Rebello (1830–1920), whose researches helped to give shape and substance to Gil Vicente's life, discovered a document of 1535 in which the poet's signature differs notably from that of the goldsmith in 1515[3]. It is, however, possible to maintain that the former signature is not that of Gil Vicente at all and that the words of the document *per seu filho Belchior Vicente* mean that Belchior signed in his father's name; or, alternatively, we can only say that Gil Vicente's handwriting had changed, a change especially frequent in artists. To those who examine all the evidence impartially there can remain very little doubt that Gil Vicente was first known at Court for his skill as goldsmith, and that he began writing verses and plays at the suggestion of his patroness, Queen Lianor.

On March 3, 1506, Vicente momentarily resumed his literary character and composed for Queen Lianor a long lay sermon, spoken before the King on the occasion of the birth of the Infante Luis (1506–55), who was himself

---

[1] The date 1509 is not barred by the reference to the *Sergas de Esplandian*, which certainly existed in an earlier edition than the earliest we now possess (1510). A certain Vasco Abul had given a girl at Alenquer a chain of gold for dancing a *ballo vylam ou mourysco* and could not get it back from the *gentil bayladeyra*. Gil Vicente contributes but a few lines: *O parecer de gil vycente neste proceso de vasco abul á rraynha dona lianor.*

[2] It is absurd to argue that during the years of his chief activity as goldsmith he had not time to produce the sixteen plays that may be assigned to the years 1502–17.

[3] *Gil Vicente* (1912), p. 11–13.

a poet and the friend and patron of men of letters. The envious feared that Vicente was playing too many parts and contended that this was no time for a sermon by a layman, but Vicente excused himself with the saying, commonly attributed to Garci Sanchez de Badajoz, that if they would permit him to play the fool this once he would leave it to them for the rest of their lives, and launched into the exposition of his text: *Non volo, volo et deficior*. His next play *Quem tem farelos?* is assigned by Senhor Braamcamp Freire to December 1508 or January 1509[1]. The reference to the *embate* in Africa in all probability alludes to the siege of Arzila in 1508. King Manuel had made preparations to set sail for an African campaign in 1501 and 1503, but the word *embate* implies something more definite. The later date (it was formerly assigned to 1505) is more suitable to the finished art of this first farce and to the fact that its success—so great that the people gave it the name by which it is still known, i.e. the first three words of the play—would be likely to cause its author to produce another farce without delay. Its successor, the *Auto da India*, acted before Queen Lianor at Almada in 1509, has not the same unity and its action begins in 1506 and ends in 1509. It displays a broader outlook and the influence of the discovery of India on the home-life of Portugal. In 1509 the fleet sailed from Lisbon under Marshal Coutinho on March 12 and *Maio* (III. 28) might be a misprint for *Março*; the *partida* alluded to, however, is that of Tristão da Cunha and Afonso de Albuquerque in 1506. It is just possible that *Quem tem farelos?* was begun in 1505 (the date of its rubric) and the *Auto da India* in 1506. Early in this year 1509 (Feb. 15) Vicente received the appointment of *Vedor* and at Christmas of the following year he produced a play at Almeirim, a favourite residence of King Manuel, who spent a part of most winters there in the pleasures of the chase[2]. This *Auto da Fé* is but a simple conversation between Faith and two peasants, who marvel at the richness of the Royal Chapel. In 1511, perhaps at Carnival[3], the *Auto das Fadas* further shows the expansion, perhaps we may say the warping, of his natural genius, for although we may rejoice in the presentation of the witch Genebra Pereira, the play soon turns aside to satirical allusions to courtiers, while the Devil gabbles in picardese. Peasants' *beirão* with a few scraps of biblical Latin had

---

[1] The dates in the rubrics are given in Roman figures and the alteration from MDV to MDIX is very slight.

[2] Cf. Bartolomé Villalba y Estaña, *El Pelegrino Curioso y Grandezas de España* [printed from MS. of last third of sixteenth century]. *Bibliófilos Españoles*, t. 23, 2 t. 1886, 9, t. 2, p. 37: 'Almerin, un lugar que los reyes de Portugal tienen para el ynvierno, con un bosque de muchas cabras, corzos y otros generos de caza.'

[3] See A. Braamcamp Freire in *Revista de Historia*, vol. XXII. p. 129.

hitherto been Vicente's only theatrical resource as regards language. The *Farsa dos Fisicos* is now[1] assigned to 1512, early in the year. It is leap year (III. 317) and Senhor Braamcamp Freire sees in the lines (III. 323):

> Voyme a la huerta de amores
> Y traeré una ensalada
> Por Gil Vicente guisada
> Y diz que otra de mas flores
> Para Pascoa tien sembrada

a reference to *O Velho da Horta*, acted before King Manuel in 1512. In August of the following year James, Duke of Braganza, set sail from Lisbon with a fleet of 450 ships to conquer Azamor:

> Foi hũa das cousas mais para notar
> Que vimos nem vio a gente passada[2].

Gil Vicente was in the most successful period of his life. In December 1512 he was chosen by the Guild of Goldsmiths to be one of the twenty-four Lisbon guild representatives and some months later he was selected by the twenty-four to be one of their four proctors, with a seat in the Lisbon Town Council. On February 4, 1513, he had become Master of the Lisbon Mint. For the departure of the fleet against Azamor he comes forward as the poet laureate of the nation and vehemently inveighs against sloth and luxury while he sings a hymn to the glories of Portugal. The play alludes to the gifts sent to the Pope in the following year and this probably led to the date of the rubric (1514), but it also refers to the royal marriages of 1521, 1525 and 1530, and we may thus assume that it was written in 1513 and touched up for a later production or for the collection of Vicente's plays. Perhaps at Christmas of this year was acted before Queen Lianor in the Convent of Enxobregas at Lisbon the *Auto da Sibila Cassandra*, hitherto placed ten years earlier. Senhor Braamcamp Freire points out that the Convent was only founded in 1509[3]. A scarcely less cogent argument for the later date is the finish of the verse and the exquisiteness of the lyrics, although the action is simple and the reminiscences of Enzina are many[4] (a fact which does not necessarily imply an early date: Enzina's echo verses are imitated in the *Comedia de Rubena*, 1521). We may note that the story of Troy is running in Vicente's head as in the *Exhortação* of 1513 (he had probably just read the *Cronica Troyana*). The last lyric, *A la guerra, caballeros*, is out

---

[1] A. Braamcamp Freire in *Rev. de Hist.* vol. XXII. p. 133–4.

[2] Luis Anriquez in *Canc. Geral*, vol. III. (1913), p. 106.

[3] See *Rev. de Hist.* vol. XXII. p. 122; vol. XXIV. p. 290.

[4] E.g. the words *ahotas* and *chapado* and the expression *en velloritas* (I. 41), cf. Enzina, *Egloga* I.: *ni estaré ya tendido en belloritas* = in clover, lit. in cowslips: *belloritas de jacinto* (*Egl.* III.).

of keeping with the rest of the play, but fighting in Africa was so frequent that it cannot help to determine the play's date. It is in this period (1512–14) that it is customary to place the death of Vicente's first wife Branca Bezerra, leaving him two sons, Gaspar and Belchior. She was buried at Evora with the epitaph:

> Aqui jaz a mui prudente
> Senhora Branca Becerra
> Mulher de Gil Vicente
> Feita terra.

This gives the *Comedia do Viuvo*, acted in 1514, a personal note, which is emphasized by the names of the widower's daughters, Paula, the name of Gil Vicente's eldest daughter, and Melicia, the name of his second wife. In the following year private grief was merged in the growing renown of Portugal in the *Auto da Fama*, which the rubric attributes to 1510, although it alludes to the siege of Goa (1510), the capture of Malaca (1511), the victorious expedition against Azamor (1513), and the attack on Aden (1513). It was acted first before Queen Lianor and then before King Manuel at Lisbon, and we may surmise that it was written or begun when the first news of Albuquerque's successes reached Lisbon and recast in 1515. The year 1516 has also been suggested, but the death of King Ferdinand the Catholic in January of that year and the death of Albuquerque in December 1515 render this date unsuitable. Even if the play was acted at Christmas 1515, there is the ironical circumstance that, at the moment when the Court was ringing with praises of the Portuguese deeds in India, the great Governor was lying dead at Goa. The date of the *Auto dos Quatro Tempos* is equally problematic. It was acted before King Manuel at the command of Queen Lianor in the S. Miguel Chapel of the Alcaçova palace on a Christmas morning. The name of the palace indicates the year 1505 or an earlier date[1], and it has been assigned to the year 1503 or 1504; but the superior development of the play's structure and even of its thought (e.g. I. 78), its resemblance to the *Triunfo do Inverno* (1529), the introduction of a French song, of the gods of Greece and of a psalm similar to that in the *Auto da Mofina Mendes* (1534)[2] and the perfection of the metre all indicate a fairly late date, while imitations of Enzina[3] are not conclusive. On the whole the intrinsic evidence counterbalances the statement of the rubric as to the Alcaçova palace and we may boldly

[1] A. Braamcamp Freire in *Rev. de Hist.* vol. XXIV. p. 290.
[2] There are, however, several such psalms in the works of Enzina.
[3] Cf. I. 85: *huele de dos mil maneras* with Enzina, *Egloga* II.: *y ervas de dos mil maneras*. In the *Auto da Alma*, probably written about this time, there are imitations of Gomez Manrique (*c.* 1415–90). Cf. the passage in the *Exhortação*.

assign this delightful piece to Christmas 1516[1], while admitting that in a rougher form it may have been presented to Queen Lianor[2] at a much earlier date.

The approximate date of the next play, the *Auto da Barca do Inferno*, is certain. This first part of Vicente's remarkable trilogy of *Barcas* was acted 'in the Queen's chamber for the consolation of the very catholic and holy Queen Dona Maria in the illness of which she died in 1517.' If we manipulate the commas so as to make the date refer to the play as well as to the Queen's death, the remedy proved fatal, for she died on March 7, but it is possible that it was acted earlier, towards the end of 1516. The subject was a gloomy one but its treatment was intended to raise many a laugh and it ends with the famous brief invocation of the Angel to the knights who had died fighting in Africa. On August 6, 1517, Vicente resigned the post of Master of the Mint in favour of Diogo Rodriguez and probably about this time he married his second wife, Melicia Rodriguez. The second and third parts of the *Barcas* trilogy were given in 1518 and 1519, but between the first and third parts Senhor Braamcamp Freire now places the *Auto da Alma*, and his scholarly suggestion[3] is amply borne out by the maturity and perfection of this beautiful play[4] and by the likelihood that Vicente when he wrote it was acquainted with Lucas Fernández' *Auto de la Pasion* (1514). The *Auto da Barca do Purgatorio* was acted before Queen Lianor on Christmas morning, 1518, at the *Hospital de Todolos Santos* (Lisbon). King Manuel had been at Lisbon in July of this year, going thence to Sintra, Collares, Torres Vedras and Almeirim, whence at the end of November he proceeded to Crato to welcome his new Queen, Dona Lianor. They returned together to Almeirim and the next months were spent there 'in great bullfights, jousts, balls and other entertainments till the beginning of Spring [May] when the King went to Evora[5].' The *Auto da Barca da Gloria* was played before his Majesty in Holy Week, 1519, and the fact that it is in Spanish and treats not of 'low figures,' but of nobles and

---

[1] That the illness of the Queen would not prevent the entertainment is proved by the fact that in the month before her death King Manuel was present at a fight between a rhinoceros and an elephant in a court in front of Lisbon's India House. We do not know if Vicente was present nor what he thought of this new thing.

[2] In December 1517 El Bachiller de la Pradilla published some verses in praise of *la muy esclarecida Señora Infanta Madama Leonor, Rey[na] de Portugal* (v. Menéndez y Pelayo, *Antología*, t. 6, p. cccxxxviii).

[3] He argues that such a form as MD & viii was never used and must be a misprint for MDxviii.

[4] Cf. also the resemblance of certain passages in the *Auto da Alma* and in the *Auto da Barca da Gloria* (1519). They must strike any reader of the two plays.

[5] Goes, *Chronica*, IV. 34.

prelates, reveals the taste of the Court and the wish to please the young Queen. In the following year (Nov. 29, 1520) Vicente was sent from Evora to Lisbon to prepare for the entry of the King and Queen into their capital (January 1521). He seems to have worked hard in arranging and directing the festivities, and in the same year (1521) he staged both the *Comedia de Rubena* and the *Cortes de Jupiter*. The latter is the only Vicente play of which we have a contemporary description. It was acted on the departure of the King's daughter, Beatriz, at the age of sixteen to espouse the Duke of Savoy. Her dowry, including precious stones, pearls and necklaces, was magnificent, and after brilliant rejoicings at Lisbon she embarked on a ship of a thousand tons in a fleet commanded by the Conde de Villa Nova. She was accompanied by the Archbishop of Lisbon and many nobles. On the evening of August 4, in the Ribeira palace 'in a large hall all adorned with rich tapestry of gold, well carpeted, with canopy, chairs and cushions of rich brocade, began a great ball in which the King our lord danced with the lady Infanta Duchess his daughter and the Queen our lady with the Infanta D. Isabel, and the Prince our lord and the Infante D. Luis with ladies they chose; and so all the courtiers danced who were going to Savoy and many other gentlemen and courtiers for a long space. And the dancing over, began an excellent and well devised comedy with many most natural and well adorned figures, written and acted for the marriage and departure of the Infanta; and with this very skilful and suitable play the evening ended[1].'

Twenty weeks after these splendid scenes and the *alegrias d'aquelas naves tam belas*[2] the King was dead. He died (13 Dec. 1521) in the full tide of apparent prosperity. As he watched the slow funeral procession passing in the night from the palace to Belem amid 600 burning torches[3] Gil Vicente must have thought of his own altered position. King Manuel had treated his sister's goldsmith generously[4] and had personally attended the acting of many of his plays. The diversion of elephant and rhinoceros had been only a momentary backsliding, and he had sat through the whole of the *Barca da Gloria*, in which a King and an Emperor fared so lamentably at the hands of the modern Silenus. But he does not appear to have done anything to secure the poet's well-being. King Manuel's sister, Vicente's faithful patroness, was, however, still alive, and he had much to hope from the new king who had grown up along with the

---

[1] Garcia de Resende, *Hida da Infanta Dona Beatriz pera Saboya* in *Chronica...del Rey Dom Ioam II*, ed. 1752, f. 99 v.

[2] Gil Vicente, *Á morte del Rei D. Manuel* (III. 347).   [3] Gil Vicente, *Romance* (III. 350).

[4] Goes says generally that King Manuel *foi muito inclinado a letras e letrados* (*Chronica*, 1619 ed., f. 342. *Favebat plurimum literis*, says Osorio, *De rebus*, 1561, p. 479).

Vicentian drama. Vicente's first literary production had celebrated his birth, at the age of nine the prince had been given a special verse in the *Auto das Fadas* (III. 111), at the age of twelve he had actually intervened in the acting of the *Comedia do Viuvo* (II. 99), although his part was confined to a single sentence. Finally, in the very year of his accession, he had been represented as a second Alexander in the *Cortes de Jupiter*, and the *Comedia de Rubena* had been acted especially for him[1]. But King João III had not the careless temperament or graceful magnificence of his father, and while he evidently trusted Vicente and showed him constant goodwill—we have the proof in the pensions received by Vicente during this reign—the favourite of one king rarely finds the same atmosphere in the *entourage* of his successor, however friendly the king himself. Thus while João III brooded over affairs of Church and State the *detractores* had more opportunity to attack the Court dramatist. On December 19 the new king was proclaimed at Lisbon and Vicente, placed too far away to hear what was said at the ceremony, invented verses which he placed on the lips of the various courtiers as they kissed hands (III. 358–64). It was not only the king but the times that had changed, and King Manuel died not a moment too soon if he wished not to see the reverse side of the brightly coloured tapestry of his reign. Vicente ends his verses with the significant words:

> Diria o povo em geral:
> Bonança nos seja dada,
> Que a tormenta passada
> Foi tanta e tam desigual.

In the following year he wrote a burlesque lamentation and testament, entitled *Pranto de Maria Parda*, 'because she saw so few branches in the streets of Lisbon and wine so dear, and she could not live without it[2].' In the late summer of 1523 in the celebrated convent of Thomar he presented one of his most famous farces before the King: *Farsa de Ines Pereira*. The critics were already gaining ground and 'certain men of good learning' doubted whether he was the author of his plays or stole them from others, a doubt suggested perhaps by the somewhat close resemblance of the *Barca da Gloria* to the Spanish *Danza de la Muerte*.

Vicente vindicated his originality by taking as his theme the proverb 'Better an ass that carries me than a horse that throws me,' and developing it into this elaborate comedy. At Christmas of the same year at

---

[1] II. 4: *Foi feita ao muito poderoso e nobre Rei D. João III. sendo principe, era de MDXXI* (rubric of *Comedia de Rubena*).

[2] II. 364. Although 'good wine needs no bush' the custom of hanging a branch above tavern doors still prevails.

Evora, in the introductory speech of the *Auto Pastoril Portugues*, placed in the mouth of a *beirão* peasant, the audience is informed that poor Gil who writes plays for the King is without a farthing and cannot be expected to produce them as splendidly as when he had the means (I. 129). He was probably disappointed that the 6 milreis which he had received that year (May 1523) was not a regular pension. His complaint fell on listening ears and in 1524 (the year of Camões' birth) he was granted two pensions of 12 and of 8 milreis, while in January 1525 he received a yet further pension of three bushels of wheat. Thus, although his possession of an estate near Torres Vedras, not far from Lisbon, has been proved to be a myth and we know that the entire fortune of his widow consisted in 1566 of ten milreis and that of his son Luis of thirty[1], and while we must remember his expenses in travelling and in the production of his plays, his financial position compares very favourably with that of Luis de Camões half a century later.

The *Fragoa de Amor*, wrongly assigned to 1525, belongs to the year 1524, the occasion being the betrothal of King João III to Catharina, sister of the Emperor Charles V[2]. The year 1525 is the most discussed date in the Vicentian chronology. Two plays are doubtfully assigned to it and we may perhaps add a third, the *Auto da Festa*, as well as the *trovas* addressed to the Conde de Vimioso. Senhor Braamcamp Freire[3] plausibly places in this year the *Farsa das Ciganas*, although the date of the rubric is 1521, the year perhaps in which the idea of this slight piece took shape in the poet's brain. There is a more definite reason for assigning *Dom Duardos* to this year. It is a play based on the romance of chivalry commonly known as *Primaleon*, of which a new edition appeared at Seville in October 1524[4], and we know from Gil Vicente's dedication that Queen Lianor († 17 Dec. 1525) was still alive[5]. Yet we are still in the region of hypothesis, for the adventures of Dom Duardos were in print since 1512 (Salamanca)[6], and we may perhaps doubt whether this 'delicious idyl[7],' the longest of Vicente's works, was ready a year after the publication of the Seville edition, although as Senhor Braamcamp Freire

---

[1] A. Braamcamp Freire in *Rev. de Hist.* vol. XXII. p. 162.

[2] *Id. ib.* vol. XXIV. p. 307. It is astonishing how slight errors in the rubrics of Vicente's plays have been permitted to survive, just as Psalm LI, of which Vicente perhaps at about this time wrote a remarkable paraphrase, still appears in all editions of his works as Ps. L.

[3] *Ib.* vol. XXIV. p. 312–3.

[4] Th. Braga, *Historia da Litteratura Portuguesa.* II. *Renascença* (1914), p. 85.

[5] J. I. Brito Rebello, *Gil Vicente* (1902), p. 64.

[6] H. Thomas, *The Palmerin Romances* (London, 1916), p. 10–12.

[7] M. Menéndez y Pelayo, *Antología*, t. 7, p. cci; *Oríg. de la Novela*, I. cclxvii: *toda la pieza es un delicioso idilio.*

points out[1], the betrothal of the Emperor Charles V to the King's sister was a suitable occasion for the production of the play[2]. The only play assigned with some certainty to 1525 is that in which the husband of Ines Pereira reappears as a rustic judge *à la Sancho Panza*: *O Juiz da Beira*, acted before the King at Almeirim.

It was a year of famine and plague at Lisbon. The fact that the verses addressed by Vicente to the Conde de Vimioso inform us that Vicente's household was down with the plague and his own life in danger (III. 38) bind these verses to no particular date, the plague being then all too common a visitation. Indeed General Brito Rebello and Senhor Braamcamp Freire both attribute this poem to 1518. His complaints of poverty would thus have begun immediately after his resignation of the lucrative post of Master of the Mint and before he had received his pensions. 'He who does not beg receives nothing,' he says, and later on in the same poem 'If hard work and merit spelt success I would have enough to live on and give and leave in my will' (III. 382–3). The general tone of these verses is more in accordance with that of his later plays[3], and the occasion was more probably that in which he composed the *Templo de Apolo*, written when he was *enfermo de grandes febres* (II. 371), and acted in January 1526[4]. In his verses he tells the Conde de Vimioso that 'I have now in hand a fine farce. I call it *A Caça dos Segredos*. It will make you very gay.' 'I call it'; but the name given by the author was more than once ousted by a popular title. This implied popularity of Gil Vicente's plays, acted before the Court and not published in a collected edition till a quarter of a century after his death, might seem unaccountable were it not for the fact that some of his pieces, printed separately, were eagerly read, and that the people might be present in fairly large numbers when his plays were represented in church or convent. We know too that plays were acted in private houses. The publication of Antonio Ribeiro Chiado's *Auto da Natural Invençam* (c. 1550) by the Conde de Sabugosa throws much light on this subject. This *auto*, acted a few years after Vicente's death, contains the description of the presentation of a play

---

[1] *Rev. de Hist.* vol. XXIV. p. 315.

[2] It should be noted that the lines in *Dom Duardos* (II. 212):

> Consuelo vete de ahi
> No perdas tiempo conmigo

are from the song in the *Comedia de Rubena* (1521):

> Consuelo vete con Dios (II. 53).

[3] Cf. *O Clerigo da Beira*: *não fazem bem [na corte] senão a quem menos faz* (III. 320); *Auto da Festa*: *os homens verdadeiros não são tidos nũa palha*, etc.

[4] *Vejo minha morte em casa* say the verses to the Conde de Vimioso; *La muerte puesta a mis lados* says the *Templo de Apolo*.

in a private house at Lisbon. The play was to begin at 10 or 11 p.m., the actors having to play first at two other private houses. So great is the interest that not only is the house crowded and its door besieged but the throng in the street outside is so thick that the players have much difficulty in forcing their way through it. The owner of the house had given 10 cruzados for the play[1]. Vicente's *Auto da Festa* was similarly acted in a private house. The most interesting of all the facts recorded by Chiado is the eagerness of the people. Uninvited persons from the crowd outside kept pressing in at the door. Thus we can easily understand how the people could give their own name to a play, fastening on words or incident that especially struck them. The Farce of the Poor Squire became *Quem tem farelos?*[2], the author's name for the *Auto da Mofina Mendes* was *Os Mysterios da Virgem* (I. 103), the *Clerigo da Beira* was also known as the *Auto de Pedreanes*[3]. Therefore when we come upon a new title of a Vicente play unknown to us we need not conclude that it is a new play.

Of the seven Vicente plays[4] placed on the Portuguese *Index* of 1551 four are known to us. The *Auto da Vida do Paço* may be identified with some probability with the *Romagem de Aggravados*[5]. If we may not identify the *Jubileu de Amores* with the *Auto da Feira* its disappearance must be accounted for by the wrath of the Church of Rome, which fell upon it when produced at Brussels in 1531[6]. The remaining play *O Auto da Aderencia do Paço* can scarcely be identified with the *Auto da Festa* on the ground that the *vilão* says (1906 ed., p. 123):

> Quem quiser ter que comer
> Trabalhe por aderencia:
> Haverá quanto quiser.
> Vosoutros que andais no paço....

especially as there was scarcely anything for the Censorship to condemn: merely the mention of the *Priol's* two sons (p. 111) and the ease with which the old woman obtains a Bull from the Nuncio (pp. 120, 124).

---

[1] *Auto da Natural Invençam* (Lisboa, 1917), pp. 64, 65, 68, 69, 70, 88, 89.

[2] *Este nome pos-lho o vulgo* (III. 4). Cf. the title *Os Almocreves*.

[3] *Rol dos livros defesos* (1551) ap. C. Michaëlis de Vasconcellos, *Notas Vicentinas*, I. p. 31. We might assume that the second part of *O Clerigo da Beira* (III. 250–9) was printed separately under the title *Auto de Pedreanes* but for the words *por causa das matinas*.

[4] *Ib.* p. 30–1.

[5] The probability is shown by the fact that the idea of their identity had occurred to me before reading the same suggestion made by Snr Braamcamp Freire in the *Revista de Historia*.

[6] See *Notas Vicentinas*, I. (1912). The *Auto da Feira* answers in some respects to Cardinal Aleandro's description of the *Jubileu de Amores*, and Rome (the Church, not the city) might conceivably have been crowned with a Cardinal's hat, but Aleandro's letter refutes this suggestion: *uno principal che parlava...fingeasi Vescovo*. Rome in the *Auto da Feira* (I. 162) is a *senhora*. One can only say that the *Auto da Feira* may perhaps have been adapted for the occasion, with an altered title, Spanish being added, to suit the foreign audience.

There is far more reason, 'in my simple conjectures,' for believing that *A Caça dos Segredos* altered its name before or after it was produced and became *A farsa chamada Auto da Lusitania.* In the burlesque passage concerning Gil Vicente in this play (III. 275–6) we learn that he was instructed for seven years and a day in the Sibyl's cave and informed by the Sibyl of the secrets which she knew about the past:

> E ali foi ensinado
> Sete anos e mais um dia
> E da Sibila informado
> Dos segredos que sabia
> Do antigo tempo passado.

If the *Trovas ao Conde de Vimioso* were written in 1525, the seven years during which Vicente hunted for secrets bring us to 1532, the date of the *Auto da Lusitania.* The necessary allusions to the birth of the Prince were inserted, but the play had been ready long before[1].

The *Auto da Festa* was probably acted in a private house at Evora. It contains scarcely an indication as to its date[2], but it has passages similar to others in the *Farsa de Ines Pereira* (1523), the *Fragoa de Amor*[3] (1524) and the *Farsa das Ciganas* (1525?)[4]. That the play was prior to the *Templo de Apolo* seems evident, and the author would be unlikely to copy from what he calls an *obra doliente* (II. 373) with Portuguese passages introduced to prop up a play originally written wholly in Spanish (*ibid.*). Nor need the anti-Spanish passages tell against the year of the betrothal of Charles V and the Infanta Isabel, for they are placed in the mouth of a *vilão* and the play was performed in private. In the *Templo de Apolo* the anti-Spanish atmosphere has not quite vanished, but the *vilão* contents himself with saying that *Deos não é castelhano*, and even so Apollo feels bound to present his excuses:

> Villano ser descortés
> No es mucho de espantar.

[1] *E como sempre isto guardasse Este mui leal autor Até que Deos enviasse O Principe nosso senhor Nam quis que outrem o gozasse* (III. 276).

[2] The familiarity with which the Nuncio is treated would be more suitable if he was the Portuguese D. Martinho de Portugal, but then the date would have to be after 1527.

[3] Cf. II. 343: *Salga esotra ave de pena...Son perdices* and *Auto da Festa*, p. 101. The latter text is corrupt (*penitas* for *peitas*, and *cousas fritas* has ousted the required rhyme *juizes*).

[4] The line *nega se m'eu embeleco* occurs here and in the *Serra da Estrella* (1527). Arguments as to date from such repetitions are not entirely groundless. Cf. *com saudade suspirando* (*Cortes de Jupiter*, 1521) and *sam suspiros de saudade* (*Pranto de Maria Parda*, 1522); *Que dirá a vezinhança?* III. 21 (1508–9), *A vezinhança que dirá?* III. 34 (1509); *Ó demo que t'eu encomendo*, III. 99 (1511), *Ó diabo que t'eu encomendo*, II. 362 (1513). The *Exhortação* (1513), which has passages similar to those in the *Farsa de Ines Pereira* (1523) and the *Pranto de Maria Parda* (1522), probably became a kind of national anthem and was touched up for each performance. Curiously, the mention of *a pedra d'estrema* in the *Pranto* and in the *Auto da Festa* might correspond to a first (1521) and second (1525) revision of the *Exhortação*.

Quem não parece esquece, says Vicente in his *trovas* to Vimioso. *Les absents ont tort.* After a quarter of a century he could no longer describe his *autos* as a new thing and he was now confronted by the formidable novelty of the hendecasyllabic metre introduced by Sá de Miranda from Italy. He felt that he had his back against the wall[1]. He made a prodigious effort to vary the themes of his plays and to produce them with increasing frequency. The year 1527 is his *annus mirabilis*. The *Sumario da Historia de Deos* and the *Dialogo sobre a Ressurreiçam* are assigned, if not to this year, to the period 1526–8[2]. The *Nao de Amores* celebrated the entry of Queen Catharina into Lisbon in 1527, and before the autumn[3] three plays, the *Divisa da Cidade de Coimbra*, the *Farsa dos Almocreves* and the *Tragicomedia da Serra da Estrella*, had been presented before the Court at the charming old town of Coimbra which ten years later definitively became the University town of Portugal. His great efforts were not unrewarded, for in the following year he received a yet further pension of 12 milreis. On his way back from Coimbra to Santarem he fell among some Spanish carriers who took advantage of the new Queen's favour to fleece the poet, and he wrote some verses of comic complaint to the King (II. 383–4). The rubric assigns to the same year the famous *Auto da Feira* (Lisbon: Christmas 1527) but Snr Braamcamp Freire[4] points out that King João did not spend Christmas of this year at Lisbon and assigns it to 1528, the year in which the celebrated Dialogues of Alfonso and Juan de Valdés saw the light. In April 1529 the *Triunfo do Inverno* celebrated the birth of the Infanta Isabel. The author introduced the play in a long lament in verse over the forgotten jollity of earlier times and then, to show that his own hand had lost none of its cunning, he gave his audience a feast of lyrical passages in the Triumphs of Winter and Spring.

In 1527 Vicente seems clearly to have aimed his allusions to the sons of priests at Francisco de Sá de Miranda, whose father was a priest and who was born at Coimbra. And now in *O Clerigo da Beira*[5] we have a priest addressing his son Francisco and telling him that

---

[1] The very success of his plays incited emulation. A play written in Latin, *Hispaniola*, was acted at the Portuguese Court before his death (Gallardo, ap. Sousa Viterbo, *A Litt. Hesp. em Portugal* (1915), p. xxiv).

[2] See A. Braamcamp Freire in *Rev. de Hist.* vol. XXIV. p. 331.

[3] Francisco Alvarez arrived at the Court at Coimbra in the late summer of 1527 and he says: *nam se tardou muito que el Rey nosso senhor se partisse com sua corte via dalmeirim. Verdadeira Informaçam* (1540), modern reprint, p. 191.

[4] *Rev. de Hist.* vol. XXV. p. 89.

[5] According to Snr Braamcamp Freire this play must be assigned to the months between September 1529 and February 1530.

a priest's son will never come to any good. On his part the grave Sá de Miranda had protested against the introduction of scenes from the Bible into the *farsas*: the allusion to Vicente was clear although his treatment of such scenes was usually reverent. Vicente still had the ear of the Court and Sá de Miranda could only lament that the new style had at first so little vogue in Portugal. That the King, when he had leisure, consulted Vicente on weightier matters than the production of Court plays is proved by a passage[1] in the letter addressed to him by the poet from Santarem. A terrible earthquake shock on Jan. 26, 1531, followed by other severe shocks, kept the people in a panic for fifty days. *Terruerant satis haec pavidam praesagia plebem*, and to make matters worse the monks of Santarem, with an eye on the new Christians, spoke of the wrath of God and announced another earthquake as calmly as if they were giving out the hour of evensong. Vicente, who in his letter to the King[2] says, like Newman's Gerontius, 'I am near to death,' assembled the monks and preached them an eloquent sermon. The prestige of the Court poet restrained their zeal and probably avoided another massacre such as he had seen at Lisbon a quarter of a century before. It was in December of this year that the *Jubileu de Amores* was acted in the house of the Portuguese Ambassador at Brussels, to the horror of Cardinal Aleandro, who almost persuaded himself that he was witnessing the sack of Rome four years earlier. It was perhaps before this that King João commanded Vicente to publish his works, but he could not be greatly perturbed that a play by Vicente had given offence to the Holy See, with which he was himself often in unpleasant relations at this time. At all events Vicente continued to produce his plays. In 1532 the birth of the long desired heir to the throne was celebrated at Lisbon, and Vicente presented the *Auto da Lusitania*, while two long plays, the *Romagem de Aggravados* and *Amadis de Gaula*, belong to the following year. The former was acted at Evora in honour of the birth of the Infante Felipe (May 1533). *Amadis de Gaula* perhaps shows some signs of weariness, and if he played the part of Amadis he would apply to himself the lines

> Que ya veis que soy pasado
> A la vida de los muertos (II. 282).

The *Auto da Cananea* was written at the request of the Abbess of Oudivellas and acted at that convent near Lisbon in 1534. It contains

---

[1] O mandei a V. A. por escrito até lhe Deos dar descanso e contentamento...pera que por minha arte lhe diga o que aqui falece (III. 388).

[2] In this letter, written in the very year of the first Bull for the introduction of the Inquisition into Portugal, Vicente uses the expression 'May I be burnt if.'

perhaps a reference to the earthquake of 1531 (I. 373). The *Auto da Mofina Mendes* may have been written some years before it was acted in the presence of the King at Evora on Christmas morning 1534: it alludes to the capture of Francis I at Pavia (1525) and to the sack of Rome (1527). Vicente had returned to Evora at least as early as August 1535, and in 1536 he produced there before the King his last play, the *Floresta de Enganos*, which may well have been a collection of farcical scenes written at various periods of his career[1]. We know that he was dead on April 16, 1540. He did not follow the Court to Lisbon in August 1537 and his death may be assigned with some plausibility to the end of 1536 at Evora[2]. The children of his second marriage were almost certainly with him, Paula and Luis, who edited his works in 1562 and were now still in their teens, and the even younger Valeria. Paula seems to have inherited her father's versatility and his musical, dramatic and literary tastes. Tradition connects her closely with him and would even assign her a part in the composition of his plays. Another and a more reliable tradition says that he was buried in the Church of S. Francisco at Evora. His life had been full and strenuous and we leave him in this quiet little town *depois da vida cansada descansando*[3].

II. CHARACTER AND IDEAS

If we were limited to the information about Gil Vicente furnished by his contemporaries, we should but know that he had introduced into Portugal *representações* of eloquent style and novel invention imitating Enzina's eclogues with great skill and wit[4], and that the mordant comic poet Gil Vicente, who hid a serious aim beneath his gaiety and was skilled in veiling his satire in light-hearted jests, might have excelled Menander, Plautus and Terence if he had written in Latin instead of in the vulgar tongue[5]. That is, we should have known nothing that we could not learn from his plays and it is to his plays that we must go if

---

[1] The line *A quien contaré mis quejas* (II. 147) is repeated from the *Trovas* addressed to King João in 1527. It is taken from a poem by the Marqués de Astorga printed in the *Cancionero General* (1511):

> ¿A quien contaré mis quexas
> Si a ti no?

Cf. *Comedia de Rubena* (II. 6): ¿*A quien contaré mi pena?* The comical rôle of the Justiça Maior may have been taken by Garcia de Resende, who added acting to his other accomplishments. He was 66, and he died at Evora in this year.

[2] See A. Braamcamp Freire in *Rev. de Hist.* vol. XXVI. p. 122–3.

[3] From Gil Vicente's epitaph written by himself.

[4] Garcia de Resende (1470–1536), *Miscellanea*, 1752 ed., f. 113.

[5] André de Resende, *Genethliacon Principis Lusitani* (1532), ap. C. Michaëlis de Vasconcellos, *Notas Vicentinas*, I. (1912), p. 17.

we would be more closely acquainted with his character and his attitude towards the problems of his day. King Manuel, says Damião de Goes, always kept at his Court Spanish buffoons as a corrective of the manners and habits of the courtiers[1]. The King may have had something of the sort in his mind in encouraging Gil Vicente, and probably he especially favoured his allusions to the courtiers; but we cannot for a moment consider that Vicente, friend and adviser of King João III, the grave town-councillor whose influence could check the fanaticism of the monks at Santarem—can we imagine them bowing before a mere mountebank, a strolling player?—was looked upon simply as a Court jester. The impression left by his plays is, rather, that of the worthy thoughtful face of Velazquez as painted in his *Las Meninas* picture, a figure closely familiar with the Court yet still somewhat aloof, *apartado,* like Gil Terron. Vicente regards himself as a *rustico peregrino* (III. 390), an *ignorante sabedor* (I. 373) as opposed to the ignorant-malicious or ignorant-presumptuous of the Court. But Vicente was no ascetic, his was a genial, generous nature, he liked to have enough to spend and give and leave in his will. Kindly and chivalrous, he was a champion of the down-trodden but had first-hand knowledge of the malice and intrigues of the peasants and of the poor in the towns. Above all he was thoroughly Portuguese. He might place his scene in Crete but in that very scene he would refer to things so Portuguese as the *janeiras* and *lampas de S. João.* Portugal is

> Pequeno e muy grandioso,
> Pouca gente e muito feito,
> Forte e mui victorioso,
> Mui ousado e furioso
> Em tudo o que toma a peito,

and he appears to have shared the popular prejudice against Spain. Did he also share the people's hostility towards the priests and the Jews? It cannot be said that the priests presented in his plays are patterns of morality. As to the Jews he knows of their corrupt practices and describes them in a late play as *a mais falsa ralé*[2]. It was during the last ten years of Vicente's life that the question of the new Christians came especially to the front (from 1525). In earlier plays Vicente seems more sympathetic towards them and the pleasant sketch of the Jewish

---

[1] *Chronica do fel. Rey Dom Emanvel,* Pt IV. cap. 84 (1619 ed., f. 341): Trazia continuadamente na sua corte choquarreiros castelhanos, com os motes & ditos dos quaes folgaua, nam porque gostasse tanto do q̃ diziam como o fazia das dissimuladas reprehensões [*jocis perstringere mores*] q̃ com geitos e palauras trocadas dauam aos moradores de sua casa fazendolhes conhecer as manhas, viços & modos que tinhão, de que se muitos tirauam & emmendauam, tomando o q̃ estes truães diziam com graças por espelho do que aviam de fazer.

[2] *Auto da Cananea* (1534).

family in Lisbon is as late as 1532[1]. In 1506, the very year of the massacre of Jews at Lisbon, he had gone to the root of the question when he declared in his lay sermon that:

> Es por demás pedir al judío
> Que sea cristiano en el corazón...
> Que es por demás al que es mal cristiano
> Doctrina de Cristo por fuerza ni ruego[2].

And twenty-five years later he said to the monks at Santarem: 'If there are some here who are still strangers to our faith it is perhaps for the greater glory of God[3].' That is to say: if you force the Jews to become Christians you will only make them hypocrites; far better to treat them frankly as Jews and not expect figs from thistles. That Vicente himself was a devout Christian and Catholic and a deeply religious man such plays as the *Auto da Alma*, the *Barcas*, the *Sumario*, the *Auto da Cananea* are sufficient proof. He had much of the Erasmian spirit but nothing in common with the Reformation. His irreverence is wholly external, it was abuses not doctrine that he attacked, the ministers of the Church and not the Church itself. He may have been in the secret of King João's somewhat stormy negotiations with the Holy See and he took the national and regalist view: in the *Auto da Feira* Mercury addresses Rome as follows:

> Nam culpes aos reis da terra,
> Que tudo te vem de cima (I. 166).

He wished to reform the Church from within. All are perversely asleep, a sleep of death[4]. Many prayers do not suffice without *almas limpas e puras*[5]. Men must be judged by their works[6]. In the *Auto da Fé* (1510) we have a simple declaration of faith:

> Fé he amar a Deos só por elle
> Quanto se pode amar,
> Por ser elle singular,
> Nam por interesse delle;
> E se mais quereis saber,
> Crer na Madre Igreja Santa
> E cantar o que ella canta
> E querer o que ella quer[7].

But four years earlier and ten before Luther's formal protest against the papal indulgences we find Vicente in his lay sermon referring to the question 'whether the Pope may grant so many pardons' and laughing

---

[1] *Auto da Lusitania.*   [2] *Sermão* (III. 346).
[3] *Carta* (III. 388).   [4] *Auto da Mofina Mendes* (I. 120, 121).
[5] *Auto da Cananea* (I. 365).   [6] *Sumario da Historia de Deos* (I. 338).
[7] I. 69. His own knowledge of the Bible was extensive and he often follows it closely, e.g. *Auto da Sibila Cassandra* (I. 47, 48 = Genesis i.).

at the hair-splitting of preachers: was the fruit that Eve ate an apple, a pear or a melon[1]? His own religion certainly had a mystical and pantheistic tendency[2]. It was as deep as was his love of Nature. He would have the hearts of men dance with jocund May[3]:

> Hei de cantar e folgar
> E bailar c'os corações,

and he had an eye for the humblest flower that blows—chicory and camomile, hedge flowerets, honeysuckle and wild roses:

> Almeirones y magarzas,
> Florecitas por las zarzas,
> Madresilvas y rosillas (I. 95. Cf. II. 29).

And he sympathized closely with what was nearest to Nature: peasants and children. Of the people of the towns he was probably less enamoured and he speaks of *a desvairada opinião do vulgo* and of the folly of pandering to it[4]. At Court he certainly had many friends. A friendly rivalry in art and letters bound him to Garcia de Resende for probably over forty years and he was no doubt on excellent terms with the *dadivoso* Conde de Penella (II. 511), the *muito jucundo* Conde de Tentugal (III. 360) and the Conde de Vimioso. High rank was no certain shelter from the shafts of Vicente's wit, but when it was a case of princes he was more careful:

> Agora cumpre atentar
> Como poemos as mãos,

as he ingenuously remarks[5]. King João II had seen to it that no class or individual should dispute the power of the throne, and now the King reigned supreme. Kings, says Vicente, are the image of God[6]. That was in 1533, when it might seem to him that the authority of the throne was more than ever necessary to cope with the confusion of the times. The King's power stood for the nation, that of a noble might mean mere private ambition or power in the hands of one unworthy, and Gil Vicente asks nobly:

> Quem não é senhor de si
> Porqué o será de ninguem?
> (Who himself cannot control
> Why should he o'er others rule?)

---

[1] III. 337, 338. His quarrel with the monks was that they did not serve the State. Cf. *Fragoa de Amor* (II. 345); *Exhortação da Guerra* (II. 367).

[2] Cf. the passage in the *Sumario da Historia de Deos* in which Abraham complains that men worship stocks and stones and have no knowledge of God, *criador dos spiritos, eternal spirito* (I. 326).

[3] III. 284. A critic upbraided Wordsworth for saying that his heart danced with the daffodils—no doubt Southey's 'my bosom bounds' was more poetical—yet Shakespeare and Vicente had used the phrase before him.

[4] *Carta* (III. 388).   [5] *Cortes de Jupiter* (II. 405).   [6] *Romagem de Aggravados* (II. 507).

He had witnessed many changes, and looking back as an old man his memory might well be overwhelmed by a period so crowded[1]. He had seen the provinces and capital of Portugal transformed by the overseas discoveries. We may be sure that he had watched with more interest than the ordinary *lisboeta* the extension of the Portuguese empire and the deeds of the unfortunate Dom Francisco de Almeida ('Tomou Quiloa e Mombaça, Parece cousa de graça Ver de que morte acabou') and the redoubtable Afonso de Albuquerque, who snatched victories from defeat in the teeth of all manner of obstruction and indifference and placed Portugal's glory on a pinnacle scarcely dreamed of even in the intoxicating moment of Gama's first return to Belem in 1499:

> Outro mundo encuberto
> Vimos então descubrir
> Que se tinha por incerto:
> Pasma homem de ouvir.

Meanwhile Vicente never lost sight of the fact that the nation's strength lay not in rich imports, however fabulous and envied, but in the good use of its own soil and capacities and in the vigour, energy and discipline of its inhabitants, and a note of warning sounded again and again in his plays as he saw the old simplicity sink and disappear before wave on wave of luxury, ambition and hollow display. He had felt the good old times, content with rustic dance and song, vanishing since 1510:

> De vinte annos a ca
> Não ha hi gaita nem gaiteiro[2].

Now no one is content: *ninguem se contenta da maneira que sohia*[3]. *Tudo bem se vai ao fundo*[4]. He especially deplored the new confusion between the classes[5]. Shepherd, page and priest all wish to serve the King, that is, to become an official and to idle for a fixed wage while the land remained unploughed. The peasants do not know what they want and *murmuram sem entender*[6]. There is slackness everywhere (*todos somos negligentes*)[7]. Portugal was suffering from a crisis similar to that of four centuries later and men were inclined to leave their professions in order to theorize or in the hope of growing rich by a short cut or by

---

[1] The preparation of his plays for the press was, he says, a burden in his old age. Some of the plays had been acted in more than one year, others had been composed years before they were acted, others had been printed separately. Hence the uncertainty of some of the rubric dates.

[2] *Triunfo do Inverno* (1529), ii. 447.

[3] *Romagem de Aggravados* (1533), ii. 524–5.

[4] *Auto Pastoril Portugues* (1523), i. 129.   [5] *Farsa dos Almocreves* (1527), iii. 219.

[6] *Triunfo do Inverno* (1529), ii. 487.   [7] *Auto da Feira* (1528), i. 175.

chance instead of by hard, steady work; and the result was a period of upheaval and disquiet. Vicente suffered like the rest. He had embodied in his plays the simple pastimes of the Portuguese people, their delight in the processions, services and dramatic displays of the Church, in the mimicry of the early *arremedillos*, in the rich fancy-dress *momos* which were an essential element at great festivities. But his drama was not classical, often it was not drama. Technically he is less dramatic than Lucas Fernández or Torres Naharro. He defied every rule of Aristotle and mingled together the grave and gay, coarse and courtly in a way faithful to life rather than to any accepted theories of the stage. While he continued to produce these natural and delightful plays all kinds of new conditions arose. It was the irony of circumstance that when the old Portuguese poetry held the field the taste of the Court for personal satire and magnificent show could scarcely appreciate at its true value the lyrical gift of Vicente; and later, after King Manuel's death, Vicente found himself confronted by a new school in which classicism carried the day, the long Italian metres superseded the merry native *redondilha* of eight syllables, and the latinisers began to transform the language and shuddered like *femmes savantes* at Vicente's barbarisms and uncouth *voquibles*. His attitude towards his critics was one of humility and good humour. It is at least good to know that Vicente with his *redondilhas* continued to triumph personally in his old age and it was only the hand of death that drove him from the scene. Nor did he cease to point out abuses: the increase of *a falsa mentira*, the corruption of justice[1], the greed for money[2] and the growth of luxury[3]. He pillories the ignorance of pilots[4] by which so many ships were lost now and later, and he seems to doubt the wisdom of keeping women shut up like nuns both before[5] and after[6] marriage. If in many respects Vicente belonged to the Middle Ages, in his curiosity and many-sidedness he was a true child of the Renaissance. He dabbled in astrology and witchcraft, loved music (he wrote tunes for some of his lyrics), poetry, reading, acting and the goldsmith's art, and maintained his zest in old age: *Mofina Mendes* was probably written when he was over sixty. Attempts to represent him as a Lutheran reformer, a deep philosopher or an authority in questions philological fall to the ground. He was a jovial

---

[1] See the *Fragoa de Amor* and the *Auto da Festa*.
[2] III. 289 (1532).
[3] II. 363 (as early as 1513).
[4] II. 467–75.
[5] III. 122.
[6] III. 148 (cf. I. 40, III. 41).

poet and a keen observer who loved his country, and when he saw its inhabitants all at sixes and sevens he would willingly have brought them back to what he called *a boa diligencia*.

III. TYPES SKETCHED IN HIS PLAYS

In Vicente's notes and sketches of the Portugal of his day we may see the master hand of the goldsmith accustomed to set jewels. His miniatures are so distinct and the types described are so various that had we no other record of the first third of the sixteenth century in Portugal we might form a very fair and singularly vivid estimate from his plays. With a comic poet we have, of course, to be on our guard. When Vicente introduces the *lavrador* who steals his neighbour's land, is he drawing from life or from Berceo's *mal labrador* or from the *Danza de la Muerte* (*fasiendo furto en la tierra agena*) or from the Bible: 'Cursed be he that removeth his neighbour's landmark'? When he presents the poverty-stricken nobleman, the dissipated priest, rustics from Beira, or negro slaves, for how much does the conventional satire of the day stand in these portraits and how much is drawn from Nature? Are they merely literary types? It is obvious that these themes were a great resource for the satirists of that time but their value to the satirist lay in their truth. The sad existence of the poor gentleman and the splendour maintained by penniless nobles are all too well attested. As to the priests, when we find King Manuel joining with King Ferdinand of Spain in a protest to the Pope to the effect that the whole of Christendom was scandalized by the dissolute life of the clergy and by the traffic in Bulls[1], and grave ecclesiastics in Spain and friends of grave ecclesiastics, like Franco Sacchetti[2] earlier in Italy, using language even more violent than that of Vicente, we need not doubt the truth of his sketches. He was perhaps more vivid than the other critics and his satire penetrated deeply for the very reason that he was a realist. There was no doubt some professional exaggeration in the language of his *beirão* rustics, but his sympathy with the peasants and his wide knowledge of the province of Beira prove that his object was not merely mockery: *zombar da gente da Beira*[3]. Many of his types are foreshadowed in the *Cancioneiro Geral*, and especially in the *Arrenegos* of Gregorio Afonso, of the household of the Bishop of Evora: the 'priest who lives like a layman,' 'the gentleman

---

[1] Goes, *Chronica do fel. Rey Dom Emanvel*, Pt I. cap. 33 (1619 ed., f. 20).

[2] E.g. *Novella* 35: sotto apparenza onesta di religione ogni vizio di gola, di lussuria e degli altri, como loro appetito desidera, sanza niuno mezzo usano; *Novella* 36: hanno meno discrezione che gli animali irrazionali.

[3] *Auto da Festa*, ed. 1906, p. 115.

who has not enough to eat,' 'the man of great estate and small income,' the *preciosos*, the *borrachas*, the *fantasticos*, the *alcouviteira*, 'the peasants placed in a position of importance.' In developing these figures Vicente was always careful to keep close to Nature. Each speaks in his own language, 'the negro as a negro, the old man as an old man.' This is carried to such a length that the Spanish Queen in the lament on the death of King Manuel is made to speak her few lines in Spanish, the rest of the poem being in Portuguese[1].

Vicente is not an easy writer because his styles are so many and his allusions so local. But we must be infinitely grateful to him for the way in which he portrays a type in a few lines and for the fact that although they are types they are evidently taken from individuals whom he had observed and who continue to live for us in his pages. His gallery of priests is for all time. Frei Paço comes, with his velvet cap and gilt sword, 'mincing like a very sweet courtier'; Frei Narciso starves and studies, tinging his complexion to an artificial yellow in the hope that his hypocritical asceticism may win him a bishopric; the worldly courtier monk fences and sings and woos; the Lisbon priest, like his confessor one of Love's train, fares well on rabbits and sausages and good red wine, even as the portly pleasure-loving Lisbon canons; the country priest resembles a kite pouncing on chickens; the ambitious chaplain accepts the most menial tasks, compared with whom the sporting priest of Beira is at least pleasantly independent; and there are the luxurious hermit, the dissipated village priest who never prayed the hours, the inconstant monk who had been carrier and carpenter and now wishes to be unfrocked in order to join more freely in dance and pilgrimage, the mad friar Frei Martinho persecuted by dogs and Lisbon *gamins*, the ambitious preacher who glosses over men's sins. If the priests·fared well in this life the satirists were determined that they should not be equally fortunate after their death. Vicente's proud Bishop is to be boiled and roasted, the grasping Archbishop is left perpetually aboiling, the ambitious Cardinal is to be devoured by dogs and dragons in a den of lions, while the sensual and simoniacal Pope is to have his flesh torn with red-hot iron. And we have—although here Vicente discreetly went to the *Danza de la Muerte* for his satire—the vainglorious and tyrannical Emperor, the Duke who had adored himself and the King who had allowed himself to be adored. There are the careless hedonistic Count

---

[1] Vicente, who could write such pure and idiomatic Portuguese, often used peculiar Spanish, not perhaps so much from ignorance as from a wish to make the best of both languages. Thus he uses the personal infinitive and makes words rhyme which he must have known could not possibly rhyme in Spanish, e.g. *parezca* with *cabeza* (Portug. *pareça* —*cabeça*). So *mucho* rhymes with *fruto*, *demueño* with *sueño*.

more given to love than to charity or churchgoing, the *fidalgo de raça*, the haughty *fidalgo de solar* with a page to carry his chair, the judge who through his wife accepts bribes from the Jews, the rhetorical goldsmith, the usurer (*onzeneiro*) with his heart in his *cassette* (*arca*)[1]. There too the pert servant-girl, the gossiping maidservant, the witch busy at night over a hanged man at the cross-roads, the faithless wife of the India-bound *lisboeta*, the Lisbon old woman copious in male-diction, her genteel daughter Isabel, the wife who in her husband's absence only leaves her house to go to church or pilgrimage, the *mal maridada* imprisoned by her husband, the peasant bride singing and dancing in skirt of scarlet, the woman superstitiously devout, the *beata alcouviteira* who would not have escaped the Inquisition had she been printed like Aulegrafia in the seventeenth century, lisping gypsies, the *alcouviteiras* Anna and Branca and Brigida, the *curandera* with her quack remedies, the poor farmer's daughter brought to be a Court lady and still stained from the winepress, the old woman desirous of a young husband, the slattern Catherina Meigengra, the market-woman who plays the *pandero* in the market-place, the peasant girls with pretentious names coming down to market basket on head from the hills, the shrew Branca and the timid wife Marta, the two irrepressible Lisbon fishwives, the voluble *saloia* who sells milk well watered and charges cruel prices for her eggs and other wares, the country priest's greedy 'wife' who eats the baptism cake and is continually roasting chestnuts, the mystical ingenuous little shepherdess Margarida who sees visions on the hills, the superior daughter of the peasant judge who had once spoken to the King, the small Beira girl keeping ducks, Lediça the affectedly ingenuous daughter of the Jewish tailor, Cezilia of Beira possessed by a familiar spirit.

Or, again, we have the ceremonious Lisbon lover Lemos, the high-flown Castilian of fearful presence and a lion's heart, however threadbare his *capa*[2], the starving gentleman who makes a *tostão* (= 5*d*.) last a month and dines off a turnip and a crust of bread, another—a sixteenth century Porthos—who imagines himself a *grand seigneur* and has not a sixpence to his name but hires a showy suit of clothes to go to the palace, another who is an intimate at Court (*o mesmo paço*) but who to satisfy a passing passion has to sell boots and viola and pawn his saddle, the poor gentle-man's servant (*moço*) who sleeps on a chest, or is rudely awakened at midnight to light the lamp and hold the inkpot while his master writes down his latest inspiration in his song-book, the incompetent Lisbon

---

[1] The miser, *o verdadeiro avaro* (III. 287), is barely mentioned. Perhaps Vicente felt that he would have been too much of an abstract type, not a living person.

[2] The boastful Spaniard appears (in Goethe's *Italienische Reise*) in the Rome Carnival at the end of the eighteenth century.

doctors with their stereotyped formulas, the frivolous persons who are bored by three prayers at church but spend nights and days listening to *novellas*, the *parvo*, predecessor of the Spanish *gracioso*, the Lisbon courtier descended from Aeneas, the astronomer, unpractical in daily life as he gazes on the stars, the old man amorous, rose in buttonhole, playing on a viola, the Jewish marriage-brokers, the country bumpkin, the lazy peasant lying by the fire, the poor but happy gardener and his wife, the quarrelsome blacksmith with his wife the bakeress, the carriers jingling along the road and amply acquainted with the wayside inns, the aspiring *vilão*, the peasant who complains bitterly of the ways of God, the *lavrador* with his plough who did not forget his prayers and was charitable to tramps but skimped his tithes, the illiterate but not unmalicious *beirão* shepherd who had led a hard life and whose chief offence was to have stolen grapes from time to time, the devout bootmaker who had industriously robbed the people during thirty years, the card-player blasphemous as the *taful* of King Alfonso's *Cantigas de Santa Maria*, the delinquent from Lisbon's prison (the *Limoeiro*) whom his confessor had deceived before his hanging with promises of Paradise, the peasant *O Moreno* who knows the dances of Beira, the negro chattering in his pigeon-Portuguese 'like a red mullet in a fig-tree,' the deceitful negro expressing the strangest philosophy in Portuguese equally strange, the rustic clown Gonçalo with his baskets of fruit and capons, who when his hare is stolen turns it like a canny peasant to a kind of posthumous account: *leve-a por amor de Deos pola alma de meus finados*, the Jew Alonso Lopez who had formerly been prosperous in Spain but is now a poor new Christian cobbler at Lisbon, the Jewish tailor who in the streets gives himself *fidalgo* airs and is overjoyed at the regard shown him by officials and who at home sings songs of battle as he sits at his work[1].

In the actions and conversation of this motley crowd of persons high and low we are given many a glimpse of the times: the beflagged ship from India lying in the Tagus, the modest dinner (*a panela cosida*) of the rich *lavrador*, the supper of bread and wine, shellfish and cherries bought in Lisbon's celebrated Ribeira market, the Lisbon Jew's dinner of kid and cucumber, the distaff bought by the shepherd at Santarem as a present for his love, the rustic gifts of acorns, bread and bacon, the shepherdess' simple dowry or the more considerable dowry of a girl somewhat higher in society (consisting of a loom, a donkey, an orchard, a mill and a mule), the migratory shepherds' ass, laden with the milk-jugs

---

[1] There are abundant signs of the cosmopolitanism of Lisbon: A Basque and a Castilian tavernkeeper, a Spanish seller of vinegar and a red-faced German friar are mentioned, while Spaniards, Jews, Moors, negroes, a Frenchman, an Italian are among Vicente's *dramatis personae*.

and bells, and with a leathern wallet, yokes and shackles, the sheepskin coats of the shepherds, bristling masks for their dogs (as a defence against wolves), loaves of bread, onions and garlic. Thus in town and village, palace and attic, house and street, on road and mountain and sea the Portugal of the early sixteenth century is clearly and charmingly conveyed to us, and we can realize better the conditions of Gil Vicente's life at Court or as he journeyed on muleback to Evora or Coimbra, Thomar or Santarem or Almeirim.

IV. ORIGINALITY AND INFLUENCE

In 1523 the 'men of good learning' doubted Vicente's originality. They might point to the imitations of Enzina or to the resemblance between the trilogy of *Barcas* and the *Danza de la Muerte* or they might reveal the origin of many a verse and phrase used by Vicente in his plays and already familiar in the song-books of Spain and Portugal. Vicente could well afford to let his critics strain at these gnats. He had the larger originality of genius and while realizing that 'there is nothing new under the sun[1]' he could transform all his borrowings into definite images or lyrical magic. (There are flashes of poetry even in the absurd *ensalada* of III. 323–4.) He was the greatest lyrical poet of his day and, in a strictly limited sense, the greatest dramatist. He is Portugal's only dramatist, without forerunners or successors, for the playwrights of the Vicentian school lacked his genius and only attain some measure of success when they closely copy their master, while the classical school produced no great drama in Portugal: it is impossible to except even Antonio Ferreira's *Ines de Castro* from this sweeping assertion. But that is not to say that Vicente stands entirely isolated, self-sufficing and self-contained. Genius is never self-sufficing. Talent may live apart in an ivory palace but genius overflows in many relations, is acted on and reacts and has the generosity to receive as well as to give. The influences that acted upon Gil Vicente were numerous: the Middle Ages and the humanism of the first days of the Renaissance, the old national Portugal with its popular traditions and the new imperial Portugal of the first third of the sixteenth century, the Bible and the *Cancioneiro de Resende*,

---

[1] It is very curious to find echoes of Enzina in Vicente's apparently quite personal prose as well as in his poetry. *No ay cosa que no esté dicha*, says Enzina, and Vicente repeats the wise quotation and imitates the whole passage. Enzina addressing the Catholic Kings speaks of himself as *muy flaca para navegar por el gran mar de vuestras alabanzas*. Vicente similarly speaks of 'crowding more sail on his poor boat.' Enzina, in his dedication to Prince Juan, mentions, like Vicente, *maliciosos* and *maldizientes*.

the whole literature of Spain and Portugal, the services of the Church, the book of Nature. But before examining how these influences work out in his plays it may be well to consider whether their sources may be yet further extended.

Court relations between Portugal and France had never entirely ceased and the 1516 *Cancioneiro* contains many allusions to the prevailing familiarity with things French. But Vicente's genius was not inspired by the Court: it would be truer to say that, while he was encouraged by Queen Lianor and the King, the Court's taste for new things, superficial fashions and personal allusions tended to thwart his genius. When he introduces a French song in his plays this does not imply any intimate acquaintance with the lyrical poetry of France but rather deference to the taste of the Court. He would pick up words of foreign languages with the same quickness with which he initiated himself into the way of witch or pilot, fishwife or doctor, but we have an excellent proof that his knowledge of neither French nor Italian was profound. We know how consistently he makes his characters speak each in his own language. Yet in the *Auto da Fama*, whereas the Spaniard speaks Spanish only, the Frenchman and Italian murder their own language and eke it out with Portuguese[1]. Vicente read what he could find to read, but we may be sure that his reading was mainly confined to Portuguese and Spanish. The very words in his letter to King João III in which he speaks of his reading are another echo of Enzina[2], and although it cannot be asserted that he was not acquainted with this or that piece of French literature and with the early French drama, it may be maintained that whatever influence France exercised upon him came mainly through Spain, whether the connecting link is extant, as in the case of the *Danza de la Muerte*, or lost, as in that of the *Sumario da Historia de Deos*. Probably Vicente knew of French *mystères* little more than the name[3]. As to the literature of Greece, Rome and Italy the conclusion is even more definite. Vicente had not read Plautus or Terence, his knowledge of *el gran poeta Virgilio* (III. 104) does not extend beyond the quotation *omnia vincit amor*. Aristotle is a name

---

[1] In this play the French *tais-toi* is written *tétoi*. In an age of few books such phonetic spelling must have been common. It has been suggested that the *vair* (grey) of early French poetry was mistaken for *vert* (green). The green eyes of the heroines in Portuguese literature from the *Cancioneiro da Vaticana* to Almeida Garrett would thus be based not on reality but, like Cinderella's glass slippers, on a confusion of homonyms (see Alfred Jeanroy, *Origines de la poésie lyrique en France*, p. 329).

[2] See his *Arte de Poesia Castellana*, ap. Menéndez y Pelayo, *Antología*, t. 5, p. 32.

[3] *Os autos de Gil Vicente resentem-se muito dos Mysterios franceses.* This was, in 1890, the opinion of Sousa Viterbo (*A Litteratura Hespanhola em Portugal* (1915), p. ix), but surely Menéndez y Pelayo's view is more correct.

et praeterea nihil. With the classical tragedy of Trissino and others he had nothing in common, and if he lived to read or see Sá de Miranda's *Cleopatra* he probably had his own very marked opinion as to its value. Dante was, of course, a closed book to him as to most of his contemporaries. With Spanish literature the case is very different. The fourteenth and fifteenth centuries were the most Spanish period of Portuguese literature. The *Cancioneiro de Resende* is nearly as Spanish as it is Portuguese. Portuguese poets were, almost without exception, bilingual. The horsemen stationed to bring the news of the wedding from Seville to Evora in 1490 were emblematic of the close relations between the two countries. Men were in continual expectation that they would come to form one kingdom[1]. King Manuel's infant son was heir to Spain and Portugal and the empires in Africa and America.

Vicente's close acquaintance with Spanish literature shows itself at every turn, and if we examine his plays we find but slight traces of the influence of any other literature. His first pieces were written in Spanish, and the Spanish is that of Enzina. Lines and phrases are taken bodily from the Spanish poet and words belonging to the conventional *sayagués* (in which there was already a Portuguese element: cf. *ollos* for *ojos*) placed on the lips of *charros* by Enzina are transferred from Salamanca to Beira. The Enzina eclogues imitated by Vicente were based on those of Virgil, but in Vicente's imitation there is no vestige of any knowledge of the classics. The only Latin that occurs is the quotation by Gil Terron of three lines from the Bible. A little later the hungry *escudero* of *Quem tem farelos?* was in all probability derived from Spanish literature, either from the Archpriest of Hita's *Libro de Buen Amor* or from some popular sketch such as that contained later in *Lazarillo de Tormes* (1554)[2]. The only French element in the *Auto da Fé* is the *fatrasie* or *enselada* 'which came from France,' but its text is not given. The classical allusions to Virgil and the Judgment of Paris in the *Auto das Fadas* are perfectly superficial. A little medical Latin is introduced in the *Farsa dos Fisicos*. *O Velho da Horta*, which opens with the Lord's Prayer, half in Latin, half in Portuguese[3], is written in Portuguese with the exception of the fragment of song and the lyric *¿Cual es la niña?* There is a reference to Macias, a name which had become a commonplace in Portuguese poetry as the type of the constant lover. Spanish influence is shown in the introduction of the *alcouviteira* Branca Gil, probably suggested by

---

[1] In Resende's *Miscellanea* the line *nõ hos quer deos jũtos ver* (1917 ed., p. 16) reads in the 1752 ed., f. 105 v. *ja hos quer.*

[2] Cf. *Tratado tercero: llevandolo a la boca começó a dar en el tan fieros bocados* (1897 ed., p. 50) and *Quem tem farelos?: e chanta nelle bocado coma cão* (I. 7).

[3] The *Canc. Geral* has a *Pater noster grosado por Luys anrryquez*, vol. III. (1913), p. 87.

Juan Ruiz' *trotaconventos* or by Celestina. The *Exhortação da Guerra* begins with humorous platitudes, *perogrulladas*, after the fashion of Enzina. Gil Terron has increased his classical lore, and Trojan and Greek heroes are brought from the underworld, the *dramatis personae* including Polyxena, Penthesilea, Achilles, Hannibal, Hector and Scipio. The influence of Enzina is still evident in the *Auto da Sibila Cassandra*, the *bellíssimo auto* wherein Menéndez y Pelayo saw the first germ of the symbolical *autos* in which Calderón excelled[1], and in the *Auto dos Quatro Tempos*. The immediate influence on the *Barcas* is plainly Spanish, this being especially marked in the *Barca da Gloria*. When the *Diabo* addresses the King:

> Nunca aca senti
> Que aprovechase aderencia
> Ni lisonjas, crer mentiras
> ...Ni diamanes ni zafiras (I. 285)

he is copying the words of Death in the *Danza de la Muerte*:

> non es tiempo tal
> Que librar vos pueda imperio nin gente
> Oro nin plata nin otro metal[2].

Vicente's Devil taxes the Archbishop with fleecing the poor (I. 294) in much the same words as those of the Spanish Death to the Dean (t. 2, p. 12). The Devil in the *Barca do Purgatorio* (I. 251) and Death (t. 2, p. 17) both reproach the *labrador* with the same offence: surreptitiously extending the boundaries of his land. It must be admitted that these signs of imitation are more direct than the French traces indicated in the introduction of the 1834 edition of Vicente's works. The whole treatment of the *Barcas* closely follows the *Danza de la Muerte*. The idea of a satirical review of the dead is of course nearly as old as literature. In the *Barca da Gloria* Vicente begins to quote Spanish *romances*[3], and this is continued on a larger scale in the *Comedia de Rubena* (cf. also the Spanish songs in the *Cortes de Jupiter*) and in *Dom Duardos*, in which reference is also made to two Spanish books, Diego de San Pedro's *Carcel de Amor* and Hernando Diaz' translation *El Pelegrino Amador*[4]. Maria Parda's will was probably suggested rather by such burlesque testaments as that of the dying mule in the *Cancioneiro de Resende* than by the

---

[1] *Antología*, t. 7, pp. clxxii, clxxiv. [2] *Antología*, t. 2, p. 6.

[3] I. 298. *Vuelta vuelta los Franceses* from the romance *Domingo era de Ramos, la Pasion quieren decir.*

[4] *Comedia de Rubena*, II. 40. The earliest known edition of the Spanish version of Jacopo Caviceo's *Il Pellegrino* (1508) is dated 1527 but that mentioned in Fernando Colón's catalogue (no. 4147) was no doubt earlier. In 1521 Vicente can already bracket the Spanish translation with the popular *Carcel de Amor* printed in 1492, and indeed it ran to many editions. Its full title was *Historia de los honestos amores de Peregrino y Ginebra*. Valdés (*Dialogo de la Lengua*) ranks *El Pelegrino* as a translation with Boscán's version of *Il Cortegiano: estan mui bien romançados.*

Testament de Pathelin. The criticism of the *homens de bom saber* seems to have turned Vicente to more peculiarly Portuguese themes in the *Farsa de Ines Pereira* and the *Auto Pastoril Portugues*, and in the *Fragoa de Amor*, written for the new Queen from Spain, he presents national types: *serranas*, pilgrims, nigger, monk, idiot. In the *Ciganas* we have a passing reference to 'the white hands of Iseult,' a lady already well known in Spanish and Portuguese literature. *Dom Duardos* is of course based entirely on a Spanish romance of chivalry. In *O Juiz da Beira* he returns to the *escudeiro* and *alcouviteira*; the figures are, however, thoroughly Portuguese with the exception of a new Christian from Castille. The title of the *Nao de Amores* already existed in Spanish literature[1]. After this we have a group of thoroughly Portuguese plays, those presented at Coimbra, the anticlerical *Auto da Feira*, the *Triunfo do Inverno*, *O Clerigo da Beira*. It is not till *Amadis de Gaula* that Vicente again has recourse to Spanish literature[2], and we may be sure that if he had known of a Portuguese text he would have written his drama in Portuguese.

Although Vicente owed much to Spanish literature we have only to compare his plays with those of Juan del Enzina or Bartolomé de Torres Naharro, or his first attempts with his later dramas to realize his genius and originality. The variety of his plays is very striking and the farce *Quem tem farelos?* (1508?), the patriotic *Exhortação* (1513), the *Barca* trilogy (1517–9), the religious *Auto da Alma* (1518), the three-act *Comedia de Rubena* (1521), the character comedy *Farsa de Ines Pereira* (1523), the idyllic *Dom Duardos* (1525?) mark new departures in the development of his genius. No doubt his plays are 'totally unlike any regular plays and rude both in design and execution[3].' Vicente divided them into religious plays (*obras de devaçam*), farces, comedies and tragi-comedies, but the kinds overlap and there is nothing to separate some of the comedies and tragicomedies from the farces, while some of the farces are religious both in subject and occasion. How artificial the division was may be seen from the rubric to the *Barca do Inferno*, which informs us that the play is counted among the religious plays because the second and third parts (*Barca do Purgatorio* and *Barca da Gloria*) were represented in the Royal Chapel, although this first part was given in the Queen's chamber, as though the subject and treatment of the three plays were not sufficient to class them together. Again, the rubric of the *Romagem de Aggravados* runs: 'The following tragicomedy is a satire.' Really only its length separates it from the early farces.

---

[1] E.g. the *Nao de Amor* of Juan de Dueñas.

[2] The Everyman-Noman theme in the *Auto da Lusitania* is, like that of *Mofina Mendes*, common to many countries and old as the hills.

[3] Henry Hallam, *Introduction to the Literature of Europe* (Paris, 1839), vol. I. p. 206.

Vicente's plays were a development of the earlier Christmas, Holy Week and Easter *representaciones*, religious shows to which special pomp was given at King Manuel's Court. When he began to write the classical drama was unknown and it is absurd to judge his work by the Aristotelean theory of the unities of time and place. His idea of drama was not dramatic action nor the development of character but realistic portrayal of types and the contrast between them. His first piece, *Auto da Visitaçam*, has not even dialogue—its alternative title is *O Monologo do Vaqueiro*—and for comic element it relies on the contrast between Court and country as shown by the herdsman's gaping wonder. The *Auto Pastoril Castelhano* contains six shepherds and contrasts the serious mystical Gil with his ruder companions.

The action of the *Auto dos Reis Magos* is as simple as that of the two preceding plays. *Quem tem farelos?* however is a quite new development. 'The argument,' says the rubric, 'is that a young squire called Aires Rosado played the viola and although his salary [as one of the Court] was very small he was continually in love.' He is contrasted with another penniless *escudeiro* who gives himself martial airs and willingly speaks of the heroic deeds of Roncesvalles, but runs away if two cats begin to fight. Only five persons appear on the stage, but with considerable skill Vicente enlarges the scene so as to include a vivid picture of the second squire as described by his servant as well as the barking of dogs, mewing of cats and crowing of cocks and the conversation of Isabel with Rosado, which is conjectured from his answers. No doubt the two *moços* owe something to Sempronio and Parmeno of the *Celestina*, but this first farce is thoroughly Portuguese and gives us a concrete and living picture of Lisbon manners. Not all the farces have this unity. The *Auto das Fadas* loses itself in a long series of verses addressed to the Court. The *Farsa dos Fisicos* has no such extraneous matter: it confines itself to the lovelorn priest and the contrast between the four doctors. The *Comedia do Viuvo* is not a farce and only a comedy by virtue of its happy ending. A merchant of Burgos laments the death of his wife and is comforted by a kindly priest and by a friend who wishes that his own wife were as the merchant's (the simple mediaeval contrast common in Vicente). Meanwhile Don Rosvel, Prince of Huxonia, has fallen in love with both the daughters of the merchant, whom he agrees to serve in all kinds of manual labour as Juan de las Brozas. His brother, Don Gilberto, arrives in search of him and a quaintly charming and technically skilful play ends with a double wedding (the Crown Prince of Portugal, present at the acting of this play, had to decide for Don Rosvel which daughter he should marry).

The *Auto da Fama* is Vicente's second great hymn to the glory of Portugal. Portuguese Fame, in the person of a humble girl of Beira, is envied and wooed in vain by Castille, France and Italy—England and Holland were then scarcely in the running—and narrates in ringing verses the deeds of the Portuguese in the East, without, however, mentioning the great name of Albuquerque, a name which inspired many of the courtiers with more fear than affection. The *Auto dos Quatro Tempos* is a pastoral-religious play, the main theme being, as its title indicates, a contrast between the four seasons. David appears as a shepherd and Jupiter also takes a considerable part in the conversation. Action there is none.

Vicente's satirical vein found excellent occasion in the ancient theme of scrutinizing the past lives of men as Death reaps them, high and low, but his profoundly religious temperament raises the *Barcas* into an atmo-sphere of sublime if gloomy splendour, which is surpassed in the *Auto da Alma*, the most perfect and consistent of his religious plays—even the symbolical character of the latter part can hardly be called a defect. In the *Comedia de Rubena* the development of Vicente's art is perhaps more superficial than real. It is divided into three long scenes or acts and is thus more like a regular comedy than his other plays. The acts, however, are isolated, the action occupies fifteen years and occurs in Castille, Lisbon and Crete. English readers of the play must be struck by its resemblance to *Pericles, Prince of Tyre*. Written fifty-five years before Lawrence Twine's *The Patterne of Painful Adventures* (1576) and eighty-seven before George Wilkins and William Shakespeare produced their play (1608), the *Comedia de Rubena* is in fact a link in a long chain beginning in a lost fifth century Greek romance concerning Apollonius of Tyre and continued after Gil Vicente's death in Timoneda's *Tarsiana* and in *Pericles*. Vicente, however, in all probability did not derive his Cismena, cold and chaste predecessor of Marina, from the *Gesta Romanorum* or the *Libro de Apolonio* but from the version in John Gower's *Confessio Amantis*, of which a translation, as we know, was early available in Portugal. After an exclusively Court piece, the *Cortes de Jupiter*, Vicente wrote the *Farsa de Ines Pereira*, in which there is more action and development of character than in his preceding, or indeed his subsequent, plays. He represents the aspirations and repentance of Ines, the 'very flighty daughter of a woman of low estate.' Despite the warnings of her sensible mother she rejects the suit of simple and uncouth Pero Marques for that of a gentleman (*escudeiro*) whose pretensions are far greater than his possessions. The mother gives them a house and retires to a small cottage. But the *escudeiro* married confirms the wisdom of the Sibyl Cassandra (i. 40). He keeps his wife shut up 'like a nun of Oudivellas.' The windows are nailed up, she is not allowed to leave the house even to go to church. Thus the hopes and ambitions of Ines Pereira de Grãa are tamed, although she was never a shrew[1]. Presently, however, the *escudeiro* resolves to cross over to Africa to win his knighthood:

> ás partes dalem
> Vou me fazer cavaleiro,

and he leaves his wife imprisoned in their house, the key being entrusted to the servant (*moço*). Ines, singing at her work, is declaring that if ever she have to choose another husband *on ne m'y prendra plus* when a letter arrives from her brother announcing that her husband, as he fled from battle towards Arzila, had been killed by a Moorish shepherd. The faithful Pero Marques again presses his suit. He is accepted and is made to suffer the whims and infidelity of the emancipated Ines. The question of women's rights was a burning one in the sixteenth century.

Vicente's versatility enabled him to laugh at his critics to the end of the chapter. In *Dom Duardos* he gave them an elaborate and very successful dramatization of a Spanish romance of chivalry. The treatment has both unity and lyrical charm. It was so successful that the experiment was repeated in 1533 with the earlier romance of *Amadis de Gaula* (1508), out of which Vicente wrought an equally skilful but less fascinating play[2]. But Vicente had not given up writing farces and the sojourn of Ines Pereira's husband in town enables the author to introduce various Lisbon types in *O Juiz da Beira*. It indeed completely resembles the early farces, while the *Auto da Festa* with its peasant scene and allegorical *Verdade* is of the *Auto da Fé* type but adds the theme of the old woman in search of a husband. The *Templo de Apolo*, composed for a special Court occasion, shows no development, but in the *Sumario* we have a fuller religious play than he had hitherto written. It proves, like *Dom Duardos*, his power of concentration and his skill in seizing on and emphasizing essential points in a long action (the period here covered is from Adam to Christ[3]). It is closely moulded on the Bible and contains, besides an exquisite *vilancete* (*Adorae montanhas*), passages of noble poetry and soaring fervour—Eve's invocation to Adam:

> Ó como os ramos do nosso pomar
> Ficam cubertos de celestes rosas (I. 314);

Job's lament 'Man that is born of woman' (I. 324); the paraphrase or

---

[1] Cf. the story *del mancebo que casó con una mujer muy fuerte et muy brava* in Don Juan Manuel's *El Conde Lucanor* (c. 1535). Shakespeare's *The Taming of the Shrew* was written exactly a century after *Ines Pereira*; the anonymous *Taming of a Shrew* in 1594.

[2] The author of a sixteenth century Spanish play published in *Biblióf. Esp.* t. 6 (1870) declares that, in order to write it, he has 'trastornado todo *Amadis y la Demanda del Sancto Grial* de pe a pa.' The result, according to the colophon, is 'un deleitoso jardin de hermosas y olientes flores,' a description which would better suit a Vicente-play.

[3] Cf. the twelfth century *Représentation d'Adam*. The *Sumario* has 18 figures. The *Auto da Feira* has 22, but over half of these consist of a group of peasants from the hills.

rather translation of 'I know that my Redeemer liveth' (I. 322). Nothing here, surely, to warrant the complaints of Sá de Miranda as to the desecration of the Scriptures. This play was followed by the *Dialogo sobre a Ressurreiçam* by way of epilogue; it is a conversation between three Jews and is treated in the cynical manner that Browning brought to similar scenes. The *Sumario* or *Auto da Historia de Deos* was acted before the Court at Almeirim and must have won the sincere admiration of the devout João III. If the courtiers were less favourably impressed they were mollified by the splendid display of the *Nao de Amores* with its much music, its Prince of Normandy and its miniature ship fully rigged. Vicente was now fighting an uphill battle and in the *Divisa da Cidade de Coimbra* he attempted a task beyond the strength of a poet and more suitable for a sermon such as Frei Heitor Pinto preached on the same subject: the arms of the city of Coimbra. Even Vicente could not make this a living play; it is, rather, a museum of antiquities and ends with praises of Court families. It is pathetic to find the merry satirist reduced to admitting (in the argument of this play) that merely farcical farces are not very refined. Yet we would willingly give the whole play for another brief farce such as *Quem tem farelos?*:

> Ya sabeis, senhores,
> Que toda a comedia começa em dolores,
> E inda que toque cousas lastimeiras
> Sabei que as farças todas chocarreiras
> Não sam muito finas sem outros primores (II. 108).

Fortunately he returned to the plain farce in *Os Almocreves*, the *Auto da Feira* and *O Clerigo da Beira* (which, however, ends with a series of Court references) with all his old wealth of satire, touches of comedy and vivid portraiture. He also returned to the pastoral play in the *Serra da Estrella*, while his exquisite lyrism flowers afresh in the *Triunfo do Inverno*, a tragicomedy which is really a medley of farces. It is not a great drama but it is a typical Vicentian piece, combining vividly sketched types with a splendid lyrical vein. Winter, that banishes the swallows and swells the voice of ocean streams, first triumphs on hills and sea and then Spring comes in singing the lovely lyric *Del rosal vengo* in the Serra de Sintra. The play ends on a serious and mystic note, for Spring's flowers wither but those of the holy garden of God bloom without fading:

> E o santo jardim de Deos
> Florece sem fenecer.

The *Auto da Lusitania* is divided into two parts, the first of which is complete in itself and gives a description of a Jewish household at

Lisbon, while the second is a medley which contains the celebrated
scene of Everyman and Noman: Everyman seeks money, worldly
honour, praise, life, paradise, lies and flattery; Noman is for conscience,
virtue, truth. In the *Romagem de Aggravados* the fashionable and
affected Court priest, Frei Paço, is the connecting link for a series of
farcical scenes in which a peasant brings his son to become a priest,
two noblemen discourse on love, two fishwives lament the excesses of
the courtiers, Cerro Ventoso and Frei Narciso betray their mounting
ambition, civil and ecclesiastic, the poor farmer Aparicianes implores
Frei Paço to make a Court lady of his slovenly daughter, two nuns
bewail their fate and two shepherdesses discuss their marriage prospects.
The *Auto da Mofina Mendes* is especially celebrated because Mofina
Mendes, personification of ill-luck, with her pot of oil is the forerunner
of La Fontaine's *Pierrette et son pot au lait*: it was perhaps suggested to
Vicente by the tale of Doña Truhana's pot of honey in *El Conde Lucanor*;
the theme of counting one's chickens before they are hatched also forms
the subject of one of the *pasos*, entitled *Las Aceitunas*, of the goldbeater
of Seville, Lope de Rueda[1]. Vicente's piece consists, like some picture of
El Greco, of a *gloria*, called, as Rueda's scenes, a *passo*, in which appear
the Virgin and the Virtues (Prudence, Poverty, Humility and Faith) and
an earthly shepherd scene. It is thus a combination of farce and religious
and pastoral play. Vicente's last play, the *Floresta de Enganos*, is composed of scenes so disconnected that one of them is even omitted in the
summary given after the first deceit: that in which a popular traditional
theme, derived directly or indirectly from a French (perhaps originally
Italian) source, *Les Cent Nouvelles Nouvelles*, is presented, akin to that
so piquantly narrated by Alarcón in *El Sombrero de Tres Picos* in the
nineteenth century, the judge playing the part of the Corregidor and the
malicious and sensible servant-girl that of the miller's wife.

In these last plays we see little or no advance: there is no attempt
at unity or development of plot. We cannot deny that the creator
of the penniless-splendid nobleman and the mincing courtier-priest
and the author of such touches as the death of Ines' husband or
the sudden ignominious flight of the judge possessed a true vein of
comedy, but he remained to the end not technically a great dramatist
but a wonderful lyric poet and a fascinating satirical observer of life.
His influence was felt throughout the sixteenth and seventeenth centuries
in Portugal, by Camões and in the plays of Chiado, Prestes and a score of
less celebrated dramatists, as well as in a considerable number of anonymous plays, but confined itself to the *auto*, which, combated by the

[1] *Obras* (1908), t. 2, p. 217–24.

followers of the classical drama and the Latin plays of the Jesuits, soon tended to deteriorate and lose its charm. In Spain his influence would seem to have been more widely felt, which is not surprising when we remember how many of his plays were Spanish in origin or language[1]. We may be sure that Lope de Rueda was acquainted with his plays and that several of them were known to Cervantes—the servant Benita insisting on telling her simple stories to her afflicted mistress is Sancho Panza to the life:

> *Benita.* Diz que era un escudero....
> *Rubena.* O quien no fuera nacida:
> ¿ Viendome salir la vida
> Paraste a contar patrañas?
> *Benita.* Pues otra sé de un carnero....

Lope de Vega was likewise certainly familiar with some of Vicente's plays. If we consider these passages in *El Viaje del Alma*, the *representación moral* contained in *El Peregrino en su Patria* (1604), we must be convinced that the trilogy of *Barcas*, the *Auto da Alma*, and perhaps the *Nao de Amores* were not unknown to him:

> Alma para Dios criada
> Y hecha a imagen de Dios, etc.;
>
> Hoy la Nave del deleite
> Se quiere hacer a la mar:
> ¿ Hay quien se quiera embarcar?;
>
> Esta es la Nave donde cabe
> Todo contento y placer[2].

The alleged imitation by Calderón in *El Lirio y la Azucena* is perhaps more doubtful. Vicente was already half forgotten in Calderón's day. In the artificial literature of the eighteenth century he suffered total eclipse although Correa Garção was able to appreciate him, nor need we see any direct influence in that of the nineteenth[3] except that on Almeida Garrett: the similar passages in Goethe's *Faust* and Cardinal Newman's *Dream of Gerontius* were no doubt purely accidental. Happily, however, we are able to point to a certain influence of the great national poet of Portugal on some of the Portuguese poets of the twentieth century. The promised edition of his plays will increase this influence and render him secure from that neglect which during three centuries practically deprived Portugal and the world of one of the most charming and inspired of the world's poets.

---

[1] The anonymous *Tragicomedia Alegórica del Paraiso y del Infierno* (Burgos, 1539) followed hard upon his death. It is not the work of Vicente, who, although in his Spanish he used *allen*, would not have translated *nas partes de alem* into an African town: *en Allen*.

[2] *3a impr.* (Madrid, 1733), p. 35; p. 37 (the 1733 text has *Oi* and *Ai*); p. 39.

[3] As late as 1870 Dr Theophilo Braga could say 'Nobody now studies Vicente' (*Vida de Gil Vicente*, p. 59).

COPILACAM

DE TODALAS OBRAS

DE GIL VICENTE, A QVAL SE
reparte em cinco Liuros. O Primeyro he de todas suas
cousas de deuaçam. O segundo as Comedias O terceyro as Tragicomedias. No quarto as Far-
las. No quinto, às obras
meudas.

(;)

¶ Vam emmendadas polo Sancto Officio,
como se manda no Cathalogo
deste Regno.

¶

¶ Foy impresso em amuy nobre & sempre leal Cidade de Lixboa, por Andres Lob·to.
Anne de M. D. Lxxxvj

¶ Foy visto polos Deputados da Sancta Inquisiçam

COM PRIVILEGIO REAL.
(.˙.)

¶ Esta taxado em papel a   reis

TITLE-PAGE OF THE SECOND (1586) EDITION OF
GIL VICENTE'S WORKS

AUTO DA ALMA

L'Angel di Dio mi prese e quel d' Inferno
Gridava: O tu dal Ciel, perchè mi privi?

DANTE, Purg. v.

Auto da Alma.

Este auto presente foy feyto aa muyto deuota raynha dona Lianor & representado ao muyto poderoso & nobre Rey dom Emmanuel, seu yrmão, por seu mandado, na cidade de Lisboa nos paços da ribeyra em a noyte de endoenças. Era do Senhor de M.D. & viij[1].

Argvmento.

Assi como foy cousa muyto necessaria auer nos caminhos estalagens pera repouso & refeyçam dos cansados caminhantes, assi foy cousa conveniente que nesta caminhante vida ouuesse hũa estalajadeyra para refeição & descanso das almas que vam caminhantes pera a eterna morada[2] de Deos. Esta estalajadeyra das almas he a madre sancta ygreja, a mesa he o altar, os mãjares as insignias da payxã. E desta perfiguraçã[3] trata a obra seguinte.

¶ Está posta hũa mesa cõ hũa cadeyra: vẽ a madre sancta ygreja cõ seus quatro doctores, Sancto Thomas, Sam Hieronymo, Sancto Ambrosio, Sancto Agostinho, & diz Agostinho.

AGOST. Necessario foy, amigos,
que nesta triste carreyra
desta vida
pera os mui perigosos perigos
dos immigos
ouuesse algũa maneyra
de guarida.
Porque a humana transitoria
natureza vay cansada

The Soul's Journey.

This play was written for the very devout Queen Lianor and played before the very powerful and noble King Manuel, her brother, by his command, in the city of Lisbon at the Ribeira palace on the night of Good Friday in the year 1508.

Argument.

As it was very necessary that there should be inns upon the roads for the repose and refreshment of weary wayfarers, so it was fitting that in this transitory life there should be an innkeeper for the refreshment and rest of the souls that go journeying to the everlasting abode of God. This innkeeper of souls is the Holy Mother Church, the table is the altar, the fare the emblems of the Passion. And this allegory is the theme of the following play.

(A table laid, with a chair. The Holy Mother Church comes with her four doctors, St Thomas, St Jerome, St Ambrose and St Augustine, who says:)

1 *St Aug.* Friends, 'twas of necessity
That upon the gloomy way
Of this our life
Some sure refuge there should be
From the enemy
And dread dangers that alway
Therein are rife.
2 Since man's spirit migratory
In the journey to its goal

---

[1] *MDXVIII.* A. Braamcamp Freire.   [2] *pera eterna morada* B.   [3] *prefiguraçã* B.

1.   *pera mui p'rigosos p'rigos* C.   *imigos* C.

em varias calmas
nesta carreyra da gloria
meritoria
foi necessario pensada
pera as almas.

¶ Pousada com mantimentos,
mesa posta em clara luz,
sempre esperando,
com dobrados mantimentos
dos tormentos
que o filho de Deos na Cruz
comprou penando.
Sua morte foy auença,
dando, por darnos parayso,
a sua vida
apreçada sem detença,
por sentença
julgada a paga em prouiso
& recebida.

¶ Ha sua mortal empresa
foy sancta estalajadeyra
ygreja madre
consolar aa sua despesa
nesta mesa
qualquer alma caminheyra
com ho padre
e o anjo custodio ayo.
Alma que lhe he encomendada
se enfraquece
& lhe vay tomando rayo
de desmayo
se chegando a esta pousada
se guarece.

¶ Vẽ o anjo custodio cõ a alma &
    diz.

Anjo. ¶ Alma humana formada
de nenhũa cousa feyta
muy preciosa,
de corrupçam separada,
& esmaltada
naquella fragoa perfeyta
gloriosa;

¶ planta neste valle posta
pera dar celestes flores
olorosas

Is oft oppressed,
Weary in this transitory
Path to glory,
An inn was needed for the soul
To stay and rest.

3 An inn provided with its fare,
In clear light a table spread
Expectantly,
And laden with a double share
Of torments rare
That the Son of God, His life-blood
Bought on the Treé.   [shed,

4 Since by the covenant of His death
He gave, to give us Paradise,
Even His life,
Unwavering He rendereth
For us His breath,
Paying the full required price
Free from all strife.

5 His work as man was to enable
Our Mother Church thus to console,
Innkeeper lowly,
And minister at this very table,
Most serviceable,
Unto every wayfaring soul,
With the Father Holy

6 And its Guardian Angel's care.
The soul to her protection given
If, weak with, sin
And yielding almost to despair,
It onward fare
And to reach this inn have striven,
Finds health within.

(*The Guardian Angel comes with the
    Soul and says:*)

7 *Angel.* Human soul, by God created
Out of nothingness yet wrought
As of great price,
From corruption separated,
Sublimated,
To glorious perfection brought
By skilled device;

8 Plant that in this valley growest
Flowers celestial for to give
Of fairest scent,

2. *pensada* A, B; *pousada* C. *passada?* cf. infra 73 and J. Ruiz *Cantar de Ciegos.*
De los bienes deste siglo No tiuemos nos *pasada.*
    3. *Pousada com alimentos?*   4. *apressada* C.   6. *em chegando?*

& pera serdes tresposta
em a alta costa
onde se criam primores
mais que rosas;
planta soes & caminheyra,
que ainda que estais vos his
donde viestes;
vossa patria verdadeyra
he ser herdeyra
da gloria que conseguis,
anday prestes.

¶ Alma bemauenturada,
dos anjos tanto querida,
nam durmais,
hum punto nam esteis parada,
que a jornada
muyto em breue he fenecida
se atentais.

ALMA. Anjo que soes minha guarda
Olhay por minha fraqueza
terreal:
de toda a parte aja resguarda
que nam arda
a minha preciosa riqueza
principal.

¶ Cercayme sempre oo redor
porque vin muy temerosa
da contenda:
Oo precioso defensor,
meu favor,
vossa espada lumiosa
me defenda.

¶ Tende sempre **mão em mim**
porque ey medo de empeçar
& de cayr.

ANJO. Pera isso sam & a isso vim
mas em fim
cumpreuos de me ajudar
a resistir.
Nam vos occupem vaydades,
riquezas nem seus debates,
olhay por vos:
que pompas, honrras, herdades,
& vaydades
sam embates & combates
pera vos.

¶ Vosso liure aluidrio,
isento, forro, poderoso,

Hence to that high hill thou goest
Where thou knowest
Even than roses graces thrive
More excellent.

9 Plant wayfaring, since thy spirit,
Scarce staying, to its first origin
Must still begone,
Thy true country is to inherit
By thy merit
That glory that thou mayest win:
O hasten on.

10 Soul that art thus trebly blest
By such angels' love attended,
Sink not asleep,
Nor one instant pause nor rest,
Thou journeyest
On a way that soon is ended
If watch thou keep.

11 *Soul.* Guardian angel, o'er me still
Keep thy ward that am so frail
And of the earth,
On all sides thy watch fulfil
That nothing kill
My true wealth nor e'er prevail
O'er its high worth.

12 Ever encompass me and shield,
For this conflict with great fear
Fills all my sense,
Noble protector in this field,
Lest I should yield,
Let thy gleaming sword be near
For my defence.

13 Still uphold me and sustain
For I fear lest I may stumble,
Fail and fall.
Angel. Therefore came I, nor in vain,
Yet amain
Must thou help me too, and humble
Resist all:

14 Even all the world's debate
Of riches and of vanity,
Seek thou for grace,
Since pomp and honour, high estate
Vainly elate,
Are but a stumbling-block to thee,
No resting-place.

15 Power uncontrolled is thine,
And an independent will

13. *a resistir* A, B, C; *e resistir* D.

vos he dado
pollo diuinal poderio
& senhorio,
que possais fazer glorioso
vosso estado.
Deuvos liure entendimento
& vontade libertada
& a memoria,
que tenhais em vosso tento
fundamento
que soes por elle criada
pera a gloria.

¶ E vendo Deos que o metal,
em que vos pos a estilar
pera merecer,
que era muyto fraco & mortal,
& por tal
me manda a vos ajudar
& defender.
Andemos a estrada nossa,
olhay nam torneis a tras
que o ĩmigo
aa vossa vida gloriosa
pora grosa.
Nam creaes a Satanas,
vosso perigo.

¶ Continuay ter cuydado
na fim de vossa jornada
& a memoria
que o spirito atalayado
do peccado
caminha sem temer nada
pera a gloria.
e nos laços infernaes
& nas redes de tristura
tenebrosas
da carreyra que passaes
nam cayaes:
sigua vossa fermosura
as gloriosas.

¶ Adiantase o Anjo e vem o diabo a ella
e diz o diabo.

¶ Tam depressa, oo delicada
alua pomba, pera onde his?
quem vos engana,
& vos leua tam cansada
por estrada

Unbound by fate:
Even so in His might divine
Did God design
That thou in glory mightst fulfil
Thy heavenly state.

16 He gave thee understanding pure,
Imparted to thee memory,
Free will is thine,
That so thou mayest e'er endure
With purpose sure,
Knowing that He has fashioned thee
To be divine.

17 And since God knew the mortal frame
Wherein He placed thee to distil,
(So to win His praise)
Was metal weak and prone to shame,
Therefore I came
Thee to protect—it was His will—
And to upraise.

18 Let us go forth upon our way.
Turn not thou back, for then indeed
The enemy
Upon thy glorious life straightway
Will make assay.
But unto Satan pay no heed
Who lurks for thee.

19 And still the goal seek thou to win
Carefully at thy journey's end,
And be it clear
That the spirit e'er at watch within
Against all sin
Upon salvation's path may wend
Without a fear.

20 In snares of Hell that shall waylay,
Dark and awful wiles among,
Thee to molest,
As thou advancest on thy way
Fall not nor stray,
But let thy beauty join the throng
Of spirits blest.

(*The Angel goes forward and the Devil
comes to the Soul and says:*)

21 *Devil*   Whither so swift thy flight,
Delicate dove most white?
Who thus deceives thee?
And weary still doth goad
Along this road,

18. *atras* B.   *imigo* B.   20.   *trestura* B.   *vem o Diabo e diz* C.

que soomente nam sentis
se soes humana?
Nam cureis de vos matar
que ainda estais em idade
de crecer.
Tempo hahi pera folgar
& caminhar,
Viuey aa vossa vontade
& a avey prazer.
¶ Gozay, gozay dos b̃es da terra,
procuray por senhorios
& aueres.
Quẽ da vida vos desterra
aa triste serra?
quem vos falla em desuarios
por prazeres?
Esta vida he descanso
doce & manso,
nam cureis doutro parayso:
quem vos põe em vosso siso
outro remanso?
ALMA. ¶ Nam me detenhaes aqui,
Deyxayme yr, q̃ em al me fundo.

DIABO. Oo descansay neste mundo,
que todos fazem assi.
Nam sam em balde os aueres,
Nam sam em balde os deleytes
& farturas*,
nam sam de balde os prazeres
& comeres,
tudo sam puros affeytes
das creaturas:
pera os hom̃es se criarão.
Dae folga a vossa possagem
doje a mais,
descansay, pois descansarão
os que passaram
por esta mesma romagem
que leuais.
O que a vontade quiser,
quanto o corpo desejar,
tudo se faça:
zombay de quem vos quiser
reprender,
querendovos marteyrar

Yea and of human sense,
Even, bereaves thee?
22 Seek not to hasten hence
Since thou hast life and youth
For further growth.
There is a time for haste,
A time for leisure:
Live at thy will and rest,
Taking thy pleasure.
23 Enjoy, enjoy the goods of Earth,
And great estates seek to possess
And worldly treasures.
Who to the hills, exiled from mirth,
Thus sends thee forth?
Who speaks to thee of foolishness
Instead of pleasures?
24 This life is all a pleasaunce fair,
Soft, debonair,
Look for no other paradise:
Who bids thee seek, with false advice,
Refuge elsewhere?
25 *Soul.* Hinder me not here nor stay,
For far other thoughts are mine.
Devil. To worldly ease thy thought
  incline
Since all men incline this way.
26 And not for nothing are delights,
And not in vain possessions sent
And fortune's prize,
And not for nought are pleasure's
And banquet-nights: [rites
All these are for man's ornament
And galliardize;
27 For mortal men is their array.
So let delight thy woes assuage,
Henceforth recline
And rest, since rest likewise had they
Who went this way,
Even this very pilgrimage
That now is thine.
28 And whatsoe'er thy body crave,
Even as thy will desire,
So let it be;
And laugh thou at the censors grave,
Whoso would have
Thee torturèd by sufferings dire

---

22. *E havei prazer* C.
26. *nam som em balde os deleytes* B.
27. *possagem* A, B; *passagem* C.

23. *& auereis?* B. *que da vida vos desterra* B.
fortunas A, B, C, D, E. *criaturas* C.

tam de graça.
Tornarame se a vos fora,
his tam triste, atribulada
que he tormenta:
senhora, vos soes senhora
emperadora,
nam deueis a ninguem nada,
sede isenta.

Anjo. Oo anday, quem vos detem?
Como vindes pera a gloria
devagar!
Oo meu Deos, oo summo bem!
Ja ninguem
nam se preza da vitoria
em se saluar.
Ja cansais, alma preciosa?
Tão asinha desmayaes?
Sede esforçada:
Oo como virieis trigosa
& desejosa,
se visseis quanto ganhaes
nesta jornada.
Caminhemos, caminhemos,
esforçay ora, alma sancta
esclarecida.

¶ Adiantase o anjo & torna Satanas.

Que vaydades & que estremos
tam supremos!
Pera que he essa pressa tanta?
Tende vida.
¶ His muy desautorizada,
descalça, pobre, perdida
de remate,
nam leuais de vosso nada
amargurada:
assi passais esta vida
em disparate.
¶ Vesti ora este brial,
metey o braço por aqui,
ora esperay.
Oo como vem tão real!
isto tal
me parece bem a mi:
ora anday.

So uselessly.

29 I would not, being thou, go forth,
So sad and troubled lies the way,
'Tis cruelty,
And thou art of imperial worth
And royal birth,
To none thou needest homage pay,
Then be thou free.

30 *Angel.* O who thus hinders thee?
On, on!
How loiterest thou on glory's path
So slowly!
O God, sole consolation!
Now is there none
Who of that victory honour hath
That is most holy.

31 Soul, already dost thou tire
Sinking so soon beneath thy burden?
Nay, soul, take heart!
Ah, with what a glowing fire
Of desire
Cam'st thou couldst thou see what
Were then thy part.   [guerdon

32 Forward, forward let us go:
Be of good cheer, O soul made holy
By this thy strife.

(*The Angel goes forward and Satan
returns.*)

Devil. But what is all this coil and
woe?
Why to and fro
Flutterest thou in haste and folly?
Nay, live thy life.

33 For very piteous is thy plight,
Poor, barefoot, ruined utterly,
In bitterness,
Carrying nothing to delight
As thine by right,
And all thy life is thus to thee
A thing senseless.

34 But don this dress, thy arm goes there,
Put it through now, even thus, now
Awhile. What grace,   [stay
What finery! I do declare
It pleases me. Now walk away
A little space.

Hũs chapins aueis mister
de Valença, muy fermosos*,
eylos aqui:
Agora estais vos molher
de parecer.
Pŏde os braços presumptuosos,
isso si,
passeayuos muy pomposa,
¶ daqui pera ali & de laa por ca,
& fantasiay.
Agora estais vos fermosa
como a rosa,
tudo vos muy bem estaa:
descansay.

     Torna o anjo a alma dizẽdo.

ANJO. ¶ Que andais aqui fazendo?

ALMA. Faço o q̃ vejo fazer
pollo mundo.
ANJO. Oo Alma, hisuos perdẽdo,
correndo vos his meter
no profundo.
Quanto caminhais auante
tanto vos tornais a tras
& a trauees,
tomastes ante com ante
por marcante
o cossayro satanas
porque querees.
¶ Oo caminhay com cuydado
que a Virgem gloriosa
vos espera:
deyxais vosso principado
desherdado,
engeytais a gloria vossa
& patria vera.
Deyxay esses chapins oɩa
& esses rabos tam sobejos,
que his carregada,
nam vos tome a morte agora
tam senhora,
nem sejais com tais desejos
sepultada.

35 So: I trow shoes are now thy need
    With a pair from Valencia, fair to see,
    I thee endow.
    Now beautiful, as I decreed,
    Art thou indeed;
    Now fold thy arms presumptuously:
    Ev'n so; and now
36 Strut airily, show off thy power,
    This way and that and up and down
    Just as thou please;
    Fair now as fairest rose in flower
    Thy beauty's dower,
    And all becomes thee as thine own:
    Now take thine ease.

(*The Angel returns to the Soul, saying:*)

37 *Angel.* What is this that thou art
    doing?
    Soul. In the world's mirror ev'n as
    I see
    I do in this.
    Angel. O soul, thou compassest thy
    And rushest forward foolishly [ruin
    To the abyss.
38 For every step that onward fares
    One step back, one step aside
    Thou takest still,
    And buyest eagerly the wares
    That pirate bears,
    Even Satan, by thee glorified
    Of thy free will.
39 O journey onward still with care
    For the Virgin with the elect
    Doth thee await:
    Thou leavest desolate and bare
    Thy kingdom rare,
    And thine own glory dost reject
    And true estate.
40 But cast these slippers now aside,
    This gaudy dress and its long train,
    Thou art all bowed,
    Lest Death come on thee unespied
    And in thy pride
    These thy desires and trappings vain
    Prove but thy shroud.

---

35. *Huns chapins aueis mister De Valença, eylos aqui* A, B, C, D, E.
36. *de la pera ca* C.
38. *marcante* A, B; *mercante* C, D.   *querês* C, D.

ALMA. ¶ Anday, day me ca essa mão:
anday vos, que eu yrey
quanto poder.

Adiãtese o anjo & torna o diabo.

DIABO. Todas as cousas cõ rezão
tem çazam.
Senhora, eu vos direy
meu parecer:
hahi tempo de folgar
& idade de crecer
& outra idade
de mandar e triumphar,
& apanhar
& acquirir prosperidade
a que poder.
¶ Ainda he cedo pera a morte:
tempo ha de arrepender
e yr ao ceo.
Pondevos a for da corte,
desta sorte
viua vosso parecer,
que tal naceo.
O ouro pera que he?
& as pedras preciosas
& brocados,
& as sedas pera que?
Tende per fee
q̃ pera as almas mais ditosas
foram dados*.
¶ Vedes aqui hum colar
douro muy bem esmaltado
& dez aneis.
Agora estais vos pera casar
& namorar:
neste espelho vos vereis
& sabereis
q̃ nam vos ey de enganar.
E poreis estes pendentes,
em cada orelha seu,
isso si,

41 *Soul.* Go forward, stretch thy hand
to save,
Go forward, I will follow thee
As best I may.

(*The Angel goes forward and the Devil
returns.*)

Devil. All things in light of reason
grave
Their seasons have.
And I to thee will, O lady,
My counsel say:
42 There is a time here for delight
And an age is given for growth,
Another age
To tread in lordly triumph's might
In the world's despite,
Gaining ease and riches both
On life's full stage.
43 It is too early yet to die,
Time later to repent on earth
And to seek Heaven.
Then cease with fashion's rule to vie,
And quietly
Enjoy the nature that at birth
To thee was given.
44 What, think'st thou, is the use for gold
And what the use for precious stones
And for brocade,
And all these silks so manifold?
Ah surely hold
That for the souls, the blessed ones,
They were all made.
45 See here a necklace in its pride
Of skilfully enamelled gold,
Here are rings ten:
Now mayst thou win the hearts of
Fit for a bride.   [men,
In this mirror thou mayst behold
Thyself and see
That I am not deceiving thee.
46 And here are ear-rings, put them on
One in each ear duly now:
Even so;

---

41. *poder* A; *puder* B, C. *Todas cousas com razão Tem sazão* C.
42. *poder* A, B; *puder* C.
43. *naceo* A, B; *nasceo* C (cf. infra 102 *nascido* A; 106 *nascido* A).
44. *dadas* A, B; *dados* C.
45. *esmaltados* B. *neste espelho & sabereis* B. *Neste espelho bem lavrado Vos vereis?*
(omitting *& sabereis—enganar*).   46. *em cada orelha o seu* B.

que as pessoas diligentes
sam prudentes:
agora vos digo eu
que vou contente daqui.

ALMA. ¶ Oo como estou preciosa,
tam dina pera seruir
& sancta pera adorar!
ANJO. Oo alma despiadosa,
perfiosa,
quem vos deuesse fugir
mais que guardar!
Pondes terra sobre terra,
que esses ouros terra sam:
oo senhor,
porque permites tal guerra
que desterra
ao reyno da confusam
o teu lauor?
¶ Nam hieis mais despejada
& mais liure da primeyra
pera andar?
Agora estais carregada
& embaraçada
com cousas que ha derradeyra
ham de ficar.
Tudo isso se descarrega
ao porto da sepultura:
alma sancta, quem vos cega,
vos carrega
dessa vaã desauentura?

ALMA. Isto nam me pesa nada
mas a fraca natureza
me embaraça.
Ja nam posso dar passada
de cansada:
tanta é minha fraqueza
& tam sem graça.
Senhor hidevos embora,
que remedio em mi nam sento,
ja estou tal.
ANJO. Sequer day dous passos ora
atee onde mora
a que tem o mantimento
celestial.
¶ Ireis ali repousar,

For things thus diligently done
Prove wisdom won,
And now I may to thee avow
That right well pleased I hence shall
go.
47 *Soul*. O how lovely is my state,
How is it for service meet,
And for holy adoration!
Angel. Cruel soul and obstinate,
Rather thereat
Should I shun thee than still treat
Of thy salvation.
48 Earth upon earth is this thy store,
Since but earth is all this gold.
O God most high,
Wherefore permittest thou such war
That, as of yore,
To Babel's kingdom from thy fold
Thy creatures hie?
49 Was it not easier journeying
At first, more free than that thou hast
With all this train,
Hampered and bowed with many a
That now doth cling   [thing
About thee, but which at the last
Must here remain?
50 All is disgorged and left behind
At the entrance to the tomb.
Who, holy soul, doth thee thus blind
Thyself to bind
With such vain misfortune's doom?
51 *Soul*. Nay, this doth scarcely on me
weigh:
It is my poor weak mortal nature
That bows me down.
So weary am I, I must stay
Nor go my way,
So void of grace, so frail a creature
Am I now grown.
52 Sir, go thy way: I cannot strive
Nor hope now further to advance,
So fallen I.
Angel. But two steps more to where
She who will give   [doth live
To thee celestial sustenance
Charitably.
53 Thither shalt thou go and rest,

47. *despiedosa* C.
50. *van* C.

49. *á derradeira* C.
52. *mim* C.

comereis algũs bocados
confortosos,
porque a hospeda he sem par
em agasalhar
os que vem atribulados
& chorosos.
ALMA. He lõge?
ANJO.   Aqui muy perto.
Esforçay, nam desmayeis
& andemos,
que ali ha todo concerto
muy certo:
quantas cousas querereis
tudo temos*.

¶ A hospeda tem graça tanta,
faruosha tantos fauores.

ALMA. Quem he ella?
ANJO. He a madre ygreja sancta,
e os seus sanctos doutores
i com ella.
Ireis di muy despejada
chea do Spirito Sancto
& muy fermosa:
ho alma sede esforçada,
outra passada,
que nam tendes de andar tãto
a ser esposa.

DIABO. ¶ Esperay, onde vos his?
Essa pressa tam sobeja
He ja pequice.
Como, vos que presumis
consentis
continuardes a ygreja
sem velhice?
Dayuos, dayuos a prazer,
q̃ muytas horas ha nos annos
que laa vem.
Na hora que a morte vier
Como xiquer
se perdoão quantos dannos
a alma tem.
Olhay por vossa fazenda:
tendes hũas scripturas
de hũs casais

And shalt taste there of that fare
New strength to borrow:
Unrivalled is that hostess blest
To give of the best
To those who weeping come to her,
Laden with sorrow.
54 *Soul.* Is it far off?
   Angel.   Nay, very near.
   Be not downcast, but now be brave,
   And let us go,
   For every remedy and cheer
   Is certain here.
   And whatsoever thou wouldst have
   We can bestow.
55 Such grace is hers that nought can
      smirch,
   Such favours will she show to thee,
   That innkeeper.
   Soul. Her name?
   Angel. The Holy Mother Church.
   And holy doctors thou shalt see
   Are there with her.
56 Joyful thence shall thy going be,
   Filled then with the Holy Spirit
   And beautified:
   O soul, take heart, courageously
   One step for thee,
   Nay, scarce one step, and thou shalt
   To be a bride.   [merit
57 *Devil.* Stay, whither art thou going
      now?
   Such haste is mere unseemly rage
   And foolishness:
   What, thou so puffed with pride,
   Thus meekly bow   [canst thou
   To go on churchward e'er old age
   Doth on thee press?
58 Let pleasure, pleasure rule thy ways,
   For many hours in years to roll
   To thee are given,
   And when death comes to end thy
   If prayer thou raise,   [days,
   Then all sins that can vex a soul
   Shall be forgiven.
59 Look to thy wealth and property:
   There is a group of houses should
   Be thine by right,

54. *muito certo?; tudo tendes* A, B, C, D, E.   56. *Siprito* B.
58. *como se quer* C.   59. *escripturas* C.

de que perdeis grande renda.
He contenda
que leyxarão aas escuras
vossos pays;
he demanda muy ligeyra,
litigios que sam vencidos
em um riso:
citay as partes terça feyra
de maneyra
como nam fiquem perdidos
& auey siso.
ALMA. Calte por amor de deos
leyxame, nam me persigas,
bem abasta
estoruares os ereos
dos altos ceos,
que a vida em tuas brigas
se me gasta.
Leyxame remediar
o que tu cruel danaste
sem vergonha,
que nam me posso abalar
nem chegar
ao logar onde gaste
esta peçonha.
ANJO. ¶ Vedes aqui a pousada
verdadeyra & muy segura
a quem quer vida.
YGREJA. Oo como vindes cansada
& carregada !
ALMA. Venho por minha ventura
amortecida.
YGREJA. Quem sois? pera onde
andais?
ALMA. Nam sey pera onde vou,
sou saluagem,
sou hũa alma que peccou
culpas mortaes
contra o Deos que me criou
aa sua imagem.
¶ Sou a triste, sem ventura,
criada resplandecente
& preciosa,
angelica em fermosura
& per natura
come rayo reluzente
lumiosa.
E por minha triste sorte

Great source of income would they
Unhappily   [be,
At thy parents' death the matter stood
In no clear light.
60 The case is simple, 'tis averred
Such lawsuits in a trice are won
At laughter's spell:
Next Tuesday let the case be heard
And, in a word,
Finish thou well what is begun.
Be sensible.
61 *Soul.* O silence, for the love of God,
Persecute me no more: thy hate
Doth it not suffice
High Heaven's heirs that it hinder
From their abode?   [should
My life to thee early and late
I sacrifice.
62 But leave me: so I may efface
The cruel wrong that shamelessly
Thou hast thus wrought;
For now I have scarce breathing-
To reach that place   [space
Where for this poison there may be
Some antidote.
63 *Angel.* See the inn: a sure retreat,
Even for all those a true home
Who would have life.
Church. O laden with sore toil and
O tired feet !   [heat !
Soul. Yea, for I destined was to come
Weary of strife.
64 *Church.* Who art thou? whither
wouldst thou win?
Soul. I know not whither, outcast,
At fortune's whim,   [fated
A soul unholy, steepèd in
Its mortal sin,
Against the God who had created
Me like to Him.
65 I am that soul ill-starred, unblest,
That by nature shone in gleaming
Robe of white,
Of angel's beauty once possessed,
Yea, loveliest,
Like a ray refulgent streaming
Filled with light.
66 And by my ill-omened fate,

61. *estrouares* B. *hereos* C.   62. *damnaste* C.   65. *como o raio* C.

& diabolicas maldades
violentas
estou mais morta que a morte,
sem deporte,
carregada de vaydades
peçonhentas.

¶ Sou a triste, sem meezinha,
peccadora abstinada
perfiosa,
pella triste culpa minha
mui mesquinha
a todo mal inclinada
& deleytosa.

Desterrey da minha mente
os meus perfeytos arreos
naturaes,
nam me prezey de prudente
mas contente
me gozey com os trajos feos
mundanaes.

¶ Cada passo me perdi
em lugar de merecer,
eu sou culpada:
auey piedade de mi
que nam me vi,
perdi meu inocente ser
& sou danada.

E por mais graueza sento
nam poderme arrepender
quanto queria,
que meu triste pensamento
sendo isento
nam me quer obedecer
como soya.

¶ Socorrey, hospeda senhora,
que a mão de Satanas
me tocou,
e sou ja de mi tam fora
que agora
nam sey se auante se a traz
nem como vou.

Consolay minha fraqueza
com sagrada yguaria,
que pereço,
por vossa sancta nobreza,
que he franqueza,

My atrocious devilries,
Sins treasonous,
More dead than death is now my
Bowed with this weight   [state
That nought can lighten, vanities
Most poisonous.

67 I am a sinner obstinate,
Perverse, that know no remedy
For this my plight,
Oppressed by guilt most obdurate,
And profligate,
Inclined to evil constantly
And all delight.

68 And I banished from my lore
All my perfect ornaments
And natural graces,
By prudence I set no store
But evermore
Rejoiced in all these vile vestments
And worldly places.

69 At each step taken in earthly cares
I further sank away from praise,
Earning but blame:
Have mercy upon one who fares
Lost unawares:
For, innocence lost, I might not raise
Myself from shame.

70 And, for my greater evil, I
Can no more repent me fully,
Since in new mood
My thoughts are mutinous and cry
For liberty,
Unwilling to obey me duly
As once they would.

71 O help me, lady innkeeper,
For Satan even now his hand
Doth on me lay,
And so grievously I err
In my despair
That I know not if I go or stand
Or backward stray.

72 Succour thou my helplessness
And strengthen me with holy fare,
For I perish,
Of thy noble saintliness
Liberal to bless,

66. *violentas* A. *& tromentas* B.
67. *mezinha* B. *obstinada* C. *a todo o mal* C; *e todo o mal* D.
68. *arreos, feos* C; *c'os trajos* C. 69. *logar* C. *damnada* C. 71. *soccorey* C.

porque o que eu merecia
bem conheço.

¶ Conheçome por culpada
& digo diante vos
minha culpa.
Senhora, quero pousada,
day passada,
pois que padeceo por nos
quem nos desculpa.
Mandayme ora agasalhar,
capa dos desemparados,
ygreja madre.

YGREJA. Vindevos aqui assentar
muy de vagar,
que os manjares são guisados
por Deos Padre.

¶ Sancto Agostinho doutor,
Geronimo, Ambrosio, Sã Thomas,
meus pilares,
serui aqui por meu amor
a qual milhor,
& tu, alma, gostaraas
meus manjares.
Ide aa sancta cosinha,
tornemos esta alma em si,
porque mereça
de chegar onde caminha
& se detinha:
pois que Deos a trouxe aqui
nam pereça.

¶ Em quanto estas cousas passam Satanas passea fazendo muytas vascas &
vem outro & diz.

¶ Como andas desasossegado.
DIABO. Arço em fogo de pesar.
OUTRO. Que ouueste?
DIABO. Ando tam desatinado
de enganado
que nam posso repousar
que me preste.
Tinha hũa alma enganada
ja quasi pera infernal
mui acesa.
OUTRO. E quem ta levou forçada?
DIABO. O da espada.
OUTRO. Ja melle fez outra tal
bulra como essa.

For knowing my deserts I dare
No hope to cherish.

73 I acknowledge all my sin
And before thee meekly thus
Forgiveness crave.
O Lady, let me now but win
Into thine inn,
Since One suffered even for us,
That He might save.

74 Bid me welcome, Mother holy,
Shield of all who are forsaken
Utterly.
Church. Enter to thy seat there
Yet come slowly,   [lowly,
For the viands thou seest were baken
By God most high.

75 Lo ye my pillars, doctor, saint,
Ambrose, Thomas and Jerome
And Augustine,
In my service wax not faint,
Nor show constraint,
And to thee, soul, shall be welcome
This fare of mine.

76 To the holy kitchen go:
Let us this frail soul restore,
That she find grace
To reach her journey's end and know
Her path, that so
By God brought hither she no more
Fail in life's race.

(*Meanwhile Satan goes to and fro,
cutting many capers, and another
devil comes and says:*)

77 *2nd D.* You're like a lion in a cage.
1st D. I'm all afire, with anger blind.
2nd D. Why, what's the matter?
1st D. To be so taken in, my rage
Can nought assuage
Nor any rest be to my mind;
For, as I flatter

78 Myself, I had by honeyed word
Deceived a certain soul, all quick
For fires of Hell.
2nd D. Who made you throw it
1st D. He of the sword. [overboard?
2nd D. He played just such another
On me as well.   [trick

74. *devagar* C.   75. *Jeronimo, Ambrosio e Thomaz* C, D.   *e qual* D.   *melhor* C, D.
76. *troxe* B.   *passeia* C.   *vem outro Diabo* C.   77. *dessocegado* C, D.

¶ Tinha outra alma ja vencida
em ponto de se enforcar
de desesperada,
a nos toda offerecida
& eu prestes pera a levar
arrastada;
e elle fella chorar tanto
que as lagrimas corriã
polla terra.
Blasfemey entonces tanto
que meus gritos retiniam
polla serra.

¶ Mas faço conta que perdi,
outro dia ganharey,
e ganharemos.

DIABO. Nam digo eu, yrmão, assi,
mas a esta tornarey
& veremos.
Tornala ey a affogar
depois que ella sayr fora
da ygreja
& começar de caminhar:
hei de apalpar
se venceram ainda agora
esta peleja.

> Alma com o Anjo.

¶ ALMA. Vos nam me desampareis,
senhor meu anjo custodio.
Oo increos
imigos, que me quereis
que ja sou fora do odio
de meu Deos?
Leyxaime ja, tentadores,
neste conuite prezado
do Senhor,
guisado aos peccadores
com as dores
de Christo crucificado,
Redemptor.

¶ Estas cousas estando a alma assentada
à mesa & o anjo junto com ella em
pee, vem os doutores com quatro bacios
de cosinha cubertos cantando Vexila
regis prodeunt*. E postos na mesa,
Sancto Agostinho diz.

79 For I had overcome a soul,
Ready to hang itself, unsteady
In its despair;
Yes, it was given to us whole
And I myself was making ready
To drag't down there.

80 And lo he made it weep and weep
So that the tears ran down along
The very ground:
You might have heard my curses deep
And cries of rage echo among
The hills around.

81 But I have hopes that what I've lost
Some other day I shall regain,
So will we all.
  1st D. I, brother, cannot share your
       trust,
But I will tempt this soul again
Whate'er befall.

82 With new promises will I woo her
When from the Church she shall have
Forth to the street   [come
Upon her journey: I will to her,
And beshrew her
If I turn not all their triumph
To defeat.

> (The Soul enters with the Angel.)

83 *Soul.* O let not thy protection fail me,
Guardian angel, help thy child.
O foes most base,
Infidels, why would you assail me
Who to my God am reconciled
And in His grace?

84 Leave me, O ye tempters, leave
Unto this most precious feast
Of Him who died,
Served to sinners for reprieve
Of those who grieve
For their Redeemer Lord, the Christ
And crucified.

> (*While the Soul is seated at the
> table and the Angel standing by her
> side, the Doctors come with four covered
> kitchen dishes, singing* Vexilla regis
> prodeunt, *and after placing them on
> the table, St Augustine says:*)

AGOST. Vos, senhora conuidada,
nesta cea soberana
celestial
aueis mister ser apartada
& transportada
de toda a cousa mundana
terreal.
Cerray os olhos corporaes,
deytay ferros aos danados
apetitos,
caminheyros infernaes,
pois buscaes
os caminhos bem guiados
dos contritos.

YGREJA. Benzey a mesa, senhor,
& pera consolaçam
da conuidada,
seja a oraçam de dor
sobre o tenor
da gloriosa payxam
consagrada.

E vos, alma, rezareis,
contemplando as viuas dores
da senhora,
vos outros respondereis
pois que fostes rogadores
atee agora.

Oraçã pa Santo Agostinho.

¶ Alto Deos marauilhoso
que o mundo visitaste
em carne humana,
neste valle temeroso
& lacrimoso
tua gloria nos mostraste
soberana;
e teu filho delicado,
mimoso da diuindade
& natureza,
per todas partes chagado
& muy sangrado
polla nossa infirmidade
& vil fraqueza.

¶ Oo emperador celeste,
Deos alto muy poderoso
essencial,
que pollo homem que fizeste
offereceste

85 *St Aug.* Lady, thou that to this feast,
Supper of celestial fare
Nobly divine,
Comest as a bidden guest,
Must now divest
Thyself of worldly thought and care
That once were thine.

86 Thou thy body's eyes must close
And in fetters sure be tied
Fierce appetite,
Treacherous guides, infernal foes:
Thy ways are those
That are a safe support and guide
For the contrite.

87 *Church.* Sir, by thee be the table blest:
In thy benedictory prayer,
To bring relief
And new strength to this our guest,
Be there expressed
The Passion's glory in despair
And all its grief.

88 Thou, O soul, with orisons,
The Virgin's sorrows contemplating
Abide even there,
And ye others make response
Since for this have you been waiting
Wrapped in prayer.

(*St Augustine's prayer:*)

89 God whose might on high appears,
Who camest to this world
In human guise,
In this vale of many fears
And sullen tears
Thy great glory hast unfurled
Before our eyes;

90 And thy Son most delicate
By His natural majesty
Of divine birth,
Ah, in blood and wounds prostrate
Is now his state
For our vile infirmity
And little worth.

91 O Thou ruler of the sky,
High God of power divine,
Enduring might,
Who for thy creature, man, to die
Didst not deny

88. *até 'gora* C, D.
90. *pela nossa* C, D.
91. *polo homem* C, E.   B omits 90 and 91.

o teu estado glorioso
a ser mortal.

¶ E tua filha, madre, esposa,
horta nobre, frol dos ceos,
Virgem Maria,
mansa pomba gloriosa
o quam chorosa
quando o seu Filho e Deos*
padecia.
Oo lagrymas preciosas,
de virginal coraçam
estilladas,
correntes das dores vossas
com os olhos da perfeyçam
derramadas!

¶ Quem hũa soo podera ver
vira claramente nella
aquella dor,
aquella pena & padecer
com que choraueis, donzella,
vosso amor.

¶ E quando vos amortecida
se lagrymas vos faltauam
nam faltaua
a vosso filho & vossa vida
chorar as que lhe ficauam
de quando orava.
Porque muyto mais sentia
pollos seus padecimentos
vervos tal,
mais que quanto padecia
lhe doya,
& dobrava seus tormentos
vosso mal.

¶ Se se podesse dizer,
se se podesse rezar
tanta dor;
se se podesse fazer
podermos ver
qual estaueis ao clauar
do Redemptor.
Oo fermosa face bella,
oo resplandor divinal,
que sentistes
quando a cruz se pos aa vella
& posto nella

Thy Godhead, and madest Thine
Our mortal plight.

92 And thy daughter, mother, bride,
Noble flower of the skies,
The Virgin blest,
Gentle Dove, when her Son died,
God crucified,
Ah what tears shed by those eyes
Her grief attest.

93 O most precious tears that well
From that virgin heart distilled
One by one,
Flowing at thy sorrow's spell
They those perfect eyes have filled
And still flow on.

94 Who but one of them might have
In it most manifestly
That grief to prove,
Even that woe and suffering grave
Which then overwhelmèd thee
For thy dear love.

95 Fainting then with grief if failed
Thy tears, yet Him they might not
Thy Life, thy Son,   [fail,
Who unto the Cross was nailed,
Even fresh tears that could avail,
In prayer begun.

96 For far greater woe was His
When He saw thee faint and languish
In thy distress,
More than His own agonies,
And doubled is
All His torture at thy anguish
Measureless.

97 For no words have ever told
No prayer or litany wailed
Such grief and loss:
Our weak thought may not enfold
Nor thee behold
As thou wert when He was nailed
Upon the Cross.

98 For to thee, O lovely face,
Wherein Heaven's beauty shone,
What woe was given
When the Cross on high they place
And thereupon

92.   *O quão chorosa Quando o seu Deos padecia* A, B, C, D, E.
93.   *com os* A, B; *c'os olhos* C, D.   94.   *podera ver* A, B; *podera haver* C, D.
96.   *vermos* B.   97.   *cravar* C.

o filho celestial
que paristes!
Vendo por cima da gente
assomar vosso conforto
tam chagado,
crauado tam cruelmente,
& vos presente,
vendo vos ser mãy do morto
& justiçado.
O rainha delicada,
sanctidade escurecida
quem nam chora
em ver morta & debruçada
a auogada,
a força de nossa vida
* [pecadora]!

AMBROSIO. Isto chorou Hyeremias
sobre o monte de Sion
ha ja dias,
porque sentio que o Messias
era nossa redempçam.
E choraua a sem ventura
triste de Jerusalem
homecida,
matando contra natura
seu Deos nascido em Belem
nesta vida.

GERONYMO. Quem vira o sancto cor-
antre os lobos humildoso   [deyro
escarnecido,
julgado pera o marteyro
do madeyro,
seu rosto aluo & fermoso
muy cuspido!

    AGOST.   Bẽze a mesa.
A bençam do padre eternal
& do filho que por nos
sofreo tal dor
& do spirito sancto, igual
Deos immortal,
conuidada, benza a vos
por seu amor.

YGREJA. ¶ Ora sus, venha agoa as
    mãos.

AGOST. Vos aveysuos de lavar

Nailèd the Son of Heaven,
Even thy Son!
99 Over the crowd's heads on high
He who was ever thy delight
Came to thy sight,
To the Cross nailèd cruelly,
Thou standing by,
Thou the mother of Him who died
There crucified!
100 O frail Queen of Holiness,
Who would not thus weep to see
Thee fainting fall
And lie there all motionless,
Thou patroness
Who dost still uphold and free
The life of all!   [miah
101 St Ambrose. Thus of yore did Jere-
On Mount Sion make lament
In days long spent,
For he knew that the Messiah
Was for our salvation sent.
102 And he mourned the misery
Of ill-starred Jerusalem,
The murderess,
Who should kill unnaturally
Her God born in Bethlehem
Our life to bless.
103 St Jerome. O the Holy Lamb to see
Humble amid the wolves' despite,
With mockery fraught,
Condemned to suffer cruelly
Upon the Tree,
And that face, so fair and white,
Thus set at nought!
    St Augustine. (He blesses the table.)
104 The Eternal Father's blessing rest,
And of the Son, who suffered thus
Even for us,
And of the Spirit holiest,
On thee our guest:
Spirit immortal, Father, Son,
The Three in One.
105 Church. Come now, bring water
    for the hands.
    St Aug. But thou must wash in
    tear on tear

---

   100. *morta debruçada* C. *de nossa vida* A, B; *da nossa vida* C, D. *pecadora?* or *e senhora?* or *nesta hora?*   101. *Mesias* B.   102. *choraua sem* B.   103. *cospido* B.
   105. *Vso aveysuos* B.

em lagrymas da culpa vossa
& bem lauada
& aueisuos de chegar
alimpar
a hũa toalha fermosa
bem laurada
co sirgo das veas puras
da Virgem sem magoa nacido
& apurado,
torcido com amarguras
aas escuras,
com grande dor guarnecido
& acabado.

¶ Nam que os olhos alimpeis.
que a nam consentirão
os tristes laços
que taes pontos achareis
da face & enues,
que se rompe o coração
em pedaços.
Vereis*, triste, laurado
[com rosto de fermosura]*
natural,
com tormentos pespontado
e figurado,
Deos criador, em figura
de mortal.

¶ Esta toalha que aqui se falla he a va-
ronica, a qual Sancto Agostinho tira
dantre os bacios & a mostra à Alma, &
a madre ygreja com os doutores lhe
fazem adoração de joelhos, cantando
Salue sancta facies, & acabando diz
a madre ygreja.

¶ Venha a primeyra yguaria.

Gero.   Esta yguaria primeyra
foy, senhora,
guisada sem alegria
em triste dia,
a crueldade cozinheyra
& matadora.
Gostala eis com salsa & sal
de choros de muyta dor,
porque os costados

Shed for thy past sins' misery,
Most thoroughly,
And then to this fair towel here
Thou mayst draw near,
A towel that is kept for thee
Worked cunningly

106 With finest silk in painlessness
From out the Holy Virgin's veins
That issuèd,
Silk that was spun in bitterness
And dark distress,
And woven with increasing pains
And finishèd.

107 Yet never shall thine eyes be dried:
This pattern sad will ever make
Thy tears downflow,
Such stitches here on either side
Doth it provide
That one's very heart must break
To see such woe.

108 Presented here thou mayest see
With lovely face most natural
—And seeing weep—
Embroiderèd with agony,
O mystery!
God fashioned, who created all,
In human shape.

(*The towel here described is the
veronica, which St Augustine takes
from among the dishes and shows to
the Soul, and the Mother Church and
the Doctors adore it on their knees,
singing Salve sancta Facies, and the
Mother Church then says:*)

109 *Church.*   Let the first viand be
brought.
St Jerome. It was preparèd joylessly
On a sad day,
With no pleasure was it fraught,
With suffering bought,
And its cook was Cruelty,
Eager to slay.

110 With seasoning of tears and shame
Must this course by thee be eaten,
Sorrowfully,

---

105.   *a limpar* A [but cf. 107. *alimpeis* (A)]; *alimpar* B; *A alimpar* C.
107.   *de face* C.   108.   *Vereis seu triste laurado Natural* A, B, C, D, E.
Esta toalha de que C.   *Veronica* C.   *a mostra* A; *amostra* B, C.   *santa facias* B.

do Messias diuinal,
sancto sem mal,
forão pollo vosso amor
açoutados.

¶ Esta yguaria em q̃ aqui se falla sam
os açoutes, & em este passo os tirã
dos bacios & os presentam a alma &
todos de joelhos adoram cantãdo Aue
flagellum, & despois diz Geronymo.

¶ Estoutro manjar segundo
he yguaria
que aueis de mastigar
em contemplar
a dor que o senhor do mundo
padecia
pera vos remediar.
foi hum tromento improuiso
que aos miolos lhe chegou
& consentio,
por remediar o siso
que a vosso siso faltou,
e pera ganhardes parayso
a sofrio.

¶ Esta yguaria segunda de que aqui se
fala he a coroa de espinhos, e em este
passo a tiram dos bacios & de joelhos
os sanctos doutores cantam Aue corona
espinearum, & acabando diz a madre
ygreja.

Venha outra do teor.

GERO. Estoutro manjar terceyro
foy guisado
em tres lugares de dor,
a qual maior,
com a lenha do madeyro
mais prezado.
Comese com gram tristeza*
porque a virgem gloriosa
o vio guisar:
vio crauar com gram crueza
a sua riqueza

Since the Messiah's holy frame,
Pure, free from blame,
Cruelly was scourged and beaten
For love of thee.

(*The viand so described consists of
the scourge which at this stage is
taken from the dishes and presented
to the Soul and all kneel and adore,
singing* Ave flagellum; *and Jerome
then says:*)

111 *St Jerome.* This second viand of
This delicacy,   [noble worth,
Must be slowly eaten by thee
In contemplation
Of what the Lord of all the earth
In agony
Sufferèd for thy salvation.

112 This new torture suddenly
He allowed to reach His brain,
That so thy wit
And sense might be restored to thee,
That perished from thee utterly,
Yea that thou Paradise mightst gain
Endured He it.

(*This second viand so described is
the crown of thorns, and at this stage
they take it from the plates, and
kneeling the holy Doctors sing* Ave
corona spinarum *and afterwards the
Mother Church says:*)

113 *Church.* Another bring in the same
      strain.
   St Jerome. This third viand that
      is brought to thee
Was prepared thrice
In places three, in each with gain
Of subtler pain,
With the wood of the Holy Tree,
Wood of great price.

114 It must be eaten sorrowfully,
Since the Virgin glorious
Saw it garnished,
Her treasure nailèd cruelly
Then did she see,

110. *em q̃ se falla* B.   *açotes* B.
112. *tormento* C.   *fala* A; *falla* B.   *espiniarum* C.   *acabado* B.
113. *theor* C.   114. *gran* C.   *tristura* A, B, C, D, E.

& sua perla preciosa
vio furar.

¶ E a este passo tira sancto Agostinho
os crauos, & todos de joelhos os adorão,
cantando Dulce lignum, dulcis clauus,
& acabada a adoraçam diz o anjo à
alma.

¶ Leixay ora esses arreos,
que estoutra nam se come assi
como cuydais:
pera as almas sam mui feos
e sam meos
con que nam andam em si
os mortais.

¶ Despe a alma o vestido & joyas que
lho imigo deu & diz Agostinho.

¶ Oo alma bem aconselhada,
que dais o seu a cujo he,
o da terra ha terra:
agora yreis despejada
polla estrada,
porque vencestes com fee
forte guerra.
YGREJA.   ¶ Venha estoutra yguaria.

GERO. A quarta yguaria he tal,
tam esmerada,
de tam infinda valia
& contia
que na mente diuinal
foy guisada,
por mysterio preparada
no sacrario virginal
muy cuberta,
da diuindade cercada
& consagrada,
despois ao padre eternal
dada em oferta.

¶ Apresenta sam Geronymo à alma hum
crucificio que tira dantre os pratos,
& os doutores o adoram cantando
Domine Jesu Christe, & acabando diz
a alma.

And her pearl most precious
Pierced and tarnished.

(*At this station St Augustine brings
the nails and all kneel and adore
them, singing* Dulce lignum, dulcis
clavus, *and when the adoration is
ended the Angel says to the Soul:*)

115 *Angel.* These trappings must thou
     lay aside,
This new fare cannot, thou must
Be eaten thus: [know,
By them are men's souls vilified
And in their pride
Puffed up with overweening show
Presumptuous.

(*The Soul casts off the dress and
jewels that the enemy gave her.*)

116 *St Augustine.* O soul, well coun-
     selled! well bestowed
To each what is of each by right,
And earth to earth:
Now shalt thou speed along thy road,
Free of this load,
Faring by faith from this stern fight
Victorious forth.

117 *Church.* To the last course I thee
     invite.
St Jerome. This fourth viand is of
So seasonèd,   [a kind
It is of value infinite,
Most exquisite,
Prepared by the Divine mind
And perfected:

118 Entrusted first in mystery
To a holy virgin came from Heaven
This secret thing,
Encompassed by divinity
And sanctity,
Then to the Eternal Father given
As offering.

(*St Jerome presents to the Soul a
Crucifix, which he takes from among
the dishes, and the Doctors adore it,
singing* Domine Jesu Christe, *and
afterwards the Soul says:*)

114.   *clausos* B.   *acabada a oração* C.
115.   *inimigo* C.   116.   *o seu a cujo he* A, B; *o seu cujo he* C, D.
118.   *oferta* A; *offerta* B.   *crucifixo* B, C.

¶ Cõ que forças, com q̃ spirito
te darey, triste, louuores
que sou nada,
vendote, Deos infinito,
tam afflito,
padecendo tu as dores
& eu culpada?

Como estaas tam quebrantado,
filho de Deos immortal!
quem te matou?
Senhor per cujo mandado
es justiçado
sendo Deos vniuersal
que nos criou?

AGOST. ¶ A fruyta deste jantar,
que neste altar vos foy dado
com amor,
yremos todos buscar
ao pomar
adonde estaa sepultado
o redemptor.

¶ E todos com a alma, cantando Te
Deum laudamus, foram adorar ho
muymento.

119 *Soul.* With what heart and mind
contrite
May I praise Thee sadly now
Who am nought,
Seeing Thee, God infinite,
To such plight
Of suffering and sorrow bow,
By my sin brought!

120 Lord, how art Thou crushed and
broken,
Thou, the Son of God, to die!
And Thy death
By whom ordered, by what token
The word spoken
Thee to judge and crucify,
Who gav'st us breath?

121 *St Aug.* For the fruit to end this
feast,
On the altar given thee thus
Lovingly,
To the orchard go we all in quest,
Where lies at rest
The Redeemer, He who died for us
And set us free.

(*And all with the Soul, singing*
Te deum laudamus, *went to adore
the tomb.*)

LAVS DEO.

119. *spirito* A, B; *sprito* C.   *tristes louvores* C, D, E.   *dios* B.
121. *fruta* B.   *a onde* C.   *redemtor* B.   *moymento* B; *moimento* C.

EXHORTAÇÃO DA GUERRA

Exhortação da Guerra†.

Interlocutores:¶Nigromante, Zebron, Danor, Diabos, Policena, Pantasilea, Archiles, Anibal, Eytor, Cepiam.

A Tragicomedia seguinte seu nome he Exortação da guerra. Foi representada ao muyto alto & nobre Rey dom Manoel o primeyro em Portugal deste nome na sua cidade de Lixboa na partida pera Azamor do illustre & muy magnifico senhor dõ Gemes Duque de Bargan.ça & de Guimarães, &c. Era de M.D.xiiij annos.

¶ *Entra primeyramente hum clerigo nigromante & diz:*

Cl. Famosos & esclarecidos
principes mui preciosos,
na terra vitoriosos
& no ceo muyto queridos,
5 sou clerigo natural
de Portugal,
venho da coua Sebila
onde se esmera & estila
a sotileza infernal.
10 E venho muy copioso
magico & nigromante,
feyticeyro muy galante,
astrologo bem auondoso.
Tantas artes diabris
15 saber quis
que o mais forte diabo
darey preso polo rabo
ao iffante Dom Luis.
Sey modos dencantamentos
20 quaes nunca soube ninguem,
artes para querer bem,
remedios a pensamentos.
Farey de hum coraçam duro
mais que muro

Exhortation to War.

Dramatis personae: A necromancer, Zebron and Danor, devils, Polyxena, Penthesilea, Achilles, Hannibal, Hector, Scipio.

The following tragicomedy is called Exhortation to War. It was played before the very high and noble King Dom Manuel I of Portugal in his city of Lisbon on the departure for Azamor of the illustrious and very magnificent Lord Dom James, Duke of Braganza, Guimarães, etc., in the year 1513.

¶ *A necromancer priest first enters and says:*

Princes of most noble worth,
To whom high renown is given,
Who, victorious on earth,
Are beloved of God in Heaven,
I a priest am and my home
Is Portugal,
From the Sibyl's cave I come
Where fumes diabolical
Are distilled and brought to birth.
In magic and necromancy
I'm a skilled practitioner,
A most accomplished sorcerer,
Well versed in astrology.
In so many a devil's art
Would I have part
That o'er the strongest I'll prevail
And just seize him by the tail
And hand him to prince Luis there.
Sorcerers of past time ne'er
Knew the enchantments that I know,
Ways of making love to grow
And of freeing from love's care.
For of hearts I will take one
Harder than stone

Era de M.D.xiiij **A.**   1513 C, D, E.
† This play was omitted in B.

25 como brando leytoayro,	And will it soft as syrup make,
e farei polo contrayro	And so change others, to changes prone,
que seja sempre seguro.	That nothing shall their firmness shake.
Sou muy grande encantador,	Truly a great wizard I
faço grandes marauilhas,	And great marvels can I work,
30 as diabolicas sillas	All the powers of Hell that lurk
sam todas em meu favor:	Favour me exceedingly,
farey cousas impossiveis	As deeds impossible shall attest
muy terribeis,	Of awful shape,
milagres muy euidentes	Miracles most manifest
35 que he pera pasmar as gentes,	Such that all shall see and gape,
visiueis & invisiueis.	Visibly and invisibly.
Farey que hũa dama esquiua	For I'll make a lady coy,
por mais çafara que seja	Though love's guerdon she defer,
quando o galante a veja	If her lover look on her,
40 que ella folgue de ser viua;	The very breath of life enjoy;
farey a dous namorados	And two lovers, love's curse under
mui penados	Kept asunder,
questem cada hum per si,	Will I leave to grieve apart,
& cousas farey aqui	And achieve by this my art
45 que estareis marauilhados.	Things at which you'll gaze in wonder.
Farey por meo vintem	For a lady most ungainly
que hũa dama muito fea	For a halfpenny at night
que de noyte sem candea	Will I cause without a light
nam pareça mal nem bem;	To look nor ill nor well too plainly.
50 e outra fermosa & bella	To another loveliest,
como estrella	As star in heaven
farey por sino forçado	Shall this destiny be given
que qualquer homem hõrrado	That of noblest men and best
nam lhe pesasse um ella.	None against her love protest.
55 Faruos ey mais pera verdes,	And the better to display
por esconjuro perfeyto,	The perfection of my spell
que caseis todos a eyto	I'll cause you all to marry well,
o milhor que vos poderdes;	That is, I mean, as best you may;
e farey da noite dia	And I'll turn night into day
60 per pura nigromanciia	All by this good art of mine,
se o sol alumear,	If the sun should chance to shine,
& farey yr polo ar	And, too, light as air shall be
toda a van fantesia.	Every foolish fantasy.
Faruos ey todos dormir	I will cause you all to sleep
65 em quanto o sono vos durar	While sleep has you in its keeping,
& faruos ey acordar	And I'll cause you to awake
sem a terra vos sentir;	Without therefore the earth quaking;
e farey hum namorado	And a lover by the thorn
bem penado	Of love forlorn
70 se amar bem de verdade	If most real be his love
que lhe dure essa vontade	I will make his fancy prove
atee ter outro cuydado.	Steadfast till it be forsworn.

25. *leituairo* C.

Faruos ey que desejeis	I will make you wish to see
cousas que estão por fazer,	Things which scarcely can be parried,
75 e faruos ey receber	And when each of you is married
na hora que vos desposeis,	Then truly shall his wedding be.
e farey que esta cidade	And I'll make this city stand
estee pedra sobre pedra,	Stone o'er stone on either hand,
e farey que quem nam medra	And that those who do not flourish
80 nunca tẽ prosperidade.	No prosperity shall nourish.
Farey per magicas rasas	For my magic art's more proof
chuuas tam desatinadas	I'll bring mighty rains whereat
que estem as telhas deytadas	All the tiles shall lie down flat
pelos telhados das casas;	Above the houses, on the roof.
85 e farey a torre da See,	And the great Cathedral tower
assi grande como he,	For all its size will I uproot
per graça da sua clima.	And despite its special power
que tenha o alicesse ao pee	Its battlements on high will put,
& as ameas em cima.	Its foundation at its foot.
90 Nam me quero mais gabar.	In my praise no more be said.
Nome de San Cebriam	In St Cyprian's name most holy,
esconjurote Satam.	Satan, I conjure thee.
Senhores não espantar!	(Gentlemen, be not afraid.)

Zeet zeberet zerregud zebet
95 oo filui soter
rehe zezegot relinzet
oo filui soter.

oo chaues das profundezas	Keys of the depths, abysses rending,
abri os porros da terra!	Open up Earth's every pore!
100 Princepe* da eterna treua	Prince of Darkness never-ending,
pareçam tuas grandezas!	Show thy great works evermore!
conjurote Satanas,	Satan, wheresoe'er thou be,
onde estaas,	I conjure thee
polo bafo dos dragões,	By the mighty dragons' breath
105 pola ira dos liões,	And the raging lions' roar
polo valle de Jurafas.	And Jehoshaphat's vale of death.
Polo fumo peçonhento	By the smoke that issueth
que sae da tua cadeyra	Poisonous from out thy chair,
e pola ardente fugueyra,	By the fire that none may slake,
110 polo lago do tormento	By the torments of thy lake,
esconjurote Satam,	From my heart right earnestly
de coraçam,	Satan, I conjure thee,
zezegot seluece soter,	Zezegot seluece soter,
conjurote, Lucifer,	Unto thee my prayer I make,
115 que ouças minha oraçam.	Lucifer, listen to my prayer!
Polas neuoas ardentes	By the mists of liquid fire
que estam nas tuas moradas,	That thy regions drear distil,
pollas poças pouoadas	By the vipers, snakes that fill
de bibaras & serpentes,	All its wells, abysses dire,
120 e pello amargo tormento	By the pangs relentlessly

100. *Princepes* A.   117. *estan* A.   118. *poças* A.   119. *viboras* C.

muy sem tento	Given by thee
que daas aos encacerados,	To the prisoners of thy pit,
pollos grytos dos danados	By the shrieks of those in it
que nunca cessam momento:	That unceasing echo still,
125 conjurote, Berzebu,	Beelzebub, I thee invite
pola ceguidade Hebrayca	By the blindness of the Jews
e polla malicia Judayca,	Who the wrong in malice choose
com a qual te alegras tu,	And thereby thy heart delight.

rezeegut Linteser

130 zamzorep tisal

siroofee nafezeri.

Vêm os diabos Zebron & Danor &	*The devils Zebron and Danor come and*
diz Zebron:	*Zebron says:*
Z. Que has tu, escomungado?	Z. What's the matter, priest accursed?
C. Oo yrmãos, venhaes embora!	P. Welcome, brothers, welcome first.
D. Que nos queres tu agora?	D. What now with us wouldst thou have?
135 C. Que me façaes hum mandado.	P. That my bidding you should do.
Z. Polo altar de Satam,	Z. By Satan's altar, this thou'lt rue,
dom vilam.	Arrogant knave.
D. Tomoo por essas gadelhas	D. Come, I'll seize him by the hair
& cortemoslhe as orelhas,	And off with his ears at least,
140 que este clerigo he ladram.	For a robber is this priest.
C. Manos, nam me façaes mal,	P. Hurt me not, good brothers, cease,
Compadres, primos, amigos!	Comrades, cousins, friends, I pray.
Z. Não te temos em dous figos.	Z. Not two figs for you we care.
C. Como vay a Belial?	P. How is Belial to-day?
145 sua corte estaa em paz?	And his court, is it at peace?
D. Dalhe aramaa hum bofete,	D. With a box o' the ear chastise him,
crismemos este rapaz	Even so will we baptise him
& chamemoslhe Zopete.	And we'll christen him a fool.
C. Ora fallemos de siso:	P. Come, let's speak more seriously:
150 estais todos de saude?	Are you all quite well and cool?
Z. Fideputa, meo almude,	Z. Villain, wineskin, Bacchus' tool,
que tẽs tu de ver com isso?	What has that to do with thee?
C. Minhas potencias relaxo	P. Nay, my powers I'll efface,
& me abaxo,	Myself abase,
155 falayme doutra maneyra.	Only speak not thus to me.
D. Sois bispo vos da Landeyra	D. Do you hold Landeira's see
ou vigayro no Cartaxo?	Or are you Cartaxo's vicar?
Z. He Cura do Lumear,	Z. He's priest of Lumear, I think,
sochantre da Mealhada,	Mealhada's precentor he,
160 acipreste de canada,	Archpriest of a pint of liquor
bebe sem desfolegar.	Since he ceases not to drink.
D. E' capelão terrantees,	D. And this chaplain of our town
bom Ingres,	Is a good Englishman, for mark,
patriarca em Ribatejo	This Ribatejo Patriarch
165 beberaa sobre hum cangrejo	Will drink even a Frenchman down,
as guelas dũ Frances.	And nothing think of it at all.

131. *Lisó fé* C.   148. *zobete* C.

Z. Danor, dime, he Cardeal
Darruda ou de Caparica?
D. Nenhũa cousa lhe fica
170 senam sempre o vaso tal,
tem um grande Arcebispado
muito honrrado
junto da pedra da estrema
onda põe a diadema
175 & a mitra o tal prelado.
Ladram, sabes o Seyxal
& Almada & pereli?
Oo fideputa alfaqui
albardeyro do Tojal.
180 C. Diabos, quereis fazer
o que eu quiser
por bem ou de outra feyçam?
D. Oo fideputa ladram
auemoste dobedecer.
185 C. Ora eu vos mando & remando
pollas virtudes dos ceos
polla potencia de Deos,
em cujo seruiço ando,
conjurouos da sua parte
190 sem mais arte
que façais o que eu mandar
polla terra & pollo ar,
aqui & em toda a parte.
Z. Como te vai com as terças?
195 E' viuo aquelle alifante
que foy a Roma tão galante?
D. Amargamte a ti estas verças?
C. Esconjurote, Danor,
por amor de sam Paulo
200 e de sam Polo.
Z. Tu não tens nenhum miolo.
C. Eu vos farey vir a dor.
Por esta madre de Deos
de tão alta dinidade,
205 & polla sua humildade,
com que abrio os altos ceos,
polas veas virginaes
emperiaes
de que Christo foi humanado.
210 Z. Que queres, escomungado?
Mandanos, nam digas mais.
C. Minha merce mãda & ordena
que tragais logo essas horas
diante destas senhoras

Z. Danor, say, is he Cardinal
Of Arruda or Caparica?
D. He has nought left thin or thick
Save always his glass of liquor
And a great Archbishopric,
An honour given but to few
Near the boundary stone, the same
On which he sets his diadem,
This prelate, and his mitre too.
Dost thou know Seixal, thou thief,
Almada and thereabouts?
Tojal packsaddler, of louts
And of villain knaves the chief.
P. Devils, will you now in brief
My bidding do
Or must I take other ways with you?
D. Cursèd robber, only say
What you'd have and we'll obey.
P. I command you instantly
By the power of the sky
And the might of God on high,
In whose service priest I am,
I conjure you in His name
That you my behests obey
Now straightway,
On the earth and in the air,
Here and there and everywhere.
Z. How are the tithes, and—another
Is the fine elephant alive   [matter—
That went to Rome for the Pope to shrive?
D. Are your feelings hurt by this
P. Danor, now I conjure thee [chatter?
By Saint Pol and by Saint Paul
Hearken to me.
Z. Your intelligence is small.
P. Then shall you hark unwillingly.
By the Mother of God most holy
And her heavenly dignity,
Her humility on earth
That had power to scale high Heaven,
And her own imperial worth
Whereby in the Virgin birth
The incarnate Christ to earth was given.
Z. Say no more, accursed knave,
We'll obey: what wouldst thou have?
P. 'Tis my will and my desire
That unto those ladies there
This very hour you should have care

167. *Cardial* C.

215 a Troyana Policena
    muyto bem atauiada
    & concertada,
    assi linda como era.
    D. Quanta pancada te dera
220 se pudera,
    mas tẽsma força quebrada.
    C. Venha por mar ou por terra
    logo muyto sem referta.
    Z. E a terça da offerta
225 tambem pagas pera a guerra?
    C. Trazei logo a Policena
    muy sem pena
    com sua festa diante.
    Z. Inda yraa outro alifante:
230 pagaraas quarto & vintena.

Vem Policena & diz:

    P. Eu que venho aqui fazer?
    Oo que gran pena me destes
    pois por força me trouxestes
    a um nouo padecer:
235 que quem viue sem ventura,
    em gram tristura
    ver prazeres lhee mais morte.
    Oo belenissima corte,
    senhora da fermosura!
240 Nam foy o paço Troyano
    dino de vosso primor:
    vejo hum Priamo mayor
    hum Cesar muy soberano,
    outra Ecuba mais alta,
245 mui sem falía,
    em poderosa, doce, humana,
    a quem por Febo & Diana
    cada vez Deos mais esmalta.
    E vos, Principe excelente,
250 dayme aluisaras liberais,
    que vossas mostras são tais
    que todo mundo he contente,
    e aos planetas dos ceos
    mandou Deos
255 que vos dessem tais fauores
    que em grandeza sejais vos
    prima dos antecessores.
    Por vos, mui fermosa flor,
    Iffante Dona Isabel
260 Foram juntos em torpel

Polyxena of Troy to bring:
Come she, for beauty's heightening,
In rich attire,
Fair as she was fair of yore.
D. With what a thrashing shouldst thou
Could I but do it.   [rue it
But thou hast taken my strength away.
P. Let her come by land or sea
Straightway and most peacefully.
Z. And as to subscriptions for the war
Hast thou any tithe to pay?
P. Without delay Polyxena bring
And joyfully
Before her shall you dance and sing.
Z. They'll send another elephant yet
And you'll have to pay the tax for it.

Polyxena comes and says:

Pol. Wherefore hither am I come?
O how great my affliction is
Since against my will you bring
Me to further suffering.
For he who lives in misery's stress
Can but borrow
From seen pleasures a new sorrow.
But what a fairy court is this
In which beauty has its home!
The palace of Troy was not your peer
Nor rival in magnificence,
I see a greater Priam here
Cesar of sovran excellence,
A Hecuba of nobler mien,
A flawless queen
In power humanely gentle: hence
Apollo's and Diana's reign
Heaven confirmeth in the twain.
And you, Prince most excellent,
Give me liberal reward:
From your promise is none debarred,
It fills all men with content,
And the planets of Heaven's abode
Had word of God
That to you be greatness sent
And fortune's favour even more
Than to those who reigned before.
And for you, most lovely flower,
Princess Dona Isabel
The Lord of Heaven in His power

221. *tens-me a* C.   238. *bellenissima* C.   260. *tropel* C.

por mandando do senhor
o ceo & sua companhia
& julgou Jupiter juiz
que fosseis Emperatriz
265 de Castella & Alemanha.
Senhor Iffante Dom Fernãdo,
vosso sino he de prudencia,
Mercurio per excelencia
fauorece vosso bando,
270 sereis rico & prosperado
e descansado,
sem cuydado & sem fadiga,
& sem guerra & sem briga:
isto vos estaa guardado.
275 Iffante Dona Breatiz,
vos sois dos sinos julgada
que aueis de ser casada
nas partes de flor de lis:
mais bem do que vos cuydais,
280 muyto mais,
vos tem o mundo guardado.
Perdey, senhores, cuydado
pois com Deos tanto priuais.
C. Que dizeis vos destas rosas,
285 deste val de fermosura?
P. Tal fora minha ventura
como ellas sam de fermosas!
Oo que corte tam lozida
& guarnecida
290 de lindezas para olhar!
quem me pudera ficar
nesta gloriosa vida!
D. Nesta vida! la acharaas.
P. Quem me trouxe a este fado?
295 D. Esse zote escomungado
te trouxe aqui onde estaas.
Perguntalhe que te quer
para ver.
P. Homem, a que me trouxeste?
300 C. Quee? ainda agora vieste
e has me de responder!
Declara a estes senhores,
pois foste damor ferida,
qual achaste nesta vida
305 que é a moor dor das dores,
e se as penas infernaes
se sam aas do amor yguaes,
ou se dam la mais tormentos
dos que ca dam pensamentos
310 e as penas que nos daes.

Marshalled in host innumerable
The sky and all its company,
And Jove as judge did then ordain
That as empress you should reign
O'er Castille and Germany.
You, O Prince Dom Ferdinand,
Since prudence is your special share
And with favourable wand
Mercury holds you in his arms,
Wealth and prosperity shall bless
In quietness
Without toil or any care,
Turmoil or loud war's alarms:
This for you the gods have planned.
For you, Princess Beatrice,
Your sure destiny it is
To be married happily
Unto France's fleur-de-lys.
And the world has more in store
For you, yea more
Than you imagine shall be given.
Princes, leave all cares of yore
Since you have the ear of Heaven.
P. What say you to the roses there
And this vale of loveliness?
Pol. Would that fortune were no less
Fair to me than they are fair!
How gleams the Court in radiancy,
What an array
Of beauty is there here to see!
O that it were given me
Ever in this life to stay!
D. In this life! Thine another school.
Pol. Who brought me to this destiny?
D. That excommunicated fool,
Thou camest here at his suggestion.
Ask him what he wants of thee,
Just to see.
Pol. Why then have you brought me
P. What, no sooner you appear [here?
Than you would begin to question!
Tell these lordlings instantly,
Since you suffered from love's wound,
What in this life here you found
The greatest of all woes to be,
Tell them if the pains of Hell
Be as deep as those of love,
Or if torments there excel
Those that here from love's thoughts well,
Griefs that every lover prove.

P. Muyto triste padecer
no inferno sinto eu
mas a dor que o amor me deu
nunca a mais pude esqueecer.
315 *C.* Que manhas, que gentileza
ha de ter o bom galante?
P. A primeyra he ser constante,
fundado todo em firmeza;
nobre, secreto, calado,
320 soffrido em ser desdañado,
sempre aberto o coração
pera receber payxão
mas nam pera ser mudado.
Ha de ser mui liberal,
325 todo fundado em franqueza,
esta he a mor gentileza
do amante natural:
porque é tam desuiada
ser o escasso namorado
330 como estar fogo em geada
ou hũa cousa pintada
ser o mesmo encorporado.
Ha de ser o seu comer
dous bocados sospirando
335 & dormir meo velando
sem de todo adormecer.
Ha de ter muy doces modos,
humano, cortessa todos,
seruir sem esperar della,
340 que quem ama com cautela
não segue a têçam dos Godos.
C. Qual he a cousa principal
porque deue ser amado?
P. Que seja mui esforçado,
345 isto he o que mais lhe val.
Porque hum velho dioso,
feo e muyto tossegoso,
se na guerra tem boa fama
com a mais fermosa dama
350 merece de ser ditoso.
Senhores guerreyros, guerreyros!
& vos senhoras guerreyras
bandeyras & não gorgueyras
lauray pera os caualeyros.
355 Que assi nas guerras Troyãs
eu mesma & minhas irmaãs
teciamos os estandartes
bordados de todas partes

Pol. Awful in intensity
Are Hell's tortures unto me,
Grievously I suffer, yet
Ne'er could I love's wound forget.
P. What the arts and qualities
That should a true lover grace?
Pol. Constancy has the first place
And resolution; and, with these,
Noble must he be, discreet,
Silent, patient of disdain
With heart e'er open to love's strain
In passion's service to compete,
But not to change and change again.
And he must be liberal,
Generous exceedingly,
Since there is no quality
That for lovers is so meet.
For to a lover avarice
Is as uncongenial
As would be a fire in ice
Or if a picture were to be
Itself and its original.
For his food he must but take
A mouthful barely, and with sighs,
And when he asleeping lies
He must still be half awake.
Very gentle-mannered he,
Humane and courteous, must be
And serve his lady without hope,
For he who loveth grudgingly
Proves himself of little scope.
P. What his qualities among
Should most bring him love for love?
Pol. That he should be brave and strong,
That will his best vantage prove.
For a man advanced in years,
Ill-favoured though be and weak,
If name famed in war he bears
Even in the fairest lady's ears
Should for him his actions speak.
On, on ye lords, to war, to war!
And ladies not as heretofore
Embroider wimples for your wear
But banners for the knights to bear.
For thus amid the wars of Troy
I and my sisters did employ
Our time and all our artifice:
Standards, with many a fair device

346. *idoso* C.   347. *muito socegado* C.

com diuisas mui loucaãs.
360 Com cantares e alegrias
dauamos nossos colares
e nossas joias a pares
per essas capitanias.
Renegay dos desfiados
365 & dos pontos enleuados
destruase aquella terra
dos perros arrenegados.
Oo quem vio Pantasileea
com quarenta mil donzellas,
370 armadas como as estrellas
no campo de Palomea.
C. Venha aqui: trazeyma ca.
Z. Deyxanos yeramaa.
C. Ora sus, questais fazendo?
375 D. O' diabo que teu encomendo
& quem tal poder te daa.

Entra Pantiselea e diz:

P. Que quereis e esta chorosa
rainha Pantasilea,
aa penada, triste, fea,
380 pera corte tam fermosa?
Porque me quereis vos ver
diante vosso poder,
rey das grandes marauilhas
que com pequenas quadrilhas
385 venceis quem quereis vencer?
Se eu, senhor, forra me vira,
do inferno solta agora,
e fora de mi senhora,
meu senhor, eu vos seruira,
390 empregara bem meus dias
em vossas capitanias,
& minha frecha dourada
fora bem auenturada
& nam nas guerras vazias.
395 Oo famoso Portugal
conhece teu bem profundo,
pois atee o Polo segundo
chega o teu poder real.
Auante, auante, senhores,
400 pois que com grandes favores
todo o ceo vos fauorece:
el Rey de Fez esmorece,
& Marrocos daa clamores.
Oo deixay de edificar
405 tantas camaras dobradas

Embroidered, did we weave for them;
And on them lavished many a gem
And gaily with glad songs of joy
Our necklaces we freely gave,
Tiara and diadem.
Then leave your points and hem-stitch
Your millinery and your lace,   [leave,
And utterly from off earth's face
These renegade dogs destroy.
O to see Penthesilea again
With forty thousand warriors,
Armed maidens gleaming like the stars
On the Palomean plain.
P. Come bring her here this very hour.
Z. Cannot you leave us one instant alone?
P. What are you doing? Come on, come on.
D. To the devil would I see you gone
And whoso gives you this power.

Penthesilea enters and says:

Pen. What would you of this hapless
Penthesilea woe-begone,   [queen
Who in tears and sorrow thus appear
Ill-favoured in this court's fair sheen?
Why should you wish to see me here
Before your high imperial throne,
Great king of marvels, who alone
With your small armies scatter still
Your victories abroad at will?
Were I now, Sir, at liberty,
From Hell's grim dominion free
And mistress of my destiny
I would serve you willingly.
All my days would I spend then
With your armies to my gain,
My golden arrow then with zest
Would serve you in a service blest
And not in useless wars and vain.
O renownèd Portugal,
Learn to know thy noble worth
Since thy power imperial
Reaches to the ends of Earth.
Forward, forward, lord and knight
Since Heaven's favours on you crowd,
Forward, forward in your might
That doth the King of Fez affright,
And Morocco cries aloud.
O cease ye eagerly to build
So many a richly furnished chamber,

375. *O' Diabo qu'eu t'encommendo* C.

Muy pintadas & douradas.	And to paint them and to gild.
Que he gastar sem prestar.	Money so spent will nothing yield.
Alabardas, alabardas!	With halberds only now remember
espingardas, espingardas!	And with rifles to excel.
410 Nam queyrais ser Genoeses	Not for Genoese fashions strive
senam muyto Portugueses	But as Portuguese to live
& morar em casas pardas.	And in houses plain to dwell.
Cobray fama de ferozes,	As fierce warriors win renown,
nam de ricos, que he perigosa,	Not for wealth most perilous,
415 douray a patria vossa	Give your country a golden crown
com mais nozes que as vozes	Of deeds, not words that mock at us.
Auante, auante Lisboa!	Forward, Lisbon! All descry
que por todo mundo soa	Thy good fortune far and nigh,
tua prospera fortuna:	And the fame thou dost inherit,
420 pois que fortuna temfuna	Since fortune raises thee on high,
faze sempre de pessoa.	Win it sturdily by merit.
Archiles, que foy daqui	Achilles when he went away
de perto desta cidade,	From near this city went,
chamay-o: diraa a verdade	Call him: you'll hear truth evident
425 se não quereis crer a mi.	If you doubt what I have said.
C. Ora sus, sus digo eu.	P. Let him come up, come up, I say.
Z. Este clerigo he sandeu.	Z. This priest has gone quite off his head.
Onde estou que o nam crismo!	I don't know what I am about
oo fideputa judeu	That I don't give the Jew a clout:
430 queres vazar o abismo?	Would you empty Hell of its dead?
Vem Archiles & diz:	*Achilles comes and says:*
A. Quando Jupiter estaua	A. When Jupiter in all his might
em toda sua fortaleza	Was seated on his throne
& seu gran poder reynaua	And in his strength ordered aright
& seu braço dominaua	By his right hand alone
435 os cursos da natureza;	The courses of the day and night;
quando Martes influya	And warrior Mars to Earth had lent
seus rayos de vencimento	His bolts of victory
& suas forças repartia;	And parted with his armament;
quando Saturno dormia	When Saturn still slept peacefully
440 com todo seu firmamento;	With all his firmament;
e quando o Sol mais lozia	When the Sun shone with clearer light
& seus rayos apuraua	And an intenser ray
& a Lũa aparecia	And the Moon's beams illumed the night,
mais clara que o meo dia;	More brightly than noonday,
445 & quando Venus cãtaua,	And Venus sang her loveliest lay;
e quando Mercurio estaua	When wisdom, that he now doth keep,
mais pronto em dar sapiencia;	Was given by Mercury,
& quando o ceo se alegraua	And mirth flashed o'er the heaven's steep
& o mar mais manso estaua	And the winds were gently hushed asleep
450 & os ventos em clemencia;	And a calm lay on the sea;
e quando os sinos estauam	When joy and fame together checked
com mais gloria & alegria	The hands of destiny
& os poolos senfeytauam	And glory's flags the poles bedecked

& as nuũes se tirauam
455 & a luz resplandecia;
e quando a alegria vera
foy em todas naturezas,
nesse dia, mes & era
quando tudo isto era
460 naceram vossas altezas.
Eu Archiles fuy criado
nesta terra muytos dias
& sam bem auenturado
ver este reyno exalçado
465 & honrrado por tantas vias.
Oo nobres seus naturaes,
por Deos nam vos descudees,
lembreuos que triumphaes;
oo prelados, nam dormais!
470 clerigos, nam murmureis!
Quando Roma a todas velas
conquistaua toda a terra
todas, donas & donzelas,
dauam suas joyas belas
475 pera manter os da guerra.
Oo pastores da Ygreja
moura a ceyta de Mafoma,
ajuday a tal peleja
que açoutados vos veja
480 sem apelar pera Roma.
Deueis devender as taças,
empenhar os breuiayros,
fazer vasos de cabaças
& comer pão & rabaças
485 por vencer vossos contrayros.
Z. Assi, assi, aramaa!
dom zote, que te parece?
C. E a mi que se me daa?
quem de seu renda nam ha
490 as terças pouco lhe empece.
A. Se viesse aqui Anibal
e Eytor e Cepiam
vereis o que vos diram
das cousas de Portugal
495 com verdade & com razam.
C. Sus Danor, e tu Zebram:
venham todos tres aqui.
D. Fideputa, rapaz, cam,
perro, clerigo, ladram!
500 Z. Mao pesar vejeu de ti.

And the heavens, by no clouds beflecked,
Gleamed in their radiancy;
When every heart with unfeigned cheer
Was merry upon Earth,
In that day and month and year,
When all these portents did appear,
Your Highnesses had birth.
Now I, Achilles, in my youth
Lived here for many days
And happy am I in good sooth
To see the kingdom's splendid growth
Honoured in countless ways.
Its noble sons these honours reap,
But let no careless strain
Prevent you what you win to keep;
Ye prelates, 'tis no time for sleep!
Ye priests, do not complain!
When mighty Rome was in full sail
Conquering all the Earth
The girls and matrons without fail,
That so the soldiers should prevail,
Gave all their jewels' worth.
Then O ye shepherds of the Church
Down, down with Mahomet's creed!
Leave not the fighters in the lurch!
For if to scourge yourselves you speed
Then Rome may spare the birch.
You should sell your chalices,
Yes and pawn your breviaries,
Turn your gourds into flasks, and e'er
Of bread and parsnips make your fare,
To vanquish thus your enemies.
Z. Aha, aha. A splendid rule!
What do you think of that, Sir Fool?
P. What is't to me? what should I care?
For he who has no revenues
Can by the tithes but little lose.
A. If hither came but Hannibal,
Hector and Scipio
You shall see what they will show
Of the things of Portugal,   [know.
What reason and truth would have you
P. Come Danor, and Zebron, hither
Bring all three of them together.
D. Rascal cleric, villain, cur,
Thief, dog, that I for you should stir!
Z. May a curse your power wither!

Vem Anibal, Eytor, Cepiam & diz
   Anibal:

A. Que cousa tam escusada
he agora aqui Anibal,
que vossa corte he afamada
per todo mundo em geral.
505 E. Nem Eytor nam faz mister.
C. Ncm tampouco Cepiam.
A. Deueis, senhores, esperar
em Deos que vos ha de dar
toda Africa na vossa mão.
510 Africa foi de Christãos,
Mouros vola tem roubada:
Capitães, pondelhas mãos,
que vos vireis mais louçãos
com famosa nomeada.
515 Oo senhoras Portuguesas,
gastay pedras preciosas,
donas, donzelas, duquesas,
que as taes guerras & empresas
sam propriamente vossas.
520 E' guerra de deuaçam
por honrra de vossa terra,
commettida com rezam,
formada com descriçam
contra aquella gente perra.
525 Fazey contas de bugalhos,
& perlas de camarinhas,
firmaes de cabeças dalhos;
isto si, senhoras minhas,
& esses que tendes daylhos.
530 Oo q̃ nam honrram vestidos
nem muy ricos atauios
mas os feytos nobrecidos,
nam briaes douro tecidos
com trepas de desuarios:
535 dayos pera capacetes.
& vos, priores honrrados,
reparti os Priorados
a soyços & soldados,
& centum pro vno accipietis.
540 A renda que apanhais
o milhor que vos podeis
nas ygrejas nam gastais,
aos proues pouca dais,
eu nam sey que lhe fazeis.
545 Day a terça do que ouuerdes
pera Africa conquistar

Hannibal, Hector and Scipio come, and
   Hannibal says:

Han. Easily you might forego
Poor Hannibal's presence here,
For your Court's fame far and near
The furthest of Earth's regions know.
Hect. Nor need Hector here appear.
S. Nor is there room for Scipio.
Han. Sirs, you should trust in God, that
All Africa presently   [he
Will reduce beneath your sway.
Africa was Christian land,
Moors have ta'en your own away.
To the work, Captains, set your hand,
For so with clearer ray shall burn
Your renown when you return.
And, O ladies of Portugal,
Spend, spend jewel and precious stone,
Duchesses, ladies, maidens, all
Since such enterprises shall
Properly be yours alone.
A religious war it is
For the honour of your land,
Against those vile enemies,
Undertaken reasonably
And with good discretion planned.
Of beads be every rosary,
Each pearl replaced by bilberry,
Brooches of the heads of leek;
Such ornaments, my ladies, seek
And those you have give every one.
For little honour now is there
In dresses and adornments fair,
Honour give noble deeds alone,
Not costly robes inwrought with gold
And pranked with trimmings manifold:
Give these now to help helmets make.
And ye, good priors, I bid you take
And divide all that you hold
Among the soldiers of the guard
And great shall be your reward.
For of the income you obtain
By whatever means you may
The churches have but little gain,
And from alms you still abstain:
How you spend it who shall say?
For the conquest of Africa
Give a tithe of your possessions,

515. *senhores Portugueses* A.

com mais prazer que poderdes,
que quanto menos tiuerdes
menos tereis que guardar.
550 Oo senhores cidadãos
Fidalgos & regedores
escutay os atambores
com ouuidos de Christãos!
E a gente popular
555 auante! nam refusar!
Ponde a vida & a fazenda,
porque pera tal contenda
ninguem deue recear.

*Todas estas figuras se ordenaram
em caracol & a vozes cantaram &
representaram o que se segue, cantando
todos:*

Ta la la la lam, ta la la la lam.
560 *A.* Auante, auante! senhores!
que na guerra com razam
anda Deos de capitam.
Cãtã. Ta la la la lam, ta la la la lam.
A. Guerra, guerra, todo estado!
565 guerra, guerra muy cruel!
que o gran Rey Dom Manoel
contra Mouros estaa viado.
Tem promettido & jurado
dentro no seu coraçam
570 que poucos lhescaparão.
Cãtã. Ta la la la lam, ta la la la lam.
Anfaiado. Sua Alteza detremina
por acrescentar a fee
fazer da Mesquita See
575 em Fez por graça diuina.
Guerra, guerra muy contina
he sua grande tençam.
Cãtã. Ta la la la lam, ta la la la lam.
A. Este Rey tam excelente,
580 muyto bem afortunado,
tem o mundo rodeado
doriente ao Ponente:
Deos mui alto, omnipotente,
o seu real coraçam
585 tem posto na sua mão.
Cãtã. Ta la la la lam, ta la la la lam.

*E com esta soyça se sayram e
fenece a susodita Tragicomedia.*

Give it, if you can, with pleasure,
For the less you have of treasure
The less need you fear oppressions.
And O rulers and noblemen,
Yea and every citizen,
Listen, listen to the drums,
Hark to them with Christian ears!
And ye people, hold not back,
Forward, forward to the attack!
Give your lives and your incomes,
For in such a conflict holy
None should harbour any fears.

*All these figures ordered themselves in
winding circles and by turns sang and
acted the following, all singing:*

Ta la la la lam, ta la la la lam.
Hannibal. On, on! go forward, lord and
Since in war waged for the right [knight,
God as Captain leads the fight.
They sing. Ta la la la lam, ta la la la lam.
H. To war, to war, both rich and poor,
To war, to war, most ruthlessly
Since the great King Manuel's wrath
Is gone forth against the Moor.
And he sworn and promised hath
In his inmost heart that he
Will destroy them from his path.
They sing. Ta la la la lam, ta la la la lam.
H. And his Highness for a sign
Of our Holy Faith's increase
Wills that at Fez by grace divine
The mosque shall a cathedral be.
War, war ever without cease
Is his purpose mightily.
They sing. Ta la la la lam, ta la la la lam.
H. This our King most excellent
And with great good fortune blest
Is lord of every continent
From the East unto the West:
And the high God omnipotent
In his gracious keeping still
Guards his royal heart from ill.
They sing. Ta la la la lam, ta la la la lam.

*And with this chorus they went out and
the above Tragicomedy ends.*

FARSA DOS ALMOCREVES

Farça dos Almocreves.

*Esta seguinte farsa foy feyta &
representada ao muyto poderoso &
excelente Rey dom Ioam o terceyro em
Portugal deste nome na sua cidade de
Coimbra na era do Sēhor de MDXXVI.
Seu fundamento he que hum fidalgo de
muyto pouca renda vsaua muyto estado,
tinha capelam seu & ouriuez seu, &
outros officiaes, aos quaes nunca
pagaua. E vendose o seu capelam
esfarrapado & sem nada de seu entra
dizendo:*

Capelã. ¶ Pois que nam posso rezar
por me ver tão esquipado
por aqui por este Arnado
quero hum pouco passear
por espaçar meu cuydado,
e grosarey o romance
de Yo me estaba en Coimbra
pois Coimbra assim nos cimbra
que nam ha quem preto alcance.
10 ¶ Yo me estaba en Coimbra
cidade bem assentada,
pelos campos de Mondego
nam vi palha nem ceuada.
Quando aquilo vi mezquinho
entendi que era cilada
contra os cauallos da corte
& minha mula pelada.
Logo tiue a mao sinal
tanta milham apanhada
20 e a peso de dinheiro:
ó mula desemparada!
Vi vir ao longo do rio
hũa batalha ordenada,
nam de gentes mas de mus,
com muita raya pisada.
A carne estaa em Bretanha
& as couves em Biscaya.

19. *milhaam* B. *milhan* C.
24. *gentes* A, B. *gente* C, D, E.

The Carriers.

*The following farce was played before the
very powerful and excellent King Dom João
III of Portugal in his city of Coimbra in
the year of the Lord 1526. Its argument is
that a nobleman with a very small income
lived in great state and had his own
chaplain, goldsmith and other officials,
whom he never paid. His chaplain seeing
himself penniless and in tatters enters,
saying:*

Chaplain. In such straits I cannot pray,
So to lessen my distress
And to win lightheartedness
I'll walk along this Sandy Way
And, the cares that on me press
To soothe, the old romance I'll gloss
"I was in Coimbra city"
Since Coimbra without pity
Brings us to such dearth and loss.
I was in Coimbra city
That is built so gracefully,
In the plains of the Mondego
Straw nor barley could I see.
Thereupon, ah me! I reckoned
'Twas a trap set artfully
For the horses of the Court
And the mule that carried me.
Ill I augured when I saw
The young maize cut so lavishly
And selling for its weight in gold:
O my mule, I grieve for thee!
In the plain along the river
I saw a host in battle free
Not of men, of mice the host was,
They were fighting furiously.
There are cabbages—in Biscay
And there's meat—in Brittany.

21. *desamparada* B.
25. *raya* A, B. *raiva* C, D, E.

Sam capelam dum fidalgo
que nam tem renda nem nada;
30 quer ter muytos aparatos
& a casa anda esfaymada,
toma ratinhos por pagẽs
anda ja a cousa danada.
Querolhe pedir licença,
pagueme minha soldada.

¶ *Chega o capelam a casa do fidalgo,
& falando com elle diz:*

Cap. ¶ Senhor, ja seraa rezam.
Fid. Auante, padre, falay.
C. Digo que em tres annos vay
que sam vosso capelam.
40 F. He grande verdade, auante.
C. Eu fora ja do ifante,
e podera ser del Rey.
F. A bofé, padre, não sey.
C. Si, senhor, que eu sou destante
Aindaque ca mempreguei.
¶ Ora pois veja, senhor,
que he o que me ha de dar,
porque alem do altar
seruia de comprador.
50 F. Nam volo ey de negar.
Fazeyme hũa petiçam
de tudo o que requereis.
C. Senhor, nam me perlongueis,
que isso nam traz concrusam
nem vejo que a quereis.
¶ Porque me fiz polo vosso
clericus & negoceatores.
F. Assi vos dey eu fauores
& disso pouco que eu posso
60 vos fiz mais que outros señores.
Ora um clerigo que mais quer
de renda nem outro bem
que darlhe homem de comer,
que he cada dia hum vintem,
& mais muyto a seu prazer?
¶ Ora a honrra que se monta:
he capelam de foam!
C. E do vestir nam fazeis conta,
& esse comer com payxam,
70 & dormir com tanta afronta
que a coroa jaz no cham

I'm chaplain to a nobleman,
Poor as a church-mouse is he;
On great show his heart is set
Although his household famished be,
Rustic louts he has for pages
And all goes disastrously.
Now will I ask leave of him
And demand my salary.

*The chaplain arrives at the nobleman's
room and converses with him thus:*

C. Sir, it is high time, I ween...
N. Say on, good padre, say on.
C. I say three years are wellnigh gone
Since your chaplain I have been.
N. Say on, for such a truth convinces.
C. And I might have been the Prince's
Yes, and might have been the King's.
N. In good sooth that's not so clear.
C. For I'm meant for higher things
Though I stayed to serve you here.
So then, sir, please to consider
What I am to gain thereby,
For besides priest's service I
Served as buyer and as bidder.
N. That I surely won't deny.
Come now, make out a petition
Of all you would have me pay.
C. Sir, put me not off, I pray,
For indeed your one condition
Seems delay and still delay.
In your service I became
Priest and man of business too.
N. Yes, and I bestowed on you
Many a favour for the same,
More than most are wont to do.
What more should a priest require
Of money or emolument
Than his meals beside the fire
—That's daily one penny spent—
All things to his heart's desire?
And besides there is the glory:
He's chaplain to Lord So-and-so.
C. Of dress you think not, nor the worry
Of meals e'er taken in a flurry,
And sleeping with my head so low
My tonsure touched the ground, and no

43. *Habofee* B.
53. *perlongueis* A, B. *prolongueis* C, D, E.
52. *o que* A, B. *quanto* C, D, E.
57. *et negociatores* C.   62. *d'outro* C.

sem cabeçal, e aa hũa hora,	Comfort nor pillow for my head,
& missa sempre de caça?	And early mass, and late to bed.
& por vos cayr em graça	And I, your favour for to win,
serviauos tambem de fora,	Served out-of-doors as well as in,
atee comprar sibas na praça;	Bought shell-fish in the market-place,
¶ E outros carregozinhos	To many an errand set my face
desonestos pera mi.	—You know, sir, it is as I say—
Isto, senhor, he assi.	That ill became my dignity.
80 & azemel nesses caminhos,	Your carrier on the highway
arre aqui & arre ali,	—Gee-up, gee-wo, the livelong day—
& ter carrego dos gatos	Was I, and charge was given me
& dos negros da cozinha	Of the kitchen-negroes and the cats,
& alimparvolos çapatos	I cleaned your boots, I brushed your hats,
& outras cousas que eu fazia.	And might add other things to these.
F. ¶ Assi fiey eu de vos	N. Yes, for so 'twas my intent
toda a minha esmolaria	To trust you with my charities,
& daueis polo amor de Deos	And for the love of God you spent,
sem vos tomar conta hum dia.	Nor asked I how the money went.
90 C. Dos tres annos que eu alego	C. For the three years of which I speak
dalaey logo sem pendenças:	I'll tell you now without ado:
mandastes dar a hum cego	To a blind man a farthing you
hum real por Endoenças.	Once bade me give in Holy Week.
F. Eu isso nam volo nego.	N. I'm not denying that it's true.
C. ¶ E logo dahi a um anno	C. And then just one year afterward,
pera ajuda de casar	An orphan's dower to help to find,
hũa orfaã mandastes dar	You bade give cloth—the roughest kind
meo couado de pano	Of Alcobaça—half a yard.
Dalcobaça por tosar.	And also, perhaps you bear in mind,
100 E nos dous annos primeyros	Three lots of fish you bade divide
repartistes tres pescadas	Among the convents round about
por todos estes mosteyros	During these first three years: supplied
na Pederneyra compradas	Were they from Pederneira, out
daquestes mesmos dinheyros.	Of that same fund must I provide.
¶ Ora eu recebi cem reaes	Now in three years I did receive
em tres annos, contay bem,	One hundred réis, and at this rate
tenho aqui meo vintem.	Just this one halfpenny they leave.
F. Padre, boa conta daes,	N. I see you are most accurate.
ponde tudo num item	But come now, without more debate,
110 & falay ao meu doutor	Make one account of everything
que elle me falaraa nisso.	And give't my secretary, he
C. Deyxe vossa Merce ysso	Will the matter to my notice bring.
pera el Rey nosso senhor,	C. O Sir, leave all that for the King
& vos falay me de siso.	Our master, and speak seriously.
Que coma, senhor, me ficastes	My services your promise was,
ysto dentro em Santarem	Sir, when we were at Santarem,
de me pagardes muy bem.	That you would pay right well for them.
F. Em quantas missas machastes?	N. How often saw you me at Mass?
das vossas digo eu porem.	—I mean when 'twas you said the same.

103. *Pedreneyra* B.   115. *coma* A. *como* B.

120 C. Que culpa vos tem çamora?
     Por vos estam ellas nos çeos.
    F. Mas tomay as pera vos
     & guarday as muytembora,
     entam paguevolas Deos.
   ¶ Que eu não gasto meus dinheyros
     em missas atabalhoadas.
    C. & vos fazeys foliadas
     & nam pagaes o gaiteyro?
     Isso sam balcarriadas.
130 se vossas merces nam ham
     cordel pera tantos nos
     vyuey vos a aquem de vos
     & nam compreis gauiam
     pois que não tendes pios.
   ¶ Uos trazeis seis moços de pee
     & acrecentaylos a capa
     coma Rey, & por merce,
     nam tendo as terras do Papa
     nem os tratos de Guine:
140 antes vossa renda encurta
     coma pano Dalcobaça.
    F. Tudo o fidalgo da raça
     em que a renda seja curta
     he per força que isso faça.
   ¶ Padre, muy bem vos entendo:
     foy sempre a vontade minha
     daruos a el Rey ou ha Raynha.
    C. Isso me vay parecendo
     bom trigo se der farinha.
150 Senhor, se misso fizer
     grande merce me faraa.
    F. Eu vos direy que seraa:
     dizey agora hum profaceo, a ver
     que voz tendes pera laa.
    C. Folgarey eu de o dizer,
     mas quem me responderaa? [lorum.
    F. Eu. C. Per omnia secula secu-
    F. Amẽ. C. Dominus vobiscum.
    F. Auante. C. Sursum corda.
160 F. Tendes essa voz tam gorda
     que pareceis Alifante
     depois de farto daçorda.
    C. ¶ Pior voz tem Simão vaz
     tesoureyro e capelam,
     & pior o Adayam

C. If that was so am I to blame?
   They have been said on your behalf.
N. O keep them, keep them for yourself,
   You're very welcome to them—so,
   God will your due reward bestow.
   My money I waste not that way
   On masses muttered anyhow.
C. What, would you have your mummeries
   And think you need no fiddler pay? [now
   This is presumption's height, I trow.
   Unless your lordship's purse possesses
   Means for pomp and state so high
   To reduce them and spend less is
   Merely not a hawk to buy
   If you are without its jesses.
   Pages six in cloaks arrayed
   Wait upon you in the street
   In state that for a king were meet.
   Yet you have not, I'm afraid,
   The Pope's lands nor Guinea's trade.
   For your revenues shrink and shrink
   Much like Alcobaça cloth.
N. Even so every noble doth
   Who to high birth small means must link.
   There's no other way, I think.
   But I see, padre, what you want,
   And my wish has always been
   To give you to the King or Queen.
C. That would be good wheat, I grant,
   If its flour could be seen.
   Sir, if that should come to pass
   At your kindness I'll rejoice.
N. Well then, without more ado,
   That so I may judge your voice,
   Sing a preface of the Mass.
C. That will I most gladly do,
   But who will the responses say?
N. I. C. Per omnia secula.
N. Amen. C. Dominus vobiscum.
N. Sing on, padre. C. Sursum corda.
N. Your voice, less soft than a recorder,
   Is thick as an elephant's that has fed
   Its fill of soup—and no more said.
C. Worse voice has Simão Vaz, I ween,
   Yet he's Treasurer and King's
   Chaplain, worse voice has the Dean

128.   *o gaiteyro* A.   *ó gaiteiro* C, D, E.
142.   *da raça* A.   *de raça* C.
157.   *Penonia* A.   *Per omnia* C.

135.   *Uos trazeis* A.   *Trazeis* C, D, E.
153.   *dizey ora* B.

que canta como alcatraz,
e outros que por hi estam.
Quereys que acabe acantiga
& vereys onde vou ter.
170 F.   Padre, eu ey de ter fadiga,
mas del Rey aueis de ser,
escusada he mais briga.
C.   ¶ Sabeis em que estaa a contenda?
direys: he meu capelam.
& el Rey sabe a vossa renda
& rirse ha, se vem aa mam,
& remetermaa aa Fazenda.
F.   Se vos foreis entoado.
C.   Que bem posso eu cantar
180 onde dam sempre pescado
& de dous annos salgado,
o pior que ha no mar?

¶ *Vem um pagem do fidalgo & diz:*

Pag.   ¶ Senhor, o oriuez see alli.
F.   Entre. Quereraa dinheyro.
Venhaes embora, caualeyro,
cobri a cabeça, cobri.
Tendes grande amigo em mi
& mais vosso pregoeyro.
Gabeyuos ontem a el Rey
190 quanto se pode gabar.
& sey que vos ha dacupar,
& eu vos ajudarey
cada vez que mi achar:
¶ Porque aas vezes estas ajudas
sam milhores que cristeis,
porque soo a fama que aueis
& outras cousas meudas
o que valem ja o sabeis.
Our.   Senhor eu o seruirey
200 & nam quero outro senhor.
F.   Sabeis que tendes milhor,
eu o disse logo a el Rey
& faz em vosso louvor,
¶ Não vos da mais q̃ vos paguẽ
que vos deyxem de pagar.
Nunca vi tal esperar
nunca vi tal auantagem
nem tal modo dagradar.

—Like a pelican *he* sings—
And others that may be seen
In the palace. Let me end
My singing and great things you'll see.
N.   I think I'm rather tired, friend.
But the King's you'll surely be,
Nor need we further effort spend.
C.   Sir, the difficulty's this:
For you'll say: 'My chaplain he,'
The King knows what your income is
And he'll laugh right merrily
And send me to the Treasury.
N.   If you had but a good ear!
C.   How sing well when 'tis your use
To give me everlasting cheer
Of stockfish salted yesteryear,
The worst that all the seas produce?

*One of the nobleman's pages comes and
says:*

Page.   My lord, the goldsmith's at the door.
N.   Show him in.—He's come for more
Money.—Come in, Sir, good-day.
Put your hat on, I implore,
I'm your great friend, you may say,
Since I e'er your praises sing.
Only last night to the King
You most highly I commended
And I know that he intended
To employ you. I'll insist
Every time I see him, for
Such mention oft advances more
Than directly to assist,
And these little things, you know,
May to a great value grow
As your name and fame have grown.
G.   No other patron would I own,
Sir, I'll serve him with all zest.
N.   Know you what I like the best
In you? (To the King I said it
And it's greatly to your credit)
That you ne'er for payment pressed
Nor your creditors molest.
Ne'er such patience did I see,
Such superiority
And anxiety to please.

---

167.   *perhi* B.   174.   *direyis* A.   180.   *honde* B.
183.   *oriuez* and infra *our.* A; *oriuz* B.   *see* A; *seee* B; *s'he* C.
191.   *de occupar* C.
198.   *ja o sabeis* A.   *ja sabeis* C.
B omits 205 and prints 206 twice.

O. Nossa conta he tam pequena,
210 & ha tanto que he deuida,
que morre de prometida,
& peçoa ja com tanta pena
que depenno a minha vida.
F. ¶ Ora olhay ese falar
como vay bem martelado!
Folgo nam vos ter pagado
por vos ouuir martelar
marteladas dauisado.
O. Senhor, beyjovolas mãos
220 mas o meu queria eu na mão.
F. Tambem isso he cortesam:
'Senhor, beyjovolas mãos,
o meu queria eu na mão.'
Que bastiães tam louçãos!
¶ Quanto pesaua o saleyro?
O. Dous marcos bem, ouro & fio.
F. Essa he a prata: & o feitio?
O. Assaz de pouco dinheyro.
F. Que val com feytio & prata?
230 O. Justos noue mil reaes.
& nam posso esperar mais
que o vosso esperar me mata.
F. Rijamente mapertaes.
E fazeisme mentiroso,
que eu gabeyuos doutro geyto
& seu tornar ao deffeito
nam seraa proueyto vosso.
O. Assi que o meu saleyro peito?
F. Elle he dos mais maos saleiros
240 que eu em minha vida comprey.
O. Ainda o eu tomarey
a cabo de tres Janeyros
que ha que volo eu fiey.
F. ¶ Jagora não he rezam:
eu nam quero que vos percais.
O. Pois porque me nam pagais?
Que eu mesmo comprey caruão
com que mencaruoiçaes.
F. Moço vayme ver que faz el Rey,
250 se parecem damas la,
este dia nam se va
em pagaraas, nam pagarey.
& vos tornay outro dia ca
se nam achardes a mi
falay com o meu Camareyro

G. Our account's so small a thing
And is so long overdue,
'Tis half dead of promises,
So that when I bring it you
I but a dead promise bring.
N. How most cunningly inlaid
And enamelled is each word!
I rejoice not to have paid
For the sake of having heard
Phrases with such skill arrayed.
G. Sir, I kiss your hands, but still
What is mine would see in mine.
N. Another courtier's phrase so fine!
'Sir, I kiss your hands, but still
What is mine would see in mine!'
Fair flowers of speech are yours at will.
What did the salt-cellar weigh?
G. A good two marks, most accurately.
N. The silver. And your work, I pray?
G. That may almost be ignored.
N. In all what may its value be?
G. Just nine thousand réis, my lord.
And I can no longer wait
For I'm killed by your delay.
N. Your insistence, Sir, is great
And I shall have told a lie
For quite differently I
Praised you. Praise may turn to gibe: you
Surely will not gain thereby.
G. With the cellar must I bribe you?
N. 'Tis of salt-cellars the worst
For which I e'er gave a shilling.
G. Though three years have passed since [first
I let you have it I am willing
To retake it even now.
N. No, no, that I won't allow
For I would not have you lose.
G. Why then pay me not my dues?
For myself the charcoal bought
With which you turn my hopes to nought.
N. Boy, go see what does the King,
And if there are ladies to be seen,
The whole day shall not pass, I ween,
In pay and won't pay: no such thing.
And you return some other day:
And if you find that I'm away
Then speak unto my Chamberlain,

236. desfeyto B.   239. B omits mais.   240. que em C.
249. ver o que faz C.   255. com o A. c'o C.

porque elle tem o dinheyro
que cadano vem aqui
da renda do meu celeyro,
e delle recebereys
260 o mais certo pagamento.
   O. E pagaisme ahi co vento
ou co as outras merces?
   F. Tomaylhe vos la o tento.

¶ *Indose o capelam vay dizendo:*
   C. ¶ Estes ham dir ao parayso?
nam creo eu logo nelle.
Eu lhes mudarey a pelle:
daqui auante siso, siso,
juro a Deos queu mabruquele.

¶ *Vem o pagem com recado e diz:*
   P. ¶ Senhor, in Rey see no paço.
270 *F.* Em q̃ casa?
   P.   Isto abasta.
   F. O recado que elle da!
ratinho es de maa casta.
   P. Abõda, bem sey eu o q̃ eu faço.
   F. Abonda! olhay o vilam.
Damas parecem per hi?
   P. Si, senhor, damas vi,
andauam pelo balcam.
   F. ¶ E quẽ erã?
   P.   Damas mesmas.
   F. Como as chamã?
   P.   Nam as chamaua nĩguẽ.
280 *F.* Ratinhos sã abãtesmas
& quem por pagẽs os tem.
Eu ey de fazer por auer
hum pagem de boa casta.
   P. Ainda eu ey de crecer,
castiço sam eu que basta
se me Deos deyxar viuer.
¶ Pois o mais deprenderey
como outros como eu peri.
   F. Pois fazeo tu assi,
290 porque has de ser del Rey,
moço da camara ainda.
   P. Boa foy logo ca vinda.
Assi que atee os pastores
ham de ser del Rey samica!

He of all moneys that accrue
Has charge and of the revenue
That yearly comes from tithe and grain:
And from him you will obtain
Most certainly what is your due.
   G. And do you pay me with parade
Of words and other bounties vain?
   N. See to it you that you are paid.

As the chaplain goes out he says:
   C. Shall such men go to paradise?
If so I'll not believe in it.
But I'll be even with them yet:
Henceforth, proof against each device,
I'll countermine them by my wit.

The page comes with a message and says:
   P. The King be in the palace, Sir.
   N. In what room?
   P.   No more I know.
   N. Low-born villain, is it so
That a message you deliver?
   P. Arrah, I know what I'm about.
   N. Arrah! just listen to the lout!
Are any ladies present there?
   P. Yes, I saw ladies, I aver,
For they upon the terrace were.
   N. Who were they?
   P.   They were ladies, Sir.
   N. How called?
   P.   My lord, no one was calling.
   N. These rustic churls are too appalling.
And serve me right for keeping such.
Henceforth I really must contrive
To have a page of better stuff.
   P. Sir, I'll grow speedily enough
To please you, yes and will do much
Provided God leaves me alive:
And the rest I'll quickly learn
As others who good wages earn.
   N. Well do so, and then I will see
How you may come to serve the King
And even page of the Chamber be.
   P. So I did well to leave my home.
Since even shepherds may become
Attendants on the King, the King!

---

257. *anno* B.
263–4. *capelam. ourives?*
269. *s'he* C.
286. *deixa* C.
288. *com os outros* B.

268. *que m'abruquele* C. B omits 268.
271. *O recado qu'elle dá! Madraço, ?*
287. *o amais* B. *o mais o* C.
292. *ca a vinda* C.

Por isso esta terra he rica
de pão, porque os lauradores
fazem os filhos paçãos:
¶ Cedo não ha dauer vilãos,
todos del Rey, todos del Rey.
300 *F.* E tu zõbas?
    P.   Nam mas antes sey
que tambem alguns Christãos
hã de deyxar a costura.
     ¶ *Torna o capelam.*
C. ¶ Vossa merce per ventura
falou ja a el Rey em mi?
F. Ainda geyto nam vi.
C. Nam seja tam longa a cura
como o tempo que serui.
F. Anda el Rey tam acupado
co este Turco, co este Papa,
310 co esta França, co esta trapa
que nam acho vao aazado
porque tudo anda solapa.
Eu entro sempre ao vestir,
porém para arrecadar
ha mister grande vagar.
Podeis me em tanto seruir
atee que eu veja lugar.
C. Senhor queria concrusam.
F. Concrusam quereis? Bem, bem,
320 concrusam ha em alguem.
C. Concrusam quer concrusam,
& nam ha concrusam em nada.
Senhor, eu tenho gastada
hũa capa & hum mantam:
pagayme minha soldada.
F. Se vos podesseis achar
a altura de Leste a Oeste,
pois nam tendes voz que preste,
perequi era o medrar.
330 *C.* & vos pagaisme co ar?
Mao caminho vejo eu este.
          ¶ *Vayse.*
P. Deueo el Rey de tomar
que luta como danado:
elle é do nosso lugar,
de moço guardaua gado
agora veo a bispar.
¶ Mas nam sinto capelam
que lhe chãte hum par de quedas,
e chamase o labaredas.

So thrives with corn the land, bereft
Of labourers, whom their fathers send
To Court their fortunes for to mend,
And soon there'll be no peasants left,
For all will on the King attend.
N. What mockery's this?
    P.   Nay, Sir, I know
That some poor Christians even so
From toil shall have deliverance.
     Re-enter the Chaplain.
C. Have you, my lord, by any chance
Yet spoken to the King of me?
N. I've had no opportunity.
C. The remedy may be delayed
Another three years, I'm afraid.
N. The King's so busy, now with France,
Now with the Turk, and now the Pope,
And other matters of high scope,
And with such careful secrecy
That I can see but little hope.
I'm always there at the levée,
But get no long talk with the King
In which to settle anything.
Meanwhile you may still serve with me
Until I find an opening.
C. Sir, I would have the matter brought
To a conclusion. *N.* To conclusion?
Yes, and perhaps better than you thought.
C. Conclusion here I see in nought,
In everything only confusion.
Sir, a cope and a chasuble too
Have I in your service quite worn out:
Pay me the wages that are due.
N. Could you now but from East to West
Discover us the latitude
So, since your voice's not of the best,
You might win the King's gratitude.
C. Sir, I perceive you do but jest:
Would you pay me with a platitude?
          (*He goes out.*)
P. The King should take him, since he's
At any price, is such a fighter: [cheap
He's from our village, and the sheep
Was in his boyhood wont to keep,
And now he's searching for a mitre.
But there's no chaplain of them all
Could ever bring him to a fall,
And Labaredas is his name.

308. *acupado* A, B. *occupado* C.   325. *minha* A, B. *a minha* C.

340 *F.* E ca chamase cotão,
mais fidalgo que os azedas.
Satisfaçam me pedia,
que he pior de fazer
que queymar toda Turquia,
porque do satisfazer
naceo a melanconia.

¶ *Vem Pero vaz, almocreue, que
traz hum pouco de fato do fidalgo &
vem tangendo a chocalhada & cantando:*

¶ A serra he alta, fria & neuosa,

vi venir serrana, gentil, graciosa.

Falando.

¶ Arre mulo namorado
350 que custaste no mercado
sete mil & nouecentos
& hum traque pera o siseyro.
Apre ruço, acrecentado
a moradia de quinhentos
paga per Nuno ribeyro.
Dix pera a paga & pera ti.
Arre, arre, arre embora
que ja as tardes sam damigo,
apre besta do roim,
360 uxtix, o atafal vay por fora
& a cilha no embigo.
Sam diabos pera os ratos
estes vinhos da candosa.

Canta.

¶ A serra he alta, fria & neuosa,

vi venir serrana, gentil, graciosa.

Fala.

¶ Apre ca yeramaa
que te vas todo torcendo
como jogador de bola.
Huxtix, huxte xulo ca,
370 que teu dou yraas gemendo
e resoprando sob a cola.
Aa corpo de mi tareja
descobrisuos vos na cama.
Parece? dix pera vossa ama,
nam criaraas tu hi bareja.

N. But here Cotão's yclept the same,
The noblest in the land withal.
Now he demands what's his by right
As though 'twere not as easy quite
For me all Turkey's lands to burn,
Since any service to requite
Gives one a melancholy turn.

*Pero Vaz, a carrier, comes with a parcel
of clothes for the nobleman and enters with
jingling of bells, singing:*

The snow is on the hills,
the hills so cold and high,
I saw a maiden of the hills,
graceful and fair, pass by.
(*Speaking:*)
Go on there, *arré*, my fine mule,
You cost me in the market-place
Seven thousand and nine hundred réis
And a kick in the eye for the tax-gatherer
Get on, my roan. And add thereto [fool.
The portion of five hundred too
That Nuno Ribeiro had to pay:
All this, my mule, was paid for you.
Get on, *arré*, upon your way,
For the afternoons now are the best of the
Get on, you brute, get on, I say, [day,
Look you the crupper's all awry
And see, right round is pulled the girth:
Candosa wines bring little mirth
To any such poor fool as I.
(*He sings:*)
The snow is on the hills,
the hills so cold and high,
I saw a maiden of the hills,
graceful and fair, pass by.
(*He speaks:*)
Curse you, go on, *arré*, I say,
And now you're going all askew
As one who would at skittles play:
Come up, my mule, *arré, arré*.
But if I once begin with you
I'll make you groan upon your way.
By my Theresa, you'd lose your load,
You would, would you, upon the road?
But I'll not give you any rest
Nor leave flies leisure to molest.

346. *melancholia* C.   *chocallada* B.
372. *Aa corpo* A.   *ao corpo* C, D, E.

369. *uxtix, uxte* C.
375. *vareja* C.

Canta.	(*He sings:*)
¶ Vi venir serrana gẽtil graciosa,	I saw a maiden of the hills,
	graceful and fair, pass by,
chegueime pera ella con grã cortesia.	And towards her then went I with great
Fala.	courtesy. (*He speaks:*)
Mandovos eu sospirar	Yes, and I would have you sigh
pola padeyra Daueiro,	For the Aveiro bakeress,
380 que haueis de chegar aa venda	For the inn you'll come to by and by
& entam ali desalbardar	And then we'll off with the packsaddle
& albardar o vendeyro	And the innkeeper we'll straddle
senam teuer que nos venda	If he have not, to slake our thirstiness,
vinho a seis, cabra a tres,	Good wine at threepence and kid at less,
pam de calo, fillhos de mãteyga,	And for hard bread soft buttermilk,
moça fermosa, lẽçoes de veludo,	A fair wench to serve and sheets of silk,
casa juncada, noyte longa,	If the floor's strewn with rushes the night
	be long,
chuua com pedra, telhado nouo,	If it hails, be the roof both new and strong,
a candea morta & a gaita a porta.	When the lamp burns dim welcome fiddler's
	strain.
390 Apre, zambro, empeçarás?	Hold up, there! At your tricks again?
Olha tu nam te ponha eu	Bandy-legged brute, shall I prevail,
oculos na rabadilha	If I rain down barnacles on your tail,
& veraas por onde vas.	To make you look where you are going.
Demo que teu dou por seu	To the Devil with you! He'll be knowing
& andaraas la de silha.	How to handle your like without fail.
¶ Chegueime a ella de grã cortesia,	'And towards her then went I with great
	courtesy:
disselhe: Señora, quereis cõpanhia?	Will you, said I, lady, of my company?'
¶ *Vem Vasco afonso, outro almocreve,*	*Vasco Afonso, another carrier, comes*
& topam se ambos no caminho & diz	*along and they meet on the road, and Pero*
Pero vaz:	*Vaz says:*
P. ¶ Ou, Vasco Afonso, onde vas?	P. Ho, Vasco Afonso, where goest thou?
V. Huxtix, per esse cham.	V. Look you, I go along the road.
400 P. Nam traes chocalhos nem nada?	P. Without thy bells nor any load?
V. Furtarão mos la detras	V. They were stolen from me even now
na venda da repeydada.	By a cursed robber at the inn.
P. Hi bebemos nos aa vinda.	P. We had a drink there as we came.
V. Cujo he o fato, Pero vaz?	V. Whose, Pero Vaz, is all this stuff?
P. Dum fidalgo, dou oo diabo	P. A nobleman's, Devil take the same,
o fato & seu dono coelle.	Him and his suit of clothes and all.
V. Valente almofreyxe traz.	V. Yes, 'tis a bundle large enough.
P. Tomo o mu de cabo a rabo.	P. It takes the mule from head to tail.
V. Par deos carrega leua elle.	V. One cannot say it's load is small.
410 P. ¶ Uxtix, agora nam paceram elles	P. Look you, now they will not graze
& la por essas charnecas	And when through open moors we pass
vem roendo as vrzeyras.	They nibble at the heather roots.

377. *pa* B.	383. *que nos* A, B. *que vos* C.
389. *a candeia morta, gaita* C.	395. *cilha* C.
397. *senhora* B.	406. *e o seu* C.

V. Leixos tu, Pero vaz, que elles
acham aqui as eruas secas
& nam comem giesteyras.
& quanto te dam por besta?
P. Nam sey, assi Deos majude.
V. Nam fizeste logo o preço?
mal aas tu de liurar desta.
420 *P.* Leyxeyo em sua virtude,
no que elle vir que eu mereço.
V. ¶ Em sua virtude o deixaste?
& trala elle com sigo
ou ha dir buscala ainda?
Oo que aramaa te fartaste!
Queres apostar comigo
que te renegues da vinda?
P. Elle pos desta maneyra
a mão na barba & me jurou
430 de meus dinheyros pagalos.
V. Essa barba era inteyra
a mesma em que te jurou
ou bigodezinhos ralos?
P. ¶ Ora Deos sabe o que faz
& o juiz de çamora:
de fidalgo he manter fee.
V. Bem sabes tu, Pero vaz,
que fidalgo ha jagora
que nam sabe se o he.
440 Como vay a ta molher
& todo teu gasalhado?
P. O gasalhado hi ficou.
V. E a molher? *P.* Fugio. *V.* Nam
pode ser.
Como estaraas magoado,
yeramaa. *P.* Bofa nam estou.
¶ Huxtix, sempre has dandar

debayxo dos souereyros?
& a mi que me da disso?
V. Per força ta de pesar
450 se rirem de ti os vendeyros.
P. Nam tenho de ver co isso.
¶ Vay, Vasco afonso, ao teu mu
que se quer deytar no cham.
V. Pesate mas desingulas.
P. Nam pesa: bem sabes tu
que as molheres nam sam
todo o verã senã pulgas.

V. Leave them, Pero Vaz, to go their ways,
For very parched is here the grass,
And they won't touch the broom's green
What is to thee for carriage given? [shoots.
P. I do not know, so help me Heaven.
V. What! didst thou not then fix a price?
Thou'st caught then in a pretty vice.
P. I left it to his good faith to pay
Whate'er he saw was due to me.
V. Left it to his good faith, you say!
And what then if he hasn't any
And has to go to look for it?
O thou hast done most foolishly:
I'll wager thee an honest penny
That thou'lt repent thy coming yet.
P. He put his hand—see here how—
Upon his beard and swore that I
Should be paid my money faithfully.
V. Was it a proper beard, look you now,
On which this oath of his was heard,
Or a mere straggling moustache?
P. Nay, as there is a God above,
A judge who will the right approve,
A nobleman will keep his word.
V. Thou knowest right well, Pero Vaz,
There are nobles now who scarcely know
Whether they're noblemen or no.
How is thy wife now? Is she well?
And thy other property?
P. That's there all right.
V. Well, and she?
P. She ran away. *V.* Impossible!
How sad thou must be feeling, why
Bad luck to it. *P.* In faith not I.
[*To his mule*] Come up there, must you
ever go
Just where the cork-trees come so low?—
What has it to do with me?
V. Thou must needs be hurt thereby
When the innkeepers laugh at thee.
P. No, that doesn't make me tremble.
Vasco Afonso, look to thy mule,
It's going to lie down on the ground.
V. Thou feelest it but canst dissemble.
P. O no, I don't. Thou know'st as a
rule
What women are all the summer round:

419. *as* B.   422. *leixaste* C.   425. *fretaste* C.
443. *fogio* B.   449. *t'ha* C.

Isto quanto aa saudade
que eu della posso ter;
460 & quanto ao rir das gentes
ella faz sua vontade:
foyse perhi a perder
& eu nã perdi os dentes.
¶ Ainda aqui estou enteyro,
Vasco afonso, como dantes,
filho de Afonso vaz
e neto de Jam diz pedreyro
& de Branca Anes Dabrantes,
nam me faz nem me desfaz.
470 Do que me fica gram noo
que teue rezam de se hir
& em parte nam he culpada;
porque ella dormia soo
& eu sempre hia dormir
cos meus muus aa meyjoada.
¶ Queria a eu yr poupando
pera la pera a velhice
como colcha de Medina
& ella mosca Fernando
480 quando vio minha pequice
foy descobrir outra mina.
V. E agora que faraas?
P. Yrey dormir aa Cornaga
e aamenhaã aa Cucanha.
E tu vay, embora vas,
que eu vou seruir esta praga
& veremos que se ganha.

¶ *Vai cantando.*

¶ Disselhe: señora q̃reis cõpanhia?
Dixeme: escudeyro segui vossa via.

490 *Pag.* Senhor, o almocreue he aq̃lle
que os chocalhos ouço eu,
este he o fato, senhor.
Fid. Ponde todos cobro nelle.
Per. Uxtix mulo do judeu.
O fato hu saa de por?
Pa. Venhaes embora, pero vaz.
Pe. Mãtenha deos vossa merce.
Pa. Viestes polas folgosas?
Pe. Ahi estiue eu oje faz
500 oyto dias pee por pee

So much for any regret that I
Might feel for her now she is gone.
And as for people's laughter, why
As was her will so has she done:
She went away to her own loss
And leaves me not one tooth the worse.
I'm hale and hearty as I was,
Vasco Afonso, no change there is:
The son still of Afonso Vaz,
Grandson of the mason Jan Diz
And Branca Annes my grandmother
Of Abrantes: nor one way nor the other
It touches me. And yet I grieve
That she was partly in the right
And was not utterly to blame,
For I was ever wont to leave
Her lonely there while every night
To sleep at the inn with my mules I came.
I wished thus that she might remain
As a refuge for my old age,
Like a Medina counterpane,
But she saw through me and alack
Must view the matter in a rage
And go off on another track.
V. And what wilt thou do now, I pray?
P. I'll sleep at Cornaga's inn to-day
And at Cucanha's to-morrow.
So get thee on upon thy way,
And I'll on this errand to my sorrow
And we'll see how it will pay.

He goes singing:

'Will you,' said I, 'lady, of my company?'
But 'Sir knight, pass on your way,' said
      she unto me.
Page. Sir, the carrier is here,
He has brought the clothes for you,
For the sound of the bells I hear.
N. Look to it all of you with care.
Pero. Hold up mule, you son of a Jew.
Where shall I put the clothes, say, where?
P. Good morrow to you, good Pero.
Pe. God keep your worship even so.
P. By the Folgosas did you go?
Pe. Yes, that way was my journey made
And to-day is just a week ago

---

465. *Afonso* B.   466. *Affonso* B.   467. *Iam diz* B. *Jan Diz* C.
470. *gram noo* A. *gran dó* C.   471. *razam* B.
484. *aa menhaa* B.   488. *señora* A, B.
491. *chocallos* B.   495. *s'ha* C.

em casa de hũas tias vossas.
Pa. Ora meu pai que fazia?
Pe. Cauaua andando o bacelo
bem cansado e bem suado.
Pa. E minha mãy?
Pe.   Leuaua o gado
la pera val de cubelo,
mal roupada que ella ia.
Huxtix, que mao lambaz.
& vossa merce que faz?
510 *Pa.* Estou louçam coma que.
Pe. E abofee creceis açaz,
saude que vos Deos dee.
Pa. ¶ Eu sou pagem de meu senhor,
se Deos quiser pagem da lança.
Pe. E hum fidalgo tanto alcança?
Isso he Demperador
ora prenda el Rey de França.
Pa. Ainda eu ey de perchegar
a caualeyro fidalgo.
520 *Pe.* Pardeos, João crespo penaluo,
que isso seria esperar
de mao rafeyro ser galgo.
¶ Mais fermoso estaa ao vilam
mao burel que mao frisado
& romper matos maninhos,
& ao fidalgo de naçam
ter quatro homẽs de recado
e leyxar laurar ratinhos;
que em Frandes & Alemanha
530 em toda França & Veneza,
que vivem por siso e manha
por nam viver em tristeza;
¶ nam he como nesta terra.
Porque o filho do laurador
casa la com lauradora
& nunca sobem mais nada;
& o filho do broslador
casa com a brosladora,
isto por ley ordenada.
540 E os fidalgos de casta
seruem os Reis & altos senhores
de tudo sem presunçam,
tam chãos q̃ pouco lhes basta:
& os filhos dos lauradores

Since in your aunts' house there I stayed.
P. What was my father doing now?
Pe. Hoeing the vines in the sweat of his
In great heat and weariness.   [brow,
P. And my mother?
Pe.   She was up the dale
Driving the herd—all in tatters her dress—
Out towards Cobelo's Vale.   [brute.
[*To the mule*] Be quiet there. The greedy
And yourself how do these times suit?
P. I'm flourishing like anything.
Pe. In faith you're growing fine and tall,
And may God give you health withal.
P. I'm my lord's page and may advance
To be the page who bears the lance.
Pe. What, is a nobleman so great?
That's for an Emperor, and the King
Of France, I see, must mind his state.
P. And more, I may go on to be
A knight of the nobility.
Pe. Nay, by the Lord, John, listen to me:
That were t'expect without good ground
A watch-dog to become a hound.
To the peasant far more honour doth
Coarse sacking than your flimsy cloth.
And to set his hand to till the soil
And for the nobleman by birth
To have men on his ways to toil
And let the rustic plough the earth.
For in Flanders and in Germany,
In Venice and the whole of France,
They live well and reasonably
And thus win deliverance
From the woes that are here to hand.
For there the peasant on the land
Doth the peasant's daughter wed,
Nor further seeks to raise his head,
And even so the skilled workmen too
Those only of their own class woo,
By law is it so orderèd.
And there the nobility
Serve kings and lords of high degree
And do so with a lowly heart
And simple, for their needs are small,
And the sons of the peasants for their part

---

503. *Cauaua andando o bacelo* A, B. *Cavando andava bacelo* C.   506. *Cobelo* C.
513. *sou* A; *sam* C [cf. 591]. *señor* B.   518. *ey de perchegar* A, B. *hei de chegar* C.   524. *bom frisado* B.   535. *casalo* B.
536. *sobem* A, B. *sabem* C.

pera todos lauram pam.
Pa. ¶ Quero hir dizer de vos.
Pe. Ora yde dizer de mi;
que se grave he Deos dos ceos
mais graves deoses ha qui.
550 *Pa.* Senhor ali vem o fato
& estaa ha porta o almocreue,
vede quem lha a de pagar
isso tal que se lhe deue.
F. ¶ Isto he com que meu mato.
quem te manda procurar?
Atenta tu polo meu
& arrecado muyto bem
& nam cures de ninguem.
Pa. Elle he dapar de Viseu
560 & homem que me pertem,
pois a porta lhabri eu.

¶ *Entra dentro o almocreue & diz:*

¶ *Pe.* Senhor, trouxe a frascaria
do vossa merce aqui.
Hi estam os mus albardados.
Fid. Essa he a mais nova arauia
d'almocreue que eu vi:
dou-te vinte mil cruzados.
Pe. Mas pagueme vossa merce
o meu aluguer, no mais,
570 que me quero logo hir.
F O aluguer quanto he?
Pe. Mil & seis centos reaes,
& isto por vos seruir.
F. ¶ Falay co meu azemel,
porque he doutor das bestas
& estrologo dos mus:
que assente em hum papel
per aualiações honestas
o que se monta, ora sus;
580 porque esta he a ordenança
& estilo de minha casa.
& se o azemel for fora,
como cuydo que he em França,
dareis outra volta aa massa
& hiruos eis por agora.
¶ Vossa paga he nas mãos.
Pe. Ja a eu quisera nos pees,
oo pesar de minha mãy!
F. E tens tu pay & yrmãos?

Sow and reap the crops for all.
P. I'll go and announce you now.
Pe. Go and announce to your heart's fill:
By the solemn God of Heaven I vow
There are gods here more solemn still.
P. Sir, they've brought the clothes for
And the carrier's at the door;   [you,
Please to tell me, Sir, therefore,
Who is to pay him what is due.
N. That's what I should like to know.
What business is it of yours? You go
And look to what they've brought for me:
Stow it away in safety
And trouble about nothing more.
P. From over against Viseu is he
And properly belongs to me
Since I it was answered the door.

The carrier comes in and says:

Pe. Sir, I've brought the goods, you see,
For your worship, they're not small,
Here they are, pack-mules and all.
N. This is the strangest carrier's jargon
That has ever come my way.
A thousand crowns for you, a bargain.
Pe. Nay, Sir, I would have you pay
Simply what you owe to me,
For I must straightway be gone.
N. And what may the carriage be?
Pe. Sixteen hundred reis: you alone
Would I charge so little, Sir.
N. Go speak with my head messenger
For he's master of the horses
And the mules' astrologer:
Let him in a neat account
Fairly reckon the amount,
What is due, and how bought, how sold,
For this customary course is
Ever followed in my household.
And if he's absent by some chance,
And I *believe* he is in France,
Then return some other day
And for the present go your way.
And your pay is in your hand.
Pe. I wish I had it in my feet.
O woe is me, O by my mother!
N. And have you a father and a brother?

549. *haqui* B. *ha aqui* C.
559. *da par* B.
576. *astrologo* C.

552. *lha a* A. *lha* B. *lhe ha* C.
562. *frescaria* B.

590 *Pe.* Pagay, senhor, não zombeis,
que sam dalem da sertãy
& nam posso ca tornar.
F. Se ca vieres aa corte
pousaraas aqui cos meus.
Pe. Nunca mais ey de fiar
em fidalgo desta sorte,
em que o mande sam Mateus.
F. ¶ Faze por teres amigos
& mais tal homem comeu
600 porque dinheyro he hum vento.
Pe. Dou eu ja oo demo os amigos
que me a mi levam o meu.

¶   *Vayse o almocreue & vem outro*
Fidalgo & diz o fidalgo primeyro:

F. 1º. ¶ Oo que grande saber vir
& que gram saber maa vontade.
F. 2º. Pois, senhor, que vos parece?
desejo de vos seruir
& nam quero q̃ venha aa cidade
hum quem nam parece esquece.
F. 1º. Paguey soma de dinheyro
610 a hum ouriuez agora
de prata que me laurou
& paguey a hum recoueiro
que he a dar dinheyros fora
a quem nam sei como os ganhou.
F. 2º. Ganhã-nos tã mal ganhados
que vos roubam as orelhas.
F. 1º. Pola hostia consagrada
& polo Deos consagrado
que os lobos nas ouelhas
620 nam dam tã crua pancada.
Polos sanctos auangelhos
e polo omnium sanctorum
que atee o meu capelam
per mesinhas de coelhos
& hũa secula seculorum
lhe dou por missa hum tostam.
¶ Não ha ja homem em Portugal
tam sogeyto em pagar
nem tam forro pera molheres.
630 *F.* 2º. Guarday vos esse bem tal
que a mi ham me de matar
bem me queres, mal me queres.
F. 1º. Per quantas damas Deos tẽ

Pe. Jest not but pay me as is meet,
For I come from beyond the moor,
Return I cannot to the Court.
N. Whenever you come to town my door
Is open: lodge with my men you must.
Pe. Never again will I put trust
In any noble of this sort,
Not though St Matthew himself exhort.
N. To making friends your thoughts
Such friends as I especially,   [incline,
For money is but vanity.
Pe. To the devil with such friends, say I,
Who cozen me of what is mine.

The carrier goes away and another
nobleman comes and the first nobleman
says:

1st N. O how well you time your visit
And your coming is most kind.
2nd N. Sir, it is not doubtful, is it?,
That to serve you I'm inclined.
And I would not have it said
Out of sight is out of mind.
1st N. A large sum of money I
To a goldsmith have just paid
For some silver he inlaid.
To a carrier too, though why
I should pay him scarce appears,
Or how he won what he obtains.
2nd N. So ill-gotten are their gains
That they rob your very ears.
1st N. Nay by the consecrated Host
And the Holy God of Heaven
Their onslaught is more fierce almost
Than that of wolves on a sheepfold even.
Why my very chaplain too
For the little work he does for me
By whatever saints there be
Yea and by the Gospels true
For his prayers I must be willing
To give him for each mass a shilling.
There's not in Portugal a man
More liable to pay than I:
Nor one who is from love so free.
2nd N. Ah keep yourself from its fell ban,
For lovers' joys and misery
I think will be the end of me.
1st N. For all the ladies upon earth

591. *sam* A; *sou* C [cf. 513]. *da Sertãy* A, B; *do sertão* C.
604. *maa* A. *me a* C. *& gran saber maa* B.   B omits 617–626.

nã daria nemigalha:	I would not give a halfpenny:
olhay que descubro isto.	Frankly I say that's what they're worth.
F. 2º. Sam tam fino em querer bem	*2nd N.* A lover gentle, you must know,
que de fino tomo a palha	As I excels in delicacy,
pola fee de Jesu Christo.	By my faith 'tis even so.
¶ Quem quereis que veja olhinhos	And who should a fair lady's eyes
640 que se nam perca por elles	Behold and not be lost in sighs?
la per hũs geytinhos lindos	And their pretty ways that lead
que vos metem em caminhos	You to toils in which indeed
& nam ha caminhos nelles	You will find no thoroughfare:
senam espinhos infindos.	Only infinite thorns and care.
F. 1º. Eu ja nam ey de penar	*1st N.* Nevermore for lady I
por amores de ninguem;	Shall be made to pine or sigh.
mas dama de bom morgado	But if she have fine estate
aqui vay o remirar,	Thither then will my eyes turn
aqui vay o querer bem,	And my heart begin to burn,
650 & tudo bem empregado.	Let the profit be but great.
¶ Que porque dance muy bem	Dance she ne'er so gracefully,
nem baylar com muyta graça,	Skilfully with nimble feet,
seja discreta, auisada,	Be she sensible, discreet,
fermosa quanto Deos tem,	And fairest of all fair to see:
senhor, boa prol lhe faça	If of her father I have no profit,
se seu pay nam tiuer nada.	Much good, I say, may she have of it.
Nam sejaes vos tam mancias,	Do not you be so lovelorn,
que isso passa ja damor	For 'tis scarcely to be borne,
& cousas desesperadas.	Love? nay madness, verily.
660 *F.* 2º. Porem la por vossas vias	*2nd N.* By your way of it, I see,
vou vos esperar, senhor,	I the husbandman discover
a rendeyro das jugadas.	And in very sooth 'twill be
¶ Porque galante caseyro	A fine story this for me
he pera por em historia.	Of the farmer turning lover.
F. 1º. Mas zombay, senhor, zombay.	*1st N.* O mock me, Sir, if mock you can.
F. 2º. Senhor, o homem inteiro	*2nd N.* Sir, the perfect gentleman
nam lha de vir ha memoria	Doth not link his lady fair
co a dama o de seu pay;	With what her father may possess.
nem ha mais de desejar	Nor descries he other scope,
670 nem querer outra alegria	Nor sighs for greater happiness
que so los tus cabellos niña:	Than 'In the tresses of thy hair,'
nam ha hi mais que esperar	For indeed is all his hope
onde he esta canteguinha,	Centred in that single song,
e todo mal he quem no tem,	And 'Sorrows to him alone belong,'
e se o disserem digão, alma minha,	And 'If they say so, let it be '
quem vos anojou meu bem.	And 'Who, my love, hath vexèd thee?'
Ey os todos de grosar	I will sing and gloss them too,
¶ ainda que sejam velhos.	All these songs both old and new.
F. 1º. Vos, senhor, vindes tão brauo	*1st N.* Sir, you are so fierce and brave

634. *nem migalha* C.	644. *enfindos* A. B omits 644.
666. *enteyro* B.	671. que so *Los tus cabellos niña* C.
675. *e se o disserem digão—Alma minha* C.	

680 que eu eyuos medo ja:
polos sanctos auangelhos
que leuais tudo ao cabo
la onde cabo nam ha.
F. 2º. Zombaes, & daes a entender
zombando que mentendeis.
Pois de vos muy alto sou,
porque deueis de saber
que se damor nam sabeis
nam podeis yr onde vou.
690 ¶ Quando fordes namorado
vireis a ser mais profundo,
mais discreto e mais sotil,
porque o mundo namorado
he la, senhor, outro mundo,
que estaa alem do Brasil.
Oo meu mundo verdadeyro!
oo minha justa batalha!
mundo do meu doce engano!
F.1º. Oo palha do meu palheyro,
700 que tenho hum mundo de palha,
palha ainda dora a hum anno;
e tenho hum mundo de trigo
para vender a essa gente:
bom cabeça tem Morale.
Nam quero damor, amigo
andar gemente & flente
in hac lachrymarum valle.
F. 2º. Voume: vos não sois sentido,
sois muy duro do pescoço,
710 não val isso nemigalha:
pesame de ver perdido
hum homem fidalgo ençosso,
pois tem a vida na palha.

That I'm half afraid of you:
By the holy books you have
A wont to carry with high hand
Even what you can't command.
2nd N. You mock me, yet 'tis but to
That as you mock you understand. [prove
For I must far above you stand,
Since if you are exempt from love
'Tis at least for you to know
That where I go you cannot go.
When you are a lover, then
A discretion more profound
And subtlety your mind may fill:
The lover's world's beyond your ken,
A different world that's to be found
In regions further than Brazil.
O my world, the only true one,
O the right I fight for oft,
Sweet illusions that pursue one!
1st N. O the straw that's in my loft!
For a world of straw is mine
That all wants for a year will meet,
And I have a world of wheat
And will sell to all beholders,
And a head upon my shoulders.
But, my friend, I will not pine
For love, nor weep throughout the years
Mourning in this vale of tears.
2nd N. Farewell, you have no sentiment
And are stiff-necked exceedingly,
All that's not worth an ancient saw.
But me it grieves to see so spent
A noble's life most witlessly,
Since he's become a man of straw.

FINIS

681. *auangelhos* A, B. *evangelhos* C.   689. *onde eu vou* C.
692. *subtil* C.   703. *vender essa essa gente* A. *a essa* B, C.
704. *bom* A, B. *boa* C.   707. *vale* A.   712. *ençosso* A. *ensoço* C.
B omits *Finis* and has: *Vanse estas figuras & acabouse esta farsa. Laus Deo*

TRAGICOMEDIA PASTORIL DA SERRA DA ESTRELLA

Tragicomedia Pastoril da Serra da Estrella.

Tragicomedia pastoril feyta & representada ao muyto poderoso & catholico Rey dom Ioam o terceyro deste nome em Portugal ao parto da serenissima & muy alta Raynha dona Caterina nossa senhora & nacimento da illustrissima iffante dona Maria, que depois foy princesa de Castella, na cidade de Coimbra na era do senhor de M.D.xxvij.

Entra logo a serra da estrela & diz:

¶ Prazer que fez abalar
tal serra comeu da estrela
faraa engrandecer o mar
e faraa baylar Castela
5 & o ceo tambem cantar.
Determino logo essora
ir a Coimbra assi inteyra
em figura de pastora,
feyta serrana da beyra
10 como quem na beyra mora.
¶ E leuarey la comigo
minhas serranas trigueyras,
cada qual com seu amigo,
& todalas ouelheyras
15 que andam no meu pacigo.
E das vacas mais pintadas
& das ouelhas meyrinhas
pera dar apresentadas
aa Raynha das Raynhas,
20 cume das bem assombradas.
¶ Sendo Raynha tamanha
veo ca aa serra embora
parir na nossa montanha
outra princesa despanha
25 como lhe demos agora,
hũa rosa imperial
como a muy alta Isabel,

Pastoral tragicomedy of the Serra da Estrella.

A pastoral tragicomedy made in honour of and played before the very powerful and catholic King Dom John III of Portugal on the delivery of the most high Queen Dona Caterina our lady and the birth of the most illustrious Infanta Dona Maria, afterwards Princess of Castille, in the city of Coimbra in the Year of the Lord 1527.

Enters the Serra da Estrella and says:

Joy that shakes and wakes the hill,
The mighty mountain-range of me,
Will increase the swelling sea
And the sky with singing fill
Till Castilla dance in glee.
And in this hour it is my will
That the whole of me, no less,
To Coimbra as a shepherdess,
A Beira peasant-girl, shall come,
Since in Beira is my home.
With me thither they who are mine,
The hill-girls of nut-brown tresses,
Each with her lover shall repair,
Yea and all the shepherdesses
Who flocks upon my pastures keep.
And the choicest of the kine
And of the merino sheep,
That I may have to offer there
A present to our Queen of Queens
Who is fairest of the fair.
Mistress she of broad demesnes
Came unto our mountain land
And among the hills hath she
Borne a new princess of Spain
That we give to her again,
Even a rose imperial
As the most high Isabel,

Esta tragecomedia pastoril foy feyta B.   com hum parvo & diz C.
2.   estrella B.   4.   Castella B.   7.   yr B.   24.   despaña B.

imagem de Gabriel,
repouso de Portugal,
30 seu precioso esperauel.
¶ Bem sabe Deos o que faz.
PARVO. Bofe nam sabe nem isto;
a virgem Maria si;
mas cantelle nam he bo
35 nega pera queymar vinhas.
SERRA. Isso has tu de dizer?
PARVO. Quem? Deos? juro a Deos
que nam faz nega o que quer.
La em Coimbra estaueu
40 quando a mesma raynha
pario mesmo em cas din Rey,
eu vos direy como foy.
Ella mesma, benzaa Deos,
estaua mesmo no paço,
45 quella, quando ha de parir,
poucas vezes anda fora.
¶ Ora a mesma camareyra
porque he mesma de Castella,
rogou aa mesma parteyra
50 que fizesse delle ella—
pere qui vay a carreyra—
sabeis porque?
Porque a mesma Empenatriz
pario mesmo Empenador
55 e agora estam auiados.
Mas quando minha mãy paria
como a virgem a liuraua
tanto se lhe dauella
que fosse aquelle como aquella
60 se nam ouos hũa vez.

¶   Vem Gonçalo, hũ pastor da serra, q̃
vem da corte & vem cantando:
¶ Volaua la pega y vayse.
Quem me la tomasse!
Andaua la pega
no meu cerrado,
65 olhos morenos, bico dourado
quem me la tomasse!
Falado.
¶ Pardeos muy aluoraçada
anda a nossa serra agora.
70 SERRA. Gonçalo, venhas embora
porque eu estou abalada
pera sair de mi fora.
Queriauos ajuntar

An image of Gabriel
For the repose of Portugal,
Its precious ward and canopy.
So clearly is God's purpose planned.
Fool. Good faith, no, not a whit he knows
But the Virgin Mary knows.
But he unto no good inclines
And only serves to burn the vines.
Serra. What a thing for thee to say!
Fool. Who? God? why, now, I swear to
That He must always have His way. [God
For I was at Coimbra, I,
At the time this very queen
In the palace bore a daughter:
I will tell you all about it.
This same queen, and may God bless her,
The queen herself was in the palace,
For, you know, on such occasions
She is rarely seen outside it.
And the Lady of the Bedchamber,
For she's from Castille, they say
At this very time began to pray
A girl, not a boy, be given her.
(Even here, see, goes our way)
And would you know the reason why?
The Empress had just before
Given birth unto an Emperor,
And they will marry by and by.
'Twas different with my mother, she
Cared not whether it might be
A boy or eke a girl by chance
But unto the Virgin Mary
Prayed she for deliverance.

Enter Gonçalo, a shepherd of the Serra,
who comes from the Court, singing:
Flying, the magpie has flown away,
O that 'twere brought to me again:
In yonder covert
'Twas mine at will,
With its dark-brown eyes
And its golden bill.
O that 'twere brought to me again!
By Heaven in fine trim to-day
Our Serra is and all aglow!
S. Come, Gonçalo, come away,
For I minded am to go,
Leaving these my haunts straightway,
Gathering you all together

34. *quant'elle* C.

53, 54. *Imperatriz, Imperador* C.

logo logo muyto asinha
75 pera yrmos visitar
nossa Senhora a Raynha,
querendo Deos ajudar.
Gonç. ¶ Eu venho agora de la
& segundo o que eu vi
80 que vamos la bem seraa:
isto crede vos quee assi:
porque dizem que a princesa,
a menina que naceo,
parece cousa do ceo,
85 hũa estrela muyto acesa
que na terra apareceo.
Serra. ¶ Gonçalo, eu te direy:
ella ja naceo em serra
e do mais fermoso Rey
90 que ha na face da terra,
e de Raynha muyto bella;
& mais naceo em cidade
muyto ditosa pareella
& de grande autoridade.
95 ¶ E mais naceo em bom dia
Martes, deos dos vencimẽtos,
& trouxeram logo os ventos
agoa que se requeria
pera todos mantimentos.
100 Parvo. Aas vezes faz Deos cousas,
cousas faz elle aas vezes,
atrauees como homem diz.
¶ Nega se meu embeleco
vay poer as pipas em seco
105 & enche dagoa o Mondego:
faraa mais hum demenesteco?
engorda os vereadores
& seca as pernas nas moças
de cima bem toos artelhos,
110 & faz os frades vermelhos
& os leygos amarelos
& faz os velhos murzelos.
¶ Enruça os mancebelhões
& nam atenta por nada.
115 Pedemlhe em Coimbra ceuada
& elle delhes mexilhões
& das solhas em cambada.
Gonç. Vos, serra, se aueis dir
com serranas & pastores
120 primeyro se ham dauyr

Forthwith and without delay
That we may all journey thither
A visit to our queen to pay
If God assist us on our way.
G. I am now come even thence
And from all that I could tell
Our going thither will be well,
Aye, 'twill be no vain pretence,
For the child of royal line,
The princess that has now had birth
Seems, they say, a thing divine,
A star that ceases not to shine
Though it has appeared on earth.
S. I'll tell thee how it is, I ween:
Her birth is in a hill-country,
Of a king fairest to be seen
Of all that are upon the earth
And of a most lovely queen.
And she is born in a city
Which will bless her and blest has been
And of great authority.
On lucky day too was she born,
Of Mars, the god of victory,
And the winds that very morn
Brought rain needed instantly
For the birth of grass and corn.
Fool. Sometimes God, it is a fact,
Sometimes, I say, God doth act
All upside down, as one might say.
For unless I'm much mistaken
Mondego will be in flood
And all the wine from the casks be taken:
Could a demon do less good?
For He so brings it about
That the aldermen grow stout
And like dry sticks girls wither away,
Purple the friars wax and red,
Yellow and jaundiced are the lay,
And lusty they whose youth is fled
While the young grow weak and grey
And for nothing doth He care.
At Coimbra when for oats they pray
Of mussels enough and e'en to spare
And fish likewise He sends straightway.
G. Serra, if you would fain go
With shepherds and with shepherdesses
First their loves of long ago

100. *faz un rey cousas* B.
109. *tós* C.

102. *atraues* B. *a través* C
116. *dá-lhe* C.

hũa manada damores
que nam querem concrudir.
¶ Eu trago na fantesia
de casar com Madanela
125 mas nam sey se querra ella
perol eu bofee queria.
  ¶ Vem Felipa pastora da serra
cãtãdo:
  ¶ A mi seguem os dous açores,
hum delles moriraa damores.
Dous açores que eu auia
130 aqui andam nesta baylia
hum delles moriraa damores.
          Falado.
Gonçalo, viste o meu gado?
dize se o viste embora.

Gonç. Venho eu da corte agora
135 & diz que lhe de recado.
Fel. Pois ja tu ca es casado,
nega que esperam por ti.
Gonç. E sem mi me casam a mi?
Ora estou bem auiado.
140 Fel. ¶ Nam ha hi nega casar logo
& fazer vida com ella
senam for com Madanela.
Gonç. Tiromeu fora do jogo.
Fel. Essa he a milhor do jogo.

145 Gonç. Essoutra sera alvarenga?
Fel. Mas Catherina meygengra.
Gonç. Antes me queime mao fogo.
  ¶ Nam vem a Meygengra a cõto,
que he descuydada perdida,
150 traz a saya descosida
e nam lhe daraa hum ponto.
Oo quantas lendẽs vi nella
e pentear nemigalha,
e por dame aquella palha
155 he mayor o riso quella.
  ¶ Varre & leyxa o lixo em casa,
come & leyxa ali o bacio,
cada dia a espanca o tio
nega porque tam devassa;
160 Madanela mata a brasa.
Nam cures de mais arenga

Must mutual agreement show
That as yet no ending blesses.
And for my part willingly
Would I Madanela wed,
That design is in my head
But I know not if she'll agree.

Enter Felipa, a shepherdess of the Serra,
singing:
Two falcons to follow me have I,
But one of them of love shall die.
Two falcons had I, and the twain
Are here with me, being of love's train,
But one of them of love shall die.
          (*Spoken:*)
F. Gonçalo, hast thou seen my sheep,
Tell me hast thou seen them now?
G. From the town I am just returned
    and trow
That I for thee thy flocks must keep.
F. Well, thou hast been married here:
They only for thy coming stay.
G. What, married ere I can appear?
Then am I in a pretty way.
F. Nay thou must marry on thy return
And must go and live with her
Unless Madanela thou wouldst prefer.
G. From the game's chance aside I turn.
F. Wouldst thou the best of them all
    thus spurn?
G. Is it, is it Alvarenga?
F. No, but Catherine Meigengra.
G. In evil fire would I rather burn.
Of Meigengra is no question here:
The greatest slattern, I assert,
Is she and if unsewn her skirt
Not a stitch will it get from her,
And though she covered be with dirt
Yet will she never comb her hair,
And at the merest word will she
Be vanquished of laughter utterly.
She sweeps and lets the sweepings lie,
She eats and will never wash the dishes,
Her uncle beats her hourly,
So laxly doth she flout his wishes.
Madanela's the apple of my eye.
And there is no more to be said

123. *phantesia* C.   125. *querera* B.
135. *reccado* C.
159. *porque* A, B, C, D, E.   *porqu'é* ?

127. *seguem dous açores* C.
152. *lendes* C.
161. *cures* A, B.   *cuides* C.

e dize tu, mana, a Meygengra
que va amassar outra massa.

Fel. ¶ Ja teu pay tem dada a mão
165 & dada a mão feyto he.
Gonç. Par deos darlhey eu de pee
comaa casca do melão.
Raivo eu de coração
damores de Madanela.
170 Fel. Meygengra he mais rica quella;
quessa nam tem nem tostam.
Gonç. Arrenega tu do argem
que me vem a dar tormento,
porque hum soo contentamento
175 val quanto ouro Deos tem.
Deos me dee quem quero bem
ou me tire a vida toda,
com a morte seja a boda
antes que outra me dem.
180 Fel. Eu me vou pee ante pee
ver o meu gado onde vay.
Gonç. E eu quero yr ver meu pay,
veremos comisto he.

¶ Vem Caterina Meygẽgra cantando:
¶ A serra es alta,
185 o amor he grande,
se nos ouuirane.
Fel. ¶ Onde vas Meygengra mana?
Cat. A novilha vou buscar,
viste ma tu ca andar?
190 Fel. Nam na vi esta somana.
Agora estora vay daqui
Gonçalo que vem da corte;
mana, pesoulhe de sorte
quando lhe faley em ti
195 como se foras a morte,
tente tamanho fastio.
Cat. Inde bem, por minha vida,
porque eu mana sam perdida
por Fernando de meu tio.
200 Seu com elle nam casar
damores mey de finar.
Aborreceme Gonçalo
como o cu do nosso galo,
nam no queria sonhar.
205 Fel. ¶ Se tu nam queres a elle
nem elle tampouco a ti.

But tell Meigengra presently
To reckon on another head.
F. Thy father has given his hand, thus clinching
The matter beyond any flinching.
G. To give her my foot would I be willing
As if she were a melon's rind,
But as for me, my heart and mind
With love of Madanela are thrilling.
F. Yet richer Meigengra thou'lt find,
For Madanela has not a shilling.
G. A curse upon money, say I,
Which only brings me fresh distress:
A single hour of happiness
'S worth all the gold beneath the sky.
God give me but the girl I love
Or deprive me of life's breath,
And my marriage be with death
If to her I faithless prove.
F. Well, I must go instantly
After my flocks and see how they fare.
G. And I to my father will repair
And find out how this thing may be.

Enter Catherina Meigengra, singing:
Lofty the mountain-height,
But stronger is love's might,
Could he but hear !
F. Whither, Meigengra, sister, away?
C. 'Tis the heifer I go to seek,
Hast thou seen it here, I pray?
F. I have not seen it all this week.
But Gonçalo is just gone hence,
Even from the Court came he
And I gave him great offence
When I spoke to him of thee,
As if thou wert a pestilence,
Such disaffection hast thou won.
C. And by my life I'm glad of it
For, sister, I have lost my wit
For Ferdinand, my uncle's son.
If I do not marry him
I will surely die of love.
But Gonçalo can only move
My thoughts, yes even in a dream,
To distaste and weariness.
F. If for him thou dost not care
He for thee cares even less.

167.   *do melão* A, B.   *de melão* C.
179.   *outra* A, B.   *outrem* C.

172.   *Arrenega tu* A, B.   *Arrenego eu* C.
196.   *tem-te* C.   197.   *Inda* C.

CAT.   Quanta selle quer a mi
negras maas nouas van delle.
Deos me case com Fernando
210 & moura logo esse dia,
porque me mate a alegria
como o nojo vay matando.
¶ Oo Fernando de meu tio
que eu vi polo meu pecado!
215 FEL.   Fernando, esse teu damado,
casaua comigo a furto.
CAT.   Dize, rogoto, ha muito?
FEL.   Este sabado passado.
CAT.   Oo Jesu, como he maluado,
220 & os homẽs cheos denganos,
que por mi vay em tres annos
que diz que he demoninhado.
¶ Felipa, gingras tu ou nam?
Isso creo que he chufar,
225 e se tu queres gingrar
nam me des no coraçam,
que o que doe nam he zõbar.
FEL.   Elle veo ter comigo
bem oo penedo da palma
230 & disse: Felipa, minhalma,
rayuo por casar com tigo;
Digo eu, digo:
Vay, vay nadar, que faz calma.
CAT. ¶ Olha tu se zombaua elle.
235 FEL.   Bem conheço eu zombaria:
vi eu, porque eu nam queria,
correr as lagrimas delle.
CAT.   Maos choros chorem por elle,
que assi chora elle comigo
240 & vayselhe o gado oo trigo
& sois nam olha parelle.
FEL. ¶ Eu vou casuso ao cabeço
por ver se vejo o meu gado.
CAT.   Tal me deyxas por meu fado
245 que do meu todo mesqueço.
Quem soubesse no começo
o cabo do que começa
porque logo se conheça
o queu jagora conheço.

¶ Vem Fernando cantando:
250 ¶ Com que olhos me olhaste
que tam bem vos pareci?
Tam asinha moluidaste?
quem te disse mal de mi?

C.   Bad luck to him through all the land
If to think of me he dare.
But if Heaven only planned
My marriage with Ferdinand
Death to me that day welcome were,
Joy's victim, not of this distress.
O Ferdinand, my uncle's son,
For thee was all this love begun!
F.   This your love, your Ferdinand,
Secretly offered me his hand.
C.   Was that long ago, I pray?
F.   It was but on last Saturday.
C.   What a villain then is he,
And men how full of all deceits,
For he these last three years repeats
That he's distraught for love of me.
Felipa, dost thou speak in jest?
I think indeed thou triflest,
But if with words thou wouldest play,
Do not play upon my heart
Since no jest is in the smart.
F.   He came to me in the heat of the day,
To the rock of the palm came he,
'Felipa, my life,' said he straightway,
'I am mad to marry thee.'
And I say, say I to him:
'Go away and have a swim.'
C.   Perhaps he was but mocking thee.
F.   Nay I know what's mockery
And because I said him No
I could see his tears downflow.
C.   Ill be the tears that are so shed,
For with me also he will weep,
And the crops may be eaten by his sheep,
He does not even turn his head.
F.   Well, I must go up the hill,
Perhaps my flock may be in sight.
C.   Thou leavest me in a plight so ill
That I've forgotten mine outright.
If one could but only know
All the end in the beginning
That one might have straightway so
Knowledge that I now am winning!

Enter Ferdinand, singing:
With what eyes thou lookedst upon me
That so fair I seemed to thee:
How have other thoughts now won thee?
Who has spoken ill of me?

231.   *com tigo* A, B.   *comtigo* C.

Cat. ¶ A que vês, Fernãdo hõrrado?
255 Ver Felipa tua senhora?
Venhas muito da maa hora
pera ti e pera o gado.
Fern. Catalina! Catalina! assi
tolhes ma fala, Catalina?
260 Olha yeramaa pera mi,
pois que me tu sees assi
carrancuda e tam mofina
quem te disse mal de mi?
Com que olhos me olhaste, &c.
265 Cat. ¶ Dize, rogoto, Fernando,
porque me trazes vendida?
Se Felipa he a tua querida
porque me andas enganando?
Fern. Eu mouro, tu estaas zombando.
270 Cat. Oo que nam zombo, Jesu.
Nam casauas coella tu?
Fern. Eu estou della chufando.
  ¶ Catalina, esta he a verdade,
nam creias a ninguem nada,
275 que tu me tens bem atada
alma & a vida & a vontade.
Cat. Pois que choraste coella
nam ha hi mais no querer.
Fern. De chorar bem pode ser
280 mas nam choraueu por ella.
  ¶ Felipa auultase contigo,
vendoa fosteme lembrar,
entam puseme a chorar
as lembranças do meu perigo.
285 Se ella o tomou por si
que culpa lhe tenho eu?
Mas este amor quem mo deu
deumo todo para ti
& bem sabes tu quee teu.
290 Cat. ¶ Oo que grande amor te tenho
& que grande mal te quero.
Fern. Ja de tudo desespero,
que ja mal nem bem nam quero.

Teu pae tem te ja casada
295 com Gonçalo dantemão
& eu fico por esse chão
sem me ficar de ti nada
senam dor de coraçom.

C. Good Ferdinand, art thou here
To see Felipa, thy lady dear?
But may thy coming even be
Ill for thy flock and ill for thee.
F. Catherina, thus wouldst thou
Deprive me of all power of speech?
Look straight at me, I beseech.
But if thus thou changest now
With lowering and angry brow,
'Who has spoken ill of me?
With what eyes thou lookedst upon me?'
C. Tell me, Ferdinand, I pray   [etc.
Why thou wouldest me betray?
If Felipa is thy love,
Why me thus with treachery prove?
F. By my life, thou'rt mocking me to-
day.
C. O no, I jest not: didst not say
That thou with her wouldst gladly wed?
F. 'Twas but for fun the words were said.
In what I say will truth be found
And believe no one else, I pray.
For as for me my life alway
And soul and will in thee are bound.
C. With weeping since thy eyes were red
Needs must be that thou lov'st her well.
F. I may have wept, I cannot tell,
But not for her my tears were shed.
Felipa's not unlike thee, so
At sight of her I thought of thee
And fell to weeping bitterly
At memory of all my woe.
And if she thought my tears did flow
For her, how should I be to blame?
For my love ever is the same
On thee, thee only to bestow,
And that it's thine well dost thou know.
C. How I hate thee, how I love thee,
Ferdinand, were it mine to prove thee!
F. Now despair I utterly,
Yes, I am most desperate,
And good and ill come all too late.
For thy father has married thee
To Gonçalo, and desolate
I here remain, alone, deserted,
Nothing of thee left to me
But to be thus broken-hearted.

261. *sês* C.
276. *alma* A. *a alma* C.

265. *rogoto* A. *rogo-te* C.
284. *do* A. *de* C.

¶ Vertaas em outro poder
300 vertaas em outro logar,
eu logo sem mais tardar
frade prometo de ser
pois os diabos quiseram
& ali me deyxaram
305 tanta de maginaçam
quanta teus olhos me deram
desdo dia dacençam.
CAT. ¶ Mas casemos, daa ca mão
& dirlhey que sam casada.
310 FERN. Ja tenho palaura dada
a Deos de religiam.
Ja nam tenho em mi nada.
CAT. Oo quantos perigos tem
este triste mar damores
315 & cada vez sam mayores
as tormentas que lhe vem.
¶ Se tu a ser frade vas
nunca me veram marido:
tu seraas frade metido,
320 porem tu me meteraas
na fim da Raynha Dido.
FERN. Nam se poderaa escusar
de casares com Gonçalo
& querendo tu escusalo
325 nam no podes acabar,
que teu pae ha dacabalo.
CAT. ¶ Se libera nos a malo!
Nunca Deos ha de querer
& Gonçalo nam me quer
330 nem eu nam quero a Gonçalo.
Eylo vem, velo Fernando?
bem em címa na portela;
diante vem Madanela,
aquella andelle buscando.
335 ¶ [FERN.] Vamolos nos espreitar
ali detras do valado
& veremos seu cuydado
se te da em que cuydar
ou se fala desuiado.

340   ¶ Vem Madanela cantando &
Gonçalo detras della.

Cantiga.

¶ Quando aqui choue & neva
que faraa na serra?

And another's shalt thou be,
Taken to another place,
And I, by the Devil's grace,
Promise that I instantly
Will a monk become: in fine
So much of thee shall be mine
In imagination's play
As was given me on that day
When thine eyes began to shine.
C. Nay, but give me thy hand instead
And I will say that I am wed.
F. Alas I have nothing now to give.
My promise is already said
That I will in a convent live.
C. How many perils mar the peace
Of this gloomy sea of love,
From day to day they still increase
And its tempests greater prove.
If a monk then thou must be
Husband mine will ne'er be seen:
If a monk thou must be, for me
Thou leavest of necessity
The fate of Dido, hapless queen.
F. Thou wilt find no sure escape
With Gonçalo not to marry,
For whatever plans thou shape
Thou wilt never round the cape
And thy father the day will carry.
C. O deliver us from ill!
May such never be my lot,
For Gonçalo loves me not,
And Gonçalo I love less still.
But there he comes, see, Ferdinand,
Above there in the mountain pass,
And Madanela goes before,
She it is that he searches for.
F. Behind this hedge here we will stand
And listen to them as they pass
And we will see what's in his mind
And if to thee he be inclined
Or if thou art given o'er.

*Enter Madanela, singing, and behind her
Gonçalo:*

(*Song:*)
When here below there's rain and snow
What will it be on the mountain-height?

299, 300. *ver-te-has* C.   308. *ca mão* A, B. *ca a mão* C.   327. *libara* B.
328. *querelo* A, B. *querê-lo* C, D, E.   332. *bem* A, B. *vem* C, D, E.

Na serra de Coimbra
345 neuaua & chouia,
que faraa na serra?
Falado.
¶ Gonçalo, tu a que vens?
Gonç. Madanela, Madanela!
350 Mad. Tornate maa hora & nella
que tam pouco empacho tẽs!
Gonç. Madanela, Madanela!
Mad. Oo decho dou eu a amargura
quasi magasta, Jesu.
355 Ora tras mi te vẽs tu?
Gonç. Pois a mi se mafigura
que nam maas de comer cru.
¶ Se tu me queres matar
por teu ter boa vontade
360 nam pode ser de verdade.
Mad. Gonçalo, torna a laurar
que isso tudo he vaidade.
Gonç. Que rezam me das tu a mi
pera nam casar comigo?
365 Eu ey de ter muyto trigo
& ey te de ter a ti
mais doce que hum pintisirgo.
¶ Nam quero que vas mondar,
nam quero que andes oo sol,
370 pera ti seja o folgar
e pera mi fazer prol.
Queres Madanela?
Mad. Gonçalo, torna a laurar
porque eu nam ey de casar
375 em toda a serra destrella
nem te presta prefiar.
¶ Catalina he muyto boa,
fermosa quanto lhabasta,
querte bem, he de boa casta,
380 & bem sesuda pessoa.
Toma tu o que te dão
em paga do que desejas.
Gonç. Ay rogote que nam sejas
aya do meu coraçam.
385 Mad. Vayte di, que paruoejas,
Gonç. ¶ Nam quero casar coella.
Mad. Nem eu tam pouco com tigo.
Vees? casuso vem Rodrigo
tras Felipa, que he aquella
390 que nam no estima num figo.

353. *eu amargura* B.
378. *lhe basta* C.

On the hills of Coimbra 'twas snowing
    and raining,
What will it be on the mountain-height?
        (*Spoken:*)
Gonçalo, what is your pretence?
G. Madanela, Madanela!
M. Go back at once, I say, go hence,
Since thou hast so little sense.
G. Madanela, Madanela!
M. What another plague is here,
What annoyance, by my soul!
What, wouldst thou now follow me?
G. I suppose I need not fear
That thou shouldst eat me whole.
But if me thou wouldest kill
Because of this my love for thee
Not serious surely is thy will.
M. Gonçalo, go back, go back to thy
For all this is but vanity.   [plough,
G. What reason canst thou give me now
To refuse to marry me?
I shall have of wheat enow
And thy life with me shall be
As a goldfinch's free from toil.
I will not have thee hoe the soil,
I will not have thee work in the sun,
But thou shalt sit and take thy ease
And by me all the work be done.
Art thou willing, Madanela?
M. Gonçalo, go back, go back to thy
With none will I marry, I avow, [plough,
In the whole Serra da Estrella,
In vain wilt thou persist and tease.
Catalina is a very good girl
And fair enough, though not a pearl,
Comes of good stock and loves thee well,
And she is very sensible.
Then take what's offered thee and so
Shalt balm of thy desire know.
G. Nay, but I pray thee do not seek
To teach my heart what way to go.
M. Go hence, if nonsense thou must
G. I say I will not marry her. [speak.
M. And I will not marry thee.
But yonder comes Rodrigo, see,
After Felipa, and I aver
That not a fig for him cares she.

354. *quasi* A, B. *qu'assi* C.

¶ Vem Rodrigo cantando:

Vayamonos ãbos, amor, vayamos,
vayamonos ambos.
Felipa & Rodrigo passaram o rio,
amor vayamonos.
395 ¶ Felipa, como te vay?
FEL. Que tẽs tu de ver co isso?
Dias ha que teu auiso
que vas gingrar com teu pay.
ROD. Nam estou eu, mana, nisso.
400 FEL. Quem te mette a ti comigo?
ROD. Felipa, olha pera ca,
dame essa mão eyaramaa.
FEL. Tirte, tirte eramaa laa,
tu que diabo has comigo?
405 ROD. ¶ Felipa, ja tu aqui es?
FEL. Rodrigo, ja tu começas?
Tu tẽs das maas vãs cabeças,
nam quero ser descortees.
ROD. Nem queyras tu er ser assi
410 grauisca & escandalosa;
mas tem graça pera mi,
como tu es graciosa
& fermosa pera ti.
FEL. Cada hum saa de regrar
415 em pedir o que he rezam:
tu pedesmo coraçam
& eu nam to ey de dar
porquee muy fora de mão.
E quanto monta a casar
420 ainda queu guarde gado
meu pay he juyz honrrado
dos melhores do lugar
& o mais aparentado.
¶ E andou na corte assaz
425 & faloulhe el Rey ja
dizendo-lhe: Affonso vaz
em fronteyra e moncarraz
como val o trigo la?
Ora eu pera casar ca,
430 Rodrigo, nam he rezam.
ROD. Se casasses com paaçom
que grande graça seraa
& minha consolaçam.
¶ Que te chame de ratinha
435 tinhosa cada mea hora,
inda que a alma me chora,

392. *vayamonos* A. *vayamos* C.
408. *descortees* A. *descortes* B. *descortez* C.

Enter Rodrigo, singing:

My love, let's be going, be going together,
Be going together.
Rodrigo and Felipa were crossing the
My love, let's be going.   [river,
How is it, Felipa, with thee?
F. And what business is that of thine?
Days past I've bidden thee thy chatter
To thy father to confine.
R. But that, my dear, does not suit me.
F. And why drag me into the matter?
R. Felipa, turn thy eyes this way
And give me that fair hand of thine.
F. Away, away with thee, I say,
What art thou to me, in the name of evil?
R. So, Felipa, thou art here, I see.
F. Rodrigo, wouldst thou begin again?
If ever there was feather-brain,
But I would not be uncivil.
R. Would then that thou mightest be
Now less shrewish and unkind.
Yet even that is to my mind,
So charming art thou unto me
So graceful and so fair to see.
F. Everyone should regulate
At reason's bidding his request,
Thou my heart requirest
But I cannot give thee that
Nor listen to thee save in jest.
And as to my marrying I wis,
Although I keep the sheep, withal
An honoured judge my father is
And by his side the rest are small,
He's best related of them all.
At Court too he's been many a day
And the king once spoke to him, to say:
'In the district of Monsarraz
And Fronteira, Affonso Vaz,
What is the price of wheat, I pray?'
So that here to marry would be for me,
Rodrigo, to act unreasonably.
R. Shouldest thou a courtier marry
What amusement unto me
And consolation that would carry!
For if as a country-lout he harry
Thee all day and for evermore, [grieve,
Would I, what though my heart should

407. *maas* A. *mais* C.
427. *moncarraz* A, B. *Monçarraz* C.

folgarey por vida minha.
Pois engeytas quem tadora;
e te diga: tirte la,
440 que me cheyras a cartaxo.
Pois te desprezas do bayxo
o alto tabaxaraa.
FEL. ¶ Quando vejo hum cortesam
com pantufos de veludo
445 & hũa viola na mão
tresandamo coraçam
& leuame a alma & tudo.
ROD. Gonçalo, vayme ajudar
aacabar minha charrua
450 & eu tajudarey aa tua.
Que estoutro sa dacabar
quando a dita vir a sua.
GONÇ. Eu sam ja desenganado
quanto monta a Madanella.
455 ROD. Deuetela dir com ella
como mami vay mal peccado
com Felipa.
GONÇ.   Assi he ella.
ROD. E tu, Rodrigo, em que estaas?
FERN. Estou em muito & em nada,
460 porque a vida namorada
tem cousas boas & maas.

    ¶ Vem hum hermitam & diz:
HERM. ¶ Fazeyme esmola, pastores,
por amor do senhor Deos.
ROD. Mas faça elle esmola a nos,
465 & seja que estes amores
se atem com senhos nos.
HERM. O casar Deos o prouee
& de Deos vem a ventura,
da ventura aa criatura
470 mas com dita he por merce
& tambem serue a cordura.
¶ Pondevos nas suas mãos
& não cureis descolher,
tomay o que vos vier
475 porque estes amores vãos
teram certo arrepender.
Filhas, aqui estais escritas,

Filhos, tomay vossa sorte,
& cada hum se comporte
480 dando graças infinitas

Rejoice, since, though I thee adore,
Me thus contemptuously dost thou leave,
And if he bid thee keep thy place
As being but of low degree:
Since thou despisest such as me
Thee shall the mighty then abase.
F. When I see a courtier fine
With his velvet slippers, and
His viola in his hand,
'Tis all up with this heart of mine
Nor can I his ways withstand.
R. Gonçalo, come help me now
At the labour of my plough
And I'll help thee anon with thine.
For as to the other 'twill be in fine
When its fortune shall allow.
G. As for Madanela, I
Have ceased at last my luck to try.
R. Ah! then the same thing it must be
As with Felipa and me.

G. Yes, 'tis even so we stand.
R. And how is't with thee, Ferdinand?
F. I am in both smiles and frowns,
And a lover's life is planned
In a maze of ups and downs.

    Enters a hermit who says:
H. Shepherds, for love of God, on me
Pray bestow your charity.
R. Rather him it now behoves
Charitable towards us to be
And tie the knots of all our loves.
H. Marrying is in God's hand
And from Him comes fortune too,
For by His especial grace
All men fortune may embrace
And good sense assists thereto.
Place yourselves beneath His sway,
Take not any thought to choose
But receive what comes your way,
For these idle loves, I say,
You'll in sure repentance lose.
Your names, my daughters, here you
    leave;
My sons, now each your lot receive:
Behave yourselves in such a sort
That you your infinite thanks shall give

456. *mami* A. *a mi* C.
469. *a creatura* C.

Desunt 462–577 in B.
477. *escriptas* C.

B.

5

a Deos & a el Rey & a corte.

¶   Tirou o ermitam da manga tres
papelinhos & os deu aos pastores,
que tomasse cada hum sua sorte &
diz Fernando:

¶ Rodrigo tome primeyro,
veremos como se guia.
ROD.   Nome da virgem Maria!
485 lede, padre, esse letreyro,
se me cega ou alumia.

Escri.   Deos & a ventura manda
que quem esta sorte ouuer
tome logo por molher
490 Felipa sem mais demanda.
ROD. ¶ Vencida tenho eu a batalha,
Felipa, mana, vem caa.
FEL.   Tirte, tirte, eramaa laa,
& tu cuydas que te valha?
495 Nunca teu olho veraa.
GONÇ.   Ora vay, Fernando, tu,
veremos que te viraa.
FERN.   Alto nome de Jesu!
lede, padre, que vay la?

Escrito.
500 ¶ A sentença he ja dada
& a sustancia della
que cases com Madanela.
MAD.   Fernando, nam me da nada,
seja muytembora & nella.
505 FERN.   Dias ha que to eu digo
& tu tinhas me fastio.
CAT.   Oo Fernando de meu tio
quem me casara com tigo!
GONÇ. ¶ Oo Madanela, yeramaa,
510 se me cayras em sorte!
CAT.   Ante eu morrera maa morte
que Fernando ficar laa
tam contrayro do meu norte.
E porem nam me da nada,
515 ja me tu a mi pareces bem,
Gonçalo.
GONÇ.   E tu a mi
Catalina; mudate di
y passea per hi alem,

To God, and to the King and Court.

*The hermit takes from his sleeve three
small written pieces of paper and gives
them to the shepherds that each may take
his lot, and Ferdinand says:*

Rodrigo shall the first lot claim.
We'll see now if he acts aright.
R.   In the Virgin Mary's name
Read it, padre, for the same
Brings to me my day or night.

The hermit reads the writing:

'By Fortune's and by God's command
Whosoever draws this lot
Shall to Felipa give his hand,
Shall do so and reason not.'
R.   I have won the victory,
Felipa, come hither to me, my dear.
F.   Away with thee, away, dost hear,
Thinkest thou this will profit thee?
Ne'er such a victory shalt thou see.
G.   Draw thy lot now, Ferdinand,
Let's see what for thee is planned.
F.   Here goes then in the name of Heaven;
Read, padre, what is written there.

The hermit reads:

'The sentence is already given
And its substance doth declare
That thou shalt Madanela wed.'
M.   Well, Ferdinand, I do not care,
If it must be so, no more be said.
F.   Many a day hast thou heard that from
But thou e'er hadst me in disdain.   [me
C.   O Ferdinand, my uncle's swain,
Would that I might marry thee!
G.   O Madanela, if only now
We had come together, I and thou.
C.   Rather might I straight expire
Than that Ferdinand should stay there
So remote from my desire.
Yet I do not greatly care,
Since to thee I am inclined,
Gonçalo.
G.   And even so,
Catalina, art thou to my mind,
But come away that I may know

---

482.   *& diz Fernando* A.   *& diz o Ermitão* C.   487.   *Escri.* A.   (*Lê o Ermitão o
escrito*) C.   498.   *alto, nome* C.   499–500.   *Escrito* A.   (*Lê o Ermitão*) C.

verey que aar das de ti.

520 FEL. ¶ Estouteu, Rodrigo, olhando,
& vou sendo ja contente.
ROD. Se de mi nam es contente
nam tey dandar mais rogando.
Eu andote namorando
525 & tu acossasme cada dia.
CAT. Inda queu isso fazia,
Rodrigo, de quando em quãdo,
muy grande bem te queria.
¶ E quando eu refusaua
530 de te tomar por amigo
nam ja porque eu nam folgaua
mas porque te examinaua
se eras tu moço atreuido.
HERM. Agoro quero eu dizer
535 o que aqui venho buscar.
Eu desejo dabitar
hũa ermida a meu prazer
onde podesse folgar.
E queriaa eu achar feyta
540 por nam cãsar em fazela,
que fosse a minha cella
antes bem larga que estreyta
& que podesse eu dançar nella.
E que fosse num deserto
545 denfindo vinho & pão,
& a fonte muyto perto
& longe a contemplação.
¶ Muyta caça & pescaria
que podesse eu ter coutada
550 & a casa temperada:
no veram que fosse fria
& quente na inuernada.
A cama muyto mimosa
& hum crauo aa cabeceyra,
555 de cedro a sua madeyra;
porque a vida religiosa
queria eu desta maneyra.
¶ E fosse o meu repousar
& dormir atee tais horas
560 que nam podesse rezar
por ouuir cantar pastoras
& outras assouiar.
Aa cea & jantar perdiz,
o almoço moxama,
565 & vinho do seu matiz,

What graces I in thee shall find.
F. Rodrigo, as I look upon thee
I begin to grow content.
R. If to that I have not won thee
By me no further prayers be spent.
For while I have courted thee
Daily hast thou flouted me.
C. Though from time to time I thus,
Rodrigo, behaved, truly
Very fond was I of thee.
And when most contemptuous
Thy wife I refused to be
'Twas not that I had no love
But, that I tested thee, to prove
The heart of thy audacity.
Hermit. Now I have a mind to say
What I came to look for here.
For my wish it is to stay
In a hermitage that may
Yield me plenty of good cheer.
Ready-made would I find it: ill
Could I all these joys fulfil
Worn out by toil and labour fell.
Wide not narrow be my cell
That I may dance therein at will;
Be it in a desert land
Yielding wine and wheat alway,
With a fountain near at hand
And contemplation far away.
Much fish and game in brake and pool
Must I have for my own preserve
And as for my house it must never swerve
From an even temperature, cool
In summer and in winter warm.
Yes, and a comfortable bed
Would not do me any harm,
All of it of cedar-wood,
A harpsichord hung at its head:
So do I find a monk's life good.
I would lie and take my rest
And sleep on far into the day
So that I could not my matins say
For noise of the whistling and the singing
Of shepherdesses' songs clear ringing.
On partridge would I sup and dine,
Of stockfish should my luncheon be
And of wine the very best.

530. *amigo* A, B, C, D, E. *marido* ?   545. *D'infindo* C.

& que a filha do juyz
me fizesse sempre a cama.
¶ E em quanto eu rezasse
esquecesse ella as ouelhas
570 & na cela me abraçasse
& mordesse nas orelhas,
inda que me lastimasse.
Irmãos pois deueis saber
da serra toda a guarida
575 prazauos de me dizer
onde poderey fazer
esta minha sancta vida.
GONÇ. ¶ Estaa alli, padre, hum
viçoso, verde, florido,   [siluado
580 com espinho tam comprido,
e vos nuu alli deytado
perderieis o proido.
Yuos, nam esteis hi mais,
porque a vida que buscais
585 nam na da Deos verdadeyro
inda que lha vos peçais.
SERRA. ¶ Ora, filhos, logo essora,
cada hum com sua esposa,
vamos ver a poderosa
590 Raynha nossa Senhora,
sem nenhum de vos por grosa,
porque he forçoso que va,
que segundo minha fama
da Raynha ey de ser ama
595 & a isso vou eu la.
¶ Que tal leyte como o meu
nam no ha em Portugal,
que tenho tanto & tal
e tam fino Deos mo deu
600 que he manteyga & nam al.
E pois ha de ser senhora
de tam grande gado & terra
quem outra ama lhe der erra,
porque a perfeyta pastora
605 ha de ser da minha serra.
GONÇ. ¶ Ha mester grandes presentes
das vilas, casaes & aldea.
SERRA. Mandaraa a vila de Sea
quinhentos queyjos resentes,
610 todos feytos aa candea,
e mais trezentas bezerras
& mil ouelhas meyrinhas
& dozentas cordeyrinhas

And the Judge's daughter should make
The bed on which I would recline. [for me
And even as my beads I tell
She should forget her flock of sheep
And embrace me in my cell
And bite my ears and make me weep:
Yes, even thus it would be well.
My brothers, since you know, I trow
The recesses of each vale and hill
Be good enough to tell me now
Where best I may so have my will
And this holy life fulfil.
G. Yonder, padre, there's a briar
All in flower, thick and green,
And its thorns are long and dire:
Naked laid thereon, I ween
You would soon lose your desire.
Go and make no further stay,
For the life you wish to live
The true God will never give
Howsoe'er for it you pray.
Serra. Come, my sons, now come away,
Each with his fair bride to-day,
That our Queen and Sovereign we
May go visit speedily,
And let none of you gainsay,
For you must go all together,
Since, if report say true, I ween
I as nurse must serve the Queen
And therefore do I go thither.
Such milk as mine you will not find
No, not in all Portugal,
So plentiful and such kind
As God has blessèd me withal:
Pure butter were not more refined.
And since she will be princess
Of such flocks and all this land,
No other nurse shall be to hand,
For the perfect shepherdess
My hill-sides alone command.
G. From every village, house and town
Great presents must with us come down.
S. The town of Sea of its store
Shall five hundred cheeses send
All home-made, and furthermore
Of calves will she send thrice five score
And of her merino sheep
A thousand, and lambs two hundred keep

Desunt 566–8 in C.   608. *Cea* C.   609. *recentes* C.   613. *duzentas* C.

taes que em nenhũas serras
615 nam se achem tam gordinhas.
¶ E Gouuea mandaraa
dous mil sacos de castanha
tam grossa, tam san, tamanha
que se marauilharaa
620 onde tal cousa se apanha.
E Manteygas lhe daraa
leyte para quatorze annos,
& Couilham muytos panos
finos que se fazem laa.
625 ¶ Mandaraam desses casaes
que estam no cume da serra
pena pera cabeçaes
toda de aguias Reaes,
naturaes mesmo da terra.
630 E os do val dos penados
& montes dos tres caminhos
que estam em fortes montados
mandarão empresentados
trezentos forros darminhos
635 pera forrar os borcados.
¶ Eu ey lhe de presentar
minas douro que eu sey
com tanto que ella ou el Rey
o mandem ca apanhar,
640 abasta que lho criey.
Gonç. E afora ainda aos presentes
auemos lhe de cantar
muyto alegres & contentes
polla Deos alumiar
645 por alegria das gentes.

Vem dous foliões do Sardoal, hum
se chama Jorge e outro Lopo, & diz
a Serra:

¶ Sois vos de Castella, manos,
ou la debayxo do estremo?
Jor. Agora nos faria o demo
a nos outros Castellanos.
650 Queria antes ser lagarto
polos sanctos auangelhos.
Serra. Donde sois?
Jor.   Do Sardoal,
& ou bebela ou vertela,
vimos ca desafiar

So fat that on no hills you'll find
Any more unto your mind.
And two thousand sacks Gouvea
Of chestnuts that there abound
Of such size, so fine and round
That all men will wonder where
Things so excellent are found.
And Manteigas will prepare
A store of milk for years twice seven,
By Covilham much fine cloth be given
That is manufactured there.
From the houses in the heather
High upon the mountain-top,
For pillows shall be sent a crop
All of royal eagles' feather
That men there are wont to gather.
From the Penados vale below
And the hills where three roads meet
That through rough mountain country go
They will send as present meet
Three hundred ermines white as snow
As edging of brocades to show.
Mines of gold too I will bring
And give all I have within
If the Queen and if the King
Order it to be brought in:
Plenty is there there to win.
G. And with presents none the less
Will we in her honour sing
With great joy and revelling
That God hath willed the Queen to bless
For her people's happiness.

*Enter two players from Sardoal, Jorge
and Lopo, and the Serra says:*

From Castille, brothers, do you hale
Or from down yonder in the vale?
J. Now in the devil's name, amen,
They would have us be Castilian men
A lizard I would rather be
By the Holy Gospels verily.
S. Well and from what land come you
then?
J. From Sardoal, and by your leave
We are come hither to defy

618. *tan grossa, tam san* B.
630. *penedos* B. *Penados* C.
645-6. Desunt *hum se chama* et *outro* in C. *Iorge* C.
649. *Castelhanos* C.

628. *Aguias reaes* B.
635. *brocados* C.
647. *extremo* C.

655 a toda a serra da estrela / The Serra our challenge to receive
a cantar & a baylar. / With us in song and dance to vie.
Rod. ¶ Soberba he isso perem / R. 'Tis a proud challenge for your ill,
pois haqui tantos pastores / For shepherds are so many here
& tam finos bayladores / And their dancing of such skill
660 que nam ham medo a ninguem. / That of none need they have fear.
Lopo. Muytos ratinhos vam la / L. Many peasants come yonder too
de ca da serra a ganhar / From the hills for sustenance
& la os vemos cantar / And we watch them sing and dance
& baylar bem coma ca / Even as up here they do:
665 & he assi desta feyçam. / Their way of it shall you see at a glance.

¶   Canta Lopo & bayla, arremedando / *Lopo sings and dances in imitation of*
os da serra. / *the men of the Serra:*

¶ E se ponerey la mano en vos / Ah, should I lay my hand on you,
Garrido amor! / Love, fair my love.
¶ Hum amigo que eu auia / A friend of mine, a friend of old,
mançanas douro menuia, / Sends unto me apples of gold,
670 Garrido amor! / How fair is love!
¶ Hum amigo que eu amaua / A friend I loved, even my friend,
mançanas douro me manda, / Apples, apples of gold doth send.
Garrido amor! / So fair is love!
¶ Mançanas douro menuia / Apples of gold he sends amain,
675 a milhor era partida, / The best of them was cleft in twain,
Garrido amor! / So fair is love!
¶ [Mançanas douro me manda, / [Apples of gold he sends to me,
a milhor era quebrada, / The best was cleft for all to see.
Garrido amor!] / How fair is love!]
         Falado. / (*Spoken:*)
680 ¶ Isso he, ou bem ou mal, / That I think is, well or ill,
assi como o vos fazeis. / How you dance on fell and hill.
Serra. Peçouolo que canteis / S. But now I would have you sing
aa guisa do Sardoal. / As in Sardoal they do.
Lopo. Esse he outro carrascal, / L. That is quite another thing,
685 esperay ora & vereis: / Wait then and I'll show it you:
¶ Ja nam quer minha senhora / Now no more my lady wills
que lhe fale em apartado. / That I speak with her alone.
Oo que mal tam alongado! / How am I now woe-begone!
¶ Minha senhora me disse / On a day my lady said
690 que me quer falar um dia / That she would fain speak with me,
agora por meu peccado / Now I for my sins atone
disseme que nam podia. / Since she says it may not be.
Oo que mal tam alongado! / How am I now woe-begone!
¶ Minha senhora me disse / For to me my lady said
695 que me queria falar, / That she fain would speak with me,
agora por meu peccado / Now I for my sins atone
nam me quer ver nem olhar. / Since me now she will not see.
Oo que mal tam alongado! / How am I now woe-begone!

655. *estrella* B.
668. *auia, havia* A, B, C, D, E. *queria* ?
660. *ham* A. *ha hi* C.
685-6. *Cantiga* B.

Agora por meu peccado	Now I for my sins atone
700 disseme que nam podia,	Since she says it may not be,
yrmey triste polo mundo	Through the world will I begone
onde me leuar a dita.	Where'er fortune carry me.
Oo que mal tam alongado!	How am I now woe-begone!

¶   Esta cantiga cantarão & baylarão de terreyro os foliões, & acabada diz Felipa:

The players sing this song, dancing together, and when it is finished Felipa says:

¶ Nam vos vades vos assi,	I pray you go not away so,
705 leixay ora a gayta vir	But wait until the fiddle come,
& o nosso tamboril,	O wait until you hear the drum,
& yreis mortos daqui	Then how to move you'll scarcely know
sem vos saberdes bolir.	So dead with dancing shall you go.
CAT. Em tanto por vida minha	C. And meanwhile by my life I ween
710 seraa bem que ordenemos	'Twere well that we our dance and song
a nossa chacotezinha	Should order here upon the green
& con ella nos yremos	And we will go with it along
ver el Rey e a Raynha.	To see the King and see the Queen.

¶   Ordenaramse todos estes pastores em chacota, como la se costuma, porem a cantiga della foy cantada de canto dorgam, & a letra he a seguinte:

All these shepherds took their places in the dance after their custom, but its song was sung to the accompaniment of the organ and with the following words:

¶ Nam me firais, madre,	O strike me not, mother,
715 que eu direy a verdade.	The truth I'm confessing.
¶ Madre, hum escudeyro	For, mother, a squire
da nossa Raynha	Of our queen all on fire
falou me damores,	With love came to woo me:
vereis que dezia,	Of what he said to me
720 eu direy a verdade.	The truth I'm confessing.
¶ Falou me damores,	He came for to woo me
vereis que dezia:	And 'O,' said he to me,
quem te me tiuesse	'Were you in my power,
desnuda em camisa!	Alone without dower!'
725 Eu direi a verdade.	The truth I'm confessing.

¶   E com esta chacota se sayram & assi se acabou.

And with this dance they went out and the play ended.

¶ LAUS DEO.

711. *chacotezinha* A, B. *chacotazinha* C.   713–4. *he a seguinte Cantiga* C.
ad fin. ¶ *Laus Deo* B.

NOTES

AUTO DA ALMA

Page 1

The *Auto da Alma*, produced probably in 1518, which in some sense forms a Portuguese pendant to the *Recuerde el alma* of Jorge Manrique (1440?–79), is a Passion play, corresponding to the modern *Stabat* on the eve of Good Friday, and was suggested, perhaps, by Juan del Enzina's *Representacion a la muy bendita pasion y muerte de nuestro precioso Redentor*. It was not, however, acted in a convent or church, but in the new riverside palace which saw so many splendid *serões* during King Manuel's reign (1495–1521). King Manuel was now in the full tide of prosperity. His sister, Queen Lianor or Eleanor (1458–1525), Gil Vicente's patroness, who so keenly encouraged Portuguese art and literature, was the widow (and first cousin) of his predecessor, King João II. The theme of the play, the contention of Angel and Devil for the possession of a human soul, was far from new. Its treatment, however, was original and the versification is clear-cut and well sustained throughout, while a deep sincerity and glowing fervour raise the whole play to the loftiest heights. The metre is mostly in verses of seven short (8848484) lines (*abcaabc*) with an occasional slight variation. There is a French version of the play, presumably in verse (see *Durendal*, No. 10: Oct. 1913: *Le Mystère de l'Âme;* tr. J. Vandervelden and Luis de Almeida Braga), but the difficult task of translating it would require, to be successful, the delicate precision of a Théophile Gautier. In his hands it might have become in French a thing of beauty and a joy for ever, as it is in the original Portuguese. As to the text, without emulating the pedantry of the critic who added a fourth season to Shelley's three, and thereby provoked a splendid outburst of wrath from Swinburne, we may assume that in passages where Vicente appears to have gone out of his way to avoid a required rhyme, this is merely a case of corruption repeated in successive editions. Thus in the *Auto Pastoril Portugues*, where *Catalina minha dama* rhymes with *toucada* we may perhaps substitute *fada* for *dama*. (Cf. *Serra da Estrella*, l. 530: *amigo* for *marido*.) So here verse 114 must read *tristeza*, not *tristura*, to rhyme with *crueza*. In 3 one of the *mantimentos* should perhaps be *alimentos*: see Lucas Fernández, *Farsas* (1867), p. 247 (cf. the two *vaydades* in 14); in 26 *fortunas* should probably read *farturas* (cf. *essas farturas* in the *Dialogo sobre a Ressurreiçam*); in 35 the words *mui fermosos*, or a single longer word, have evidently dropped out; in 54 *tendes* was perhaps an alteration by some critic who did not realize that the Angel might naturally associate itself with the Church (or with the Soul) and say *temos*; the last line of 100 was perhaps the word *pecadora* or *e senhora* (cf. Fr. Luis de León, *Los Nombres de Cristo*, Bk I: *mi única abogada y señora*); in 108 also a line is missing and a rhyme required for *figura* (*lavrado* must go with *Deos*, *triste* with *vereis*, omitting *seu*). On the other hand it is hardly necessary to alter 42 or 45 (although here *esmaltado* is in the air) or 46 so as to make them exactly fit the metre.

1 *perigos dos immigos*, cf. *Os Trabalhos de Jesus*, 1665 ed. p. 94: *o caminho do Ceo he cercado de inimigos e perigos para o perder. Qualibus in tenebris vitae quantisque periclis Degitur hoc aevi quodcunque est!*

7 Cf. Newman, *The Dream of Gerontius*, l. 292 *et seq.*:

> O man, strange composite of heaven and earth,
> Majesty dwarfed to baseness, fragrant flower, etc.

7–10 These exquisite verses have something of the scent and perfection of wild flowers, and that mystic rapture which is not to be found in Goethe's more worldly *Faust*. We may, if we like, call the *Auto da Alma* (as also the witch-scene in the *Auto das Fadas*) a 16th century *Faust*, but really no parallel can be drawn between the two plays. The ethereal beauty of Vicente's lyrical *auto*, carved in delicate ivory, is far less varied and human: it has scarcely a touch of the cynicism and not a touch of the coarseness of Goethe's splendid work cast in bronze. It can be compared at most with such lyrical passages as *Christ ist erstanden* or *Ach neige, Du Schmerzenreiche, Dein Antlitz gnädig meiner Not*, and as a whole is a mere lily of the valley by the side of a purple hyacinth.

9 *Planta sois e caminheira.* Cf. the white-flowered 'wayfaring tree.'

16–17 This passage resembles those in the Spanish plays *Prevaricación de Adán* and *La Residencia del Hombre* quoted in the *Revista de Filología Española*, t. IV (1917), No. 1, p. 15–17.

17 Cf. *The Dream of Gerontius*, l. 280 *et seq.*: 'Then was I sent from Heaven to set right, etc.'

18 *porá grosa*, attack, criticize, gloss. (= *glosar*. Cf. the modern 'to grouse.')

35 Cf. Antonio Prestes, *Auto dos Cantarinhos* (*Obras*, 1871 ed. p. 457): *todo Valença em chapins*. The *chapim* was rather a high-heeled shoe than a slipper. The reference is to the Spanish city Valencia del Cid. Cf. Fr. Juan de la Cerda ap. R. Altamira, *Historia de España*, III, 728: 'En una mujer ataviada se ve un mundo: mirando los chapines se verá a Valencia'; Alonso Jerónimo de Salas Barbadillo in *El Cortesano Descortés* (1621) speaks of 'un presente de chapines valencianos'; and in *La Pícara Justina* (1912 ed. vol. I, p. 70) we have 'un chapin valenciano.'

38 *marcante.* In the *Auto da Feira* the Devil is similarly a *bufarinheiro* (pedlar) and *mercante*.

43 *a for da corte. For* = *foro* (v. Gonçalvez Viana, *Apostilas*, vol. I, p. 353).

58 Cf. Plato, *Respublica*, 365: ἀδικητέον καὶ θυτέον ἀπὸ τῶν ἀδικημάτων, κ.τ.λ. Vicente in his plays often inculcates the need of something more than a formal religion.

xiquer. Cf. *Auto da Barca do Inferno: Isto hi xiquer irá.*

59–60 These two verses are in the true spirit of Goethe's Mephistopheles.

62 *esta peçonha.* Would Vicente have written thus (cf. 66 and *Obras*, III, 344, sermon addressed to Queen Lianor; and also Garcia de Resende, *Miscellanea*, 1917 ed. p. 50) of the soul had there been the slightest gossip or suspicion that his patroness, Queen Lianor, had poisoned her husband? (See the most interesting studies in *Critica e Historia*, por Anselmo Braamcamp Freire, vol. I. Lisbon, 1910.)

71 Cf. *The Dream of Gerontius*, l. 210–1:

> Nor do I know my attitude,
> Nor if I stand or lie or sit or kneel.

73 *day passada* = *perdoai, dai licença.* Cf. Jorge Ferreira de Vasconcellos, *Eufrosina*, II, 5. 1616 ed. f. 79 v.

77 In Basque *pastorales* one of the main attributes of the devils and the wicked is that they are never quiet on the stage. In the *Auto da Cananea* (1534), a play in many ways resembling the *Auto da Alma*, the line *Como andas desosegado* recurs, addressed by Belzebu to Satanas. It is the 'incessant pacing to and fro' of *The Dream of Gerontius* (l. 446). In its beauty and intensity as a whole and in many details Cardinal Newman's *The Dream of Gerontius* is strikingly similar to the *Auto da Alma*. But in it the strife is o'er, the battle won, and the sanctified soul, rising refreshed from sleep with a feeling of 'an inexpressive lightness and sense of freedom,' passes serenely, accompanied by its guardian angel, above the 'sullen howl' of the demons in the middle region. Cf. *Calte por amor de Deus, leixai-me, não me persigais* with 'But hark! upon my sense Comes a fierce hubbub which would make me fear *Could I be frighted*' (l. 395–7).

80 Cf. Amador Arraez, *Dialogos*, No. 1, 1604 ed. f. lv.: *S. Jeronimo diz que é grande o reino, potencia e alçada das lagrimas...atormentam mais aos Demonios que a pena infernal.*

84 The author of the *Vexilla regis* hymn was Venantius Fortunatus (530–600).

95 Cf. Antonio Feo, *Trattados Quadragesimais* (1609), II, f. 23: *assy na Cruz como no monte Oliueto chorou porque vio vir a quem ouuera de chorar.*

97 Cf. Gomez Manrique, *Fechas para la Semana Santa* (ap. M. Pelayo, *Antología*, t. III, p. 92).

108 Cf. Juan del Enzina, *Teatro* (1893), p. 39: *Veis aqui donde vereis Su figura figurada Del original sacada.*

116 *dais o seu a cujo he*, cf. *Triunfo do Inverno*: *Porque se devem de dar As cousas a cujas são*; *C. Res.* I (1910), p. 64: *dar o seu a cujo hee.*

121 Cf. Gomez Manrique, *Fechas* (*Antolog.* t. III, p. 93):

> Y vamos, vamos al huerto
> Do veredes sepultado
> Vuestro fijo muy prouado
> De muy cruda muerte muerto.

EXHORTAÇÃO DA GUERRA

PAGE 23

The expedition to capture from the Moors the important town of Azamor in N.W. Africa consisted of over 400 ships (Luis Anriquez in his poem in the *Cancioneiro Geral* says 450) and a force of 18,000 soldiers, of which 3000 were provided by James, Duke of Braganza, who commanded the expedition. It set sail from Lisbon on the 17th of August, 1513. (Damião de Goes and Osorio say the 17th, Luis Anriquez the 15th, which was evidently the day (the Feast of the Assumption) fixed for departure.) It was entirely successful and the news of the fall of Azamor caused great rejoicings both at Lisbon and Rome. The play was evidently touched up afterwards, for it includes the sending of the elephant to Rome (1514) and the marriages of the princesses. It is barely possible that it was written after the victory, in which case the words *na partida* would be retrospective and the date given in the 1st edition was not a slip. Parts of the play suit 1514 better than 1513. Tristão da Cunha's special mission (cf. lines 195–6) to the Pope (with Garcia de Resende for secretary) left early in 1514 and entered Rome on March 12. One of the objects of the mission was to obtain a grant of the tithes (ll. 194, 224) for the Crown to use for the war in Africa. (The request was granted but King Manuel subsequently renounced them in return for 150,000 gold coins.) The exhortations of l. 351 *et seq.*, l. 514 *et seq.*, l. 559 *et seq.* are better suited to a time when more men and money were needed actively to continue the war than when an army of 18,000 was equipped and ready to leave. The Pope in 1514 promised indulgences to all those who should contribute money for the African war and also granted King Manuel a portion of church property in Portugal (cf. ll. 475–84 and 535–48) for the same object (l. 546: *pera Africa conquistar*). The King's aim is now to build a cathedral in Fez (l. 573–4). There is no mention of Azamor. This was the first of the great patriotic outbursts (cf. the *Auto da Fama* and other plays) in which Vicente appears not as a satirist or religious reformer but as an enthusiastic imperialist, and which still delight and stir his countrymen.

18 Prince Luis (1506–55), one of the most gallant, talented and interesting of Portuguese *infantes*, was no doubt present at the *serão* and would be delighted by this reference. (The youngest princes, Afonso, born in 1509, and Henrique, born in 1512, are not mentioned. They both became Cardinals and the latter King of Portugal, 1578–80.) The princes are similarly addressed in the *Cortes de Jupiter* in 1521.

46 Mercury opens the *Auto da Feira* with a similar string of absurdities (suggested by Enzina's *perogrulladas*), e.g. *Que se o ceo fora quadrado Não fora redondo, Senhor; E se o sol fora azulado D'azul fora seu cor.* (If square the sky were found then it would not be round, and if the sun were blue then blue would be its hue.) *Os disparates de 'Joan de Lenzina'* (Ferreira, *Ulys.* IV, 7) were well-known in Portugal.

94, 113, 129 No meaning is to be squeezed out of these cabbalistic words.

116   We have an even more detailed description in the *Sumario da Historia de Deos*:

> A furna das trevas, ponte de navalhas,
> o lago dos prantos, a horta dos dragos,
> os tanques da ira, os lagos da neve,
> os raios ardentes, sala dos tormentos,
> varanda das dores, cozinha dos gritos,
> Açougue das pragas, a torre dos pingos,
> o valle das forcas.

125   Vicente was more tolerant than most contemporary writers who inveighed against the blindness and malice of the Jews.

132   The necromancer evokes spirits which he is unable to control. He calls them brothers but they answer in effect: 'Du gleich'st dem Geist den du begreif'st, nicht mir.'

151   The *almude* = 12 gallons.

156   Cabrela e Landeira is a village near Montemôr-o-Novo. Cf. *Sum. da Hist. de Deos*:

> *Satanas:*   Sabes Rio-frio e toda aquela terra,
> aldea Gallega, a Landeira e Ranginha
> e de Lavra a Coruche? Tudo é terra minha.

157   Cartaxo, a small town in the district of Santarem.

158   The village of Lumiar is now connected with Lisbon by a tramway.

159   Mealhada, a parish in the district of Aveiro.

162   Cf. *uva terrantes* (indigenous).

164   Ribatejo = the country along the river Tejo (Tagus). Cf. *Auto da Feira*: *Vai-te ao sino do Cranguejo, Signum Cancer, Ribatejo*.

168   Arruda dos Vinhos and Caparica are villages in a vine-growing district on the left bank of the Tagus opposite Lisbon, near Almada.

173   *estrema* = *marco* (Sp. *mojon*). Cf. *Auto da Festa*, ed. Conde de Sabugosa (1906), p. 110: *Este he da pedra do estremo*.

174   *diadema* is usually masculine, but Antonio Vieira has it both ways.

176   Seixal (2500–3000 inh.) in the district of Almada.

177   Almada, formerly Almadãa (Arab = the mine, but as Englishmen settled there in the 12th century it was later given the fanciful derivation All made or All made it), a town of 10,000 inh., opposite Lisbon on the left bank of the Tagus.

179   Tojal (= whin-moor, gorse-common), a small village near Olivaes (= olive groves), in the Lisbon district.

195   The impression produced by the arrival in Rome of King Manuel's elephant, panther and other magnificent gifts was vividly described by several writers. Cf. Damião de Goes, *Chron. de D. Manuel*, Pt 3, cap. 55, 56, 57 (1619 ed. f. 223 v.–227). According to Ulrich von Hutten the elephant 'fuit mirabile animal, habens longum rostrum in magna quantitate; et quando vidit Papam tunc geniculavit ei et dixit cum terribili voce *bar, bar, bar*' (apud Theophilo Braga, *Gil Vicente e as Origens do Theatro Nacional* (1898), p. 191). Cf. also Manuel Bernardez, *Nova Floresta*, v, 93–4. The head of this celebrated elephant forms the background to a portrait of Tristão da Cunha (head of the embassy to the Pope) reproduced in Senhor Joaquim de Vasconcellos' edition of Francisco de Hollanda's *Da Pintura Antigua* (Porto, 1918).

229   In 1517 among other exotic presents a rhinoceros was sent to the Pope. It was however shipwrecked and drowned on the way. It had the honour of being drawn by Albrecht Dürer.

238   Vicente seems to have coined this intensive of *bellisima*.

243–4   Cesar = King Manuel. Hecuba = his second wife, Queen Maria, daughter of Ferdinand and Isabella of Spain.

249   Prince João, born in 1502, afterwards King João III (1521–57).

259   The Infanta Isabel (1503–39) married her first cousin the Emperor Charles V, and in her honour on that occasion Vicente composed his *Templo de Apolo* (1526). Her

marriage may have already been planned in 1513, but more probably Vicente altered the passage when he was preparing the 1st edition of his works during the last months of his life. Gil Vicente more than once refers to her great beauty. Her portrait by Titian in the Madrid Prado fully bears out his praises and the expression on her face places this among the most fascinating portraits of women. The Empress is sitting by a window looking on to a beautiful country of woods and blue mountains, in her hand is a book; but one feels that she is thinking of neither book nor scenery but that her thoughts go back in *saudade* to the soft air and merry days of Lisbon. It might indeed be a picture of *Saudade*. There is a slight flush on her pale oval face. Her almond-shaped eyes are grey-green, her nose delicately aquiline. In the eyes and in the general expression there is a look of undeniable sadness. Her dress of plum, cherry-pink, gold and brown gives a gorgeously mellow effect and the curtain at the back is plum-brown. If the colouring seems at first too rich this is due to the criminal gold frame which clashes with the dress and the chestnut-golden hair. In a dark frame the picture would be twice as beautiful. The Empress' dress gleams with pearls and she has a jewel with pearls—set perhaps by Gil Vicente—in her hair, large pearl earrings and a necklace of large pearls. She died at Toledo at the age of 36 and lies in the grim Pantheon of the Kings in the Escorial crypt.

266   Of Prince Fernando, born in 1507, Damião de Goes, who knew him personally, says: 'assi na mocidade como depois de ser homem foi de bom parecer e bem disposto, muito inclinado a letras e dado ao estudo das historias verdadeiras e imigo das fabulosas. ...Era colerico e apressado em seus negocios e muito animoso, com mostra e desejo de se achar em algun grande feito de guerra, mas nem o tempo nem o estudo do Regno deram pera isso lugar' (*Chron. de D. Manuel*, II, xix). Cf. Osorio, *De Rebvs Emmanvelis* (1571), p. 18ϑ: 'Fuit in antiquitate pervestiganda valde curiosus: maximarum rerum studio flagrabat multisque virtutibus illo loco dignis praeditus erat.'

275   Princess Beatrice as a matter of fact married Charles, Duke of Savoy, and on the occasion of her departure from Lisbon by sea with a magnificent suite Vicente wrote the *Cortes de Jupiter* (1521) with the *romance*:

> Niña era la Ifanta,   Doña Beatriz se dezia,
> Nieta del buen Rei Hernando,   el mejor rei de Castilla,
> Hija del Rei Don Manuel   y Reina Doña Maria, etc.

284   Cf. the *Auto das Fadas* (with which this play has many points of resemblance): *Feiticeira* (ao principe e infantes): *ó que joias esmaltadas, ó que boninas dos ceos, ó que rosas perfumadas!*

331–2   Cf. *Divisa da Cidade de Coimbra*: *Vai delas a eles tão grande avantagem... como haverá...do vivo a hũa imagem.*

341   *Godos*, Goths, i.e. of ancient race, 'Norman blood.'

346   For *dioso*=*idoso* v. *C. Geral*, vol. II (1910), p. 153.   Fernam Lopez, *Chron. J. I.* Pt. 2, cap. 10, has *deoso*.

384   *pequenas quadrilhas.* When Afonso de Albuquerque began his glorious career (1509–15) there were in India but a few hundred Portuguese fighting men, and most of these badly armed. The whole population of Portugal during this time of fighting and discovery in N.-West, West and East Africa and India is by some calculated at a million and a half, by others at between two and three millions.

416   Prov. *mais são as vozes que as nozes.*

418   For this line cf. Pedro Ferrus: *Que por todo el mundo suena* (ap. Menéndez y Pelayo, *Antologia*, t. I, p. 159 and Enzina, *Egloga*, v (*ib.* t. VII, p. 57)).

420   *pois que...pessoa*, a homely version of Goethe's *Was du ererbt von deinen Vätern hast Erwirb' es um es zu besitzen.*

470–4   These lines are translated from the Spanish poet Gomez Manrique (1415?–1490?). See Menéndez y Pelayo, *Antologia*, t. VII, p. ccx.

Cf. Jorge Ferreira de Vasconcellos, *Ulysippo*, v, 7: *Vos quando vos tirarem de Ansias e passiones mias e quando Roma conquistava.*

487 *dom zote.* Cf. supra *zopete* and Sp. *zote, zopo, zopenco, zoquete* (a dolt); low Latin *sottus*; Dutch *zot*; Fr. *sot*; Eng. *sot* (*bebe sem desfolegar*). *Zote* occurs twice in the *Auto Pastoril Portugues*: *muito gamenho* (cf. Fr. *gamin*) *zote* and *Auto da Fé*, l. 5.

534 *trepas* is the Span. form (Port. *tripas*?).

538 *soyços* the old, *soldados* the new, word for 'soldiers.' Cf. Lucas Fernández, *Farsas* (1867), p. 89: *Entra el soldado, o soizo, o infante.*

559 This rousing chorus fitly ends a play from every page of which breathes the most ardent patriotism. Small wonder that King Sebastião (1557–78), with his visions of conquest and glory, read Vicente with pleasure as a boy.

561 Cf. Gaspar Correa, *Lendas da India*, IV, 561–2: *o Governador logo sobio e o frade diante dele bradando a grandes brados, dizendo: 'O fieis Christãos, olhai para Christo, vosso capitão, que vai diante'* (1546).

FARSA DOS ALMOCREVES

PAGE 37

This is one of the most famous of those lively farces with which Gil Vicente for a quarter of a century delighted the Portuguese Court and which still hold the reader by their vividness and charm. Its fame rests on the portraiture of the poverty-stricken but magnificent nobleman who has been a favourite object of satire with writers in the Peninsula since the time of Martial, and who in a poem of the *Cancioneiro Geral* is described in almost the identical words of Vicente's prefatory note:

> o gram estado
> e a renda casi nada
> (*Arrenegos que que fez Gregoryo Affonsso*).

An alternative title of the play is *Auto do Fidalgo Pobre*, but the extremely natural present-ment of the two carriers in the second part justifies the more popular name. The Court, fleeing from plague at Lisbon, was in the celebrated little university town of Coimbra on the Mondego and here Gil Vicente in the following year staged his *Divisa da Cidade de Coimbra*, the *Farsa dos Almocreves*, and (in October) the *Tragicomedia da Serra da Estrella* and Sá de Miranda, in open rivalry, produced his *Fabula do Mondego*. But Gil Vicente was not to be silenced by the introduction of the new poetry from Italy and to these two years, 1526 and 1527, belong no less than seven (or perhaps eight) of his plays. Yet what a difference in his own position and in the state of the nation since his first farce—*Quem tem farelos?* twenty years before! The magnificent King Manuel was dead, and his son, the more care-ridden João III, was on the throne:

> tão ocupado
> co'este Turco, co'este Papa
> co'esta França.

There was plague and famine in the land. The discovery of a direct route to the East and its apparently inexhaustible wealth had not brought prosperity to the Portuguese pro-vinces. There the chief effect had been to make men discontented with their lot and to lure away even the humblest workers to seek their fortune and often to find death or a far less independent poverty:

> até os pastores
> hão de ser d'el-Rei samica.

The result was that the old rustic jollity which Vicente had known so well in his youth was dying out, and the very songs of the peasants took a plaintive air:

> E no mais triste ratinho
> s'enxergava hũa alegria
> que agora não tem caminho.
> Se olhardes as cantigas

do prazer acostumado
todas tem som lamentado,
carregado de fadigas,
longe do tempo passado.
O d' então era cantar
e bailar como ha de ser,
o cantar pera folgar,
o bailar pera prazer,
que agora é mao d'achar[1].

Nor could it be expected that the rich *parvenu*, the mushroom courtier, the *fidalgo* 'que *não sabe se o é*,' the palace page fresh from keeping goats in the *serra*, the Court chaplain anxious to hide his humble origin, would greatly relish Vicente's plays which satirized them and in which rustic scenes and songs and memories appeared at every turn. It was much like mentioning the rope in the house of the hanged, and these dainty and sophisticated persons would turn with relief to the revival of the more decorous ancient drama inaugurated by Trissino in Italy and in Portugal by Sá de Miranda.

3 *este Arnado*. Cf. Bernardo de Brito, *Chronica de Cister*, III, 18: 'se foi [Afonso Henriquez] ao longo do Mondego por um campo q̃ então e no tempo de agora se chama o Arnado, trocado ja pelas enchentes do rio de campo cuberto de flores em um areal esteril e sem nenhũa verdura.' Cf. *Cancioneiro da Vaticana*, No. 1014: 'en Coimbra caeu ben provado, caeu en Runa ata en o Arnado.'

7 See the Spanish *romance* (ap. Menéndez y Pelayo, *Antología*, t. VIII, p. 124): 'Yo me estaba allá en Coimbra que yo me la hube ganado.'

8, 9 The sense of these two obscure lines is apparently: 'Since Coimbra so chastises us that we are left without a penny.' Ruy Moniz in the *Canc. Geral*, vol. II (1910), p. 142, has *çimbrar ou casar*. In Spanish *cimbrar* = 'to brandish a rod,' 'to bend.' In the *Auto del Repelon*, printed in 1509, Enzina has: *El palo bien assimado Cimbrado naquella tiesta* (*Teatro* (1893), p. 236) and Fernández (p. 25) *No vos cimbre yo el cayado*. Cf. Antonio Prestes, *Autos* (ed. 1871), p. 211: *E o vilão vindo me zimbra: reprender-me!* and João Gomes de Abreu (*C. Ger.* vol. IV (1915), p. 304) *seraa rrijo çimbrado*. *preto* = *real preto*, contrasted with the white (i.e. silver) *real*.

12 *Pelos campos de Mondego cavaleiros vi somar* were two very well-known lines apparently belonging to a real historical Portuguese *romance* on the death of Ines de Castro. They occur in Garcia de Resende's poem on her death. See C. Michaëlis de Vasconcellos, *Estudos sobre o romanceiro peninsular*.

13 Cf. *Tragicomedia da Serra da Estrella* (1527): *Pedem-lhe em Coimbra cevada E elle dá-lhe mexilhões*.

19 *milham*, green maize cut young for fodder.

32 *ratinhos*, peasants from Beira. They play a large part in Portuguese comedy.

80 *azemel* = *almocreve*. Both words are of Arabic origin. Cf. *almofreixe* infra.

93 *Endoenças* = *indulgentiae*. *Semana de Endoenças* = Holy Week.

103 In the *Auto da Lusitania* Vicente says jestingly, perhaps in imitation of the Spanish *romances*, that he was born at Pederneira (a small sea-side town in the district of Leiria). He mentions it again in the *Cortes de Jupiter* and in the *Templo de Apolo*.

109 Cf. Alvaro Barreto in *Cancioneiro Geral*, vol. I (1910), p. 322: *poẽ me tudo em hũũ item*.

120 It was the plea of Arias Gonzalo that the inhabitants of Zamora were not answerable for the guilt of Vellido Dolfos who had treacherously killed King Sancho:

¿Qué culpa tienen los viejos? ¿qué culpa tienen los niños?
¿qué culpa tienen los muertos...?

129 *balcarriadas*. Cf. *Auto das Fadas: Venhas muitieramá com tuas balcarriadas:*

---

[1] *Triunfo do Inverno* (1529), l. 13–25.

Auto da Festa: *tão grão balcarriada; Auto da Barca do Purgatorio: Nunca tal balcarriada Nem maré tão desastrada.* Couto, *Asia*, VII, 5, vii: *Tal balcarriada* (act of folly) *foi esta.* The *Canc. Geral*, vol. IV (1915), p. 370, has the form *barquarryadas.*

134 Cf. *Auto da Lusitania*: *um aito bem acordado Que tenha ave e piós* (=well-proportioned).

135 The numerous servants of the starving *fidalgos* are satirized by Nicolaus Clenardus and others. Like the English as described by a German in the 18th century they were 'lovers of show, liking to be followed wherever they go by whole troops of servants' (*A Journey into England*, by Paul Hentzer. Trans. Horace Walpole, 1757). Clenardus in his celebrated letter from Evora (1535) says that a Portuguese is followed by more servants in the streets than he spends sixpences in his house. He mentions specifically the number eight.

141 Alcobaça is the town famous for its beautiful Cistercian convent.

161 *Alifante.* Cf. infra, *avangelho. A* for *e* is still common in Galicia: e.g. *mamoria* (memory). Cf. Span. Basque *barri* (new), for Fr. Basque *berri.*

165 The Dean was Diogo Ortiz de Vilhegas († 1544) successively Bishop of São Tomé (1534) and Ceuta (1540). See A. Braamcamp Freire in *Revista de Historia*, No. 25 (1918), p. 3.

224 *bastiães=bestiães*, figures in relief. Gomez Manrique has *bestiones* in this sense.

247 In Antonio Prestes' play *Auto do Mouro Encantado* the golden apples prove to be pieces of coal. So Mello in his *Apologos Dialogaes* speaks of the treasure of *moiras encantadas* which all turns to coal.

269 *In Rey*, the popular form of *El-Rei* (the king) is frequent also in the plays of Simão Machado, who died about a century after Vicente.

272 It is tempting to add the word *madraço* (fool, ignoramus) for the sake of the rhyme. If *O recado que elle dá* were spoken very fast the line would bear the addition.

293 Here, as often, the deeper purpose of Vicente's satire appears beneath his fun. The growing depopulation of the provinces was becoming painfully evident to those who cared for Portugal.

302 Jorge Ferreira, *Ulysippo*, III, 5: *não haveria corpo, por mais que fosse de aço milanes, que podesse sofrer quanta costura lhe seria necessaria;* ib. III, 7: *temos muita costura esta noite; muita costura e tarefa;* Antonio Vieira, *Cartas*: *tambem aqui teremos costura* (1 de agosto de 1673).

310 *trapa* in Port. = 'a gin,' 'a trap,' but in Sp., as perhaps here, = 'noise,' 'uproar.'

327 Cf. *Farsa dos Fisicos*: *Praticamos ali O Leste e o Oeste e o Brasil* and III, 377; Chiado, *Auto da Natural Invençam*, ed. Conde de Sabugosa (1917), p. 74.

348 The carrier comes along singing snatches of a *pastorela* of which we have other examples, of more intricate rhythm, in the *Cancioneiro da Vaticana* and the poems of the Archpriest of Hita and the Marqués de Santillana. A modern Galician *cantiga* says that

> O cantar d'os arrieiros
> E um cantariño guapo:
> Ten unha volta n'o medio
> Para dicir 'Arré macho.'

(Pérez Ballesteros, *Cancionero Popular Gallego*, vol. II, p. 215.)

355 Cf. *O Clerigo da Beira*: *Nuno Ribeiro Que nunca paga dinheiro E sempre arreganha os dentes;* and *Ah Deos! quem te furtasse Bolsa, Nuna Ribeiro. Homem vai buscar dinheiro, A todo ele disse: Ja dinheiro feito é.*

360 *uxtix, uxte.* Ferreira de Vasconcellos, *Eufrosina*, II, 4: *Tanto me deu por uxte como por arre.*

atafal. Cf. *Barca do Purgatorio* (I, 258): *amanhade-lhe o atafal* (not *amanhã dé-lhe*).

363 Candosa, a village of some 1400 inh. in the district of Coimbra.

369 *xulo=chulo, picaro.* The derivation of *chulo* is uncertain (v. Gonçalvez Viana, *Apostilas*, vol. I (1906), p. 299). While Dozy derives it from Arabic *xul*, A. A. Koster suggests the same origin as that of Fr. *joli*, It. *giulivo*, Catalan *joliu* [=gay. Cf. Eng. *jolly* and the Portuguese word used by D. João de Castro: *joliz*], viz. the Old German word *jol*

(gaiety). Vid. *Quelques mots espagnols et portugais d'origine orientale (Zeitschrift für rom. Philologie*, Bd. 38 (1914), S. 481-2). The Valencian form for July (*Choliol*) may strengthen this view.

372 Tareja is the old Portuguese form of Theresa.

375 *bareja = mosca varejeira.*

379 Aveiro. A town of about 7500 inh., 40 miles S. of Oporto. It was nearly taken by the Royalists in 1919.

398 For the naturalness of this conversation cf. that of the peasants Amancio Vaz and Deniz Lourenço in the *Auto da Feira.*

410 Pero Vaz' point is that the mules will not stop to feed in the cool shade of the trees but do so in the shelterless *charneca.*

429 Cf. the act of D. João de Castro (1500-48) as before him of Afonso de Albuquerque in pawning hairs of his beard, and the proverb *Queixadas sem barbas não merecem ser honradas.*

435 *O juiz de çamora.* In the *romance Ya se sale Diego Ordoñez* Arias Gonzalo of Zamora says: 'A Dios pongo por juez porque es justo su juicio.' So that the judge of Zamora = God.

438-9 No one was better situated than Gil Vicente to criticize—and suffer the slights of—the brand-new nobility of the Portuguese Court. The nearer they were to the plough the more disdainful were they likely to be to a mere goldsmith and poet.

454 *desingulas* (=*dissimulas*). Cf. *Auto Pastoril Portugues: não o deffengules mais.* Duarte Nunes de Leão, *Origem da Lingva Portvgvesa* (1606), cap. 18, includes *dissingular* (=dissimular) among the *vocabulos que vsão os plebeios ou idiotas que os homens polidos não deuem vsar.*

467 For the form Diz cf. *Auto das Fadas*: Estevão Dis, and *O Juiz da Beira*: Anna Dias, Diez, Diz (=Diaz).

473 Pero Vaz evidently did not know the *cantiga:*

> A molher do almocreve
> Passa vida regalada
> Sem se importar se o marido
> Fica morto na estrada.

Cf. the Galician quatrain (Pérez Ballesteros, *Canc. Pop. Gall.* II, 219):

> A vida d'o carreteiro
> É unha vida penada,
> Non vai o domingo á misa
> Nin dorme n'a sua cama.

478 Vicente refers to the Medina fair in the *Auto da Feira* and again in *O Juiz da Beira: morador en Carrion Y mercader en Medina.*

498 *Folgosas.* There are two small villages in Portugal called Folgosa, but reference here is no doubt to an inn or small group of houses.

506 Vicente several times refers to *Val de Cobelo*, e.g. *Comedia de Rubena: E achasse os meus porquinhos Cajuso em Val de Cobelo*, and the shepherd in the *Auto da Barca do Purgatorio: estando em Val de Cobelo.*

529-30 Cf. Sá de Miranda, 1885 ed., No. 108, l. 261: *Inda hoje vemos que em França Vivem nisto mais á antiga*, etc. Couto (*Dec.* v, vi, 4) speaking of the mingling of classes, says: 'no nosso Portugal anda isto mui corrupto.'

537 Cf. *Comedia de Rubena: E broslados* (=bordados) *uns letreiros Que dizem Amores Amores.*

559 The ancient town of Viseu or Vizeu (9000 inh.) in Beira has now sunk from its former importance.

560 *pertem* for *pertence.*

565 *arauia = algaravia.* So *ingresia, germania*, etc. (cf. the French word *charabia*).

586 Cf. *O Juiz da Beira*: *pois tem a morte na mão* (=not 'there is death in that hand' as was said of Keats, but 'he is at death's door').

591 The original reading *da sertãy* (rhyming with *mãy* in l. 588) is confirmed by the *Auto da Lusitania*: *rendeiro na Sertãe*. The town of Certã in the district of Castello Branco now has some 5000 inh.

603 Cf. Jorge Ferreira, *Aulegrafia*, I, 4: *Ó senhor, grão saber vir.*

657 *tam mancias*, i.e. *Macias, o Namorado*, the prince of lovers. For the form *Mancias* cf. *palanciana* used for *palaciana.*

671 *los tus cabellos niña.* Cf. Ferreira de Vasconcellos, *Aulegrafia*, f. 113: *Sob los teus cabelos, ninha, dormiria.*

675 Cf. Jorge Ferreira, *Eufrosina. Prologo*: *Eu por mim digo com a cantiga se o dizem digão*, etc.; *Cortes de Jupiter*: *Cantará c'os atabaques: Se disserão digão, alma minha* and Barbieri, *Cancionero Musical*, No. 127: *Si lo dicen digan, Alma mia*, etc. E wrongly gives the words *alma minha* to the next quotation.

676 Cf. *Auto da India*: *Quem vos anojou, meu bem, Bem anojado me tem.*

707 Cf. *Auto das Fadas*: *Son los suspiros que damos In hac vita lachrymarum.*

713 Camões, *Filodemo*, IV, 4, has *tudo ierei numa palha*, 'I will not care a straw' (cf. Vicente in the *Auto da Festa*: *Que os homens verdadeiros não são tidos numa palha*), but here the meaning is different.

TRAGICOMEDIA PASTORIL DA SERRA DA ESTRELLA
PAGE 55

It is remarkable that just at the time when Sá de Miranda had returned to Portugal with the new metres from Italy and was frankly contemptuous of Gil Vicente's rough mirth and rustic verse, Gil Vicente felt his position strong enough to present this lengthy play before the King and Court at Coimbra on occasion of the birth of the King's daughter Maria. There is no action in the play, and King Manuel would perhaps have yawned at these shepherds' quarrels, relieved not at all by the *parvo's* wit or the hermit's grossness and only occasionally by a touch of lyric poetry; but perhaps these simple scenes were welcome to the growing artificiality of the Court. For us the beautiful *cossante Um amigo que eu havia* stands out like a single orange gleaming from a dark-foliaged tree. The interest lies in the customs of the shepherds and their snatches of song and in the intimate knowledge of the Serra da Estrella shown by the author.

10 The Serra da Estrella, the highest mountain-range in Portugal (6500 ft), is in the province of Beira.

17 *meyrinhas = maiorinho* (merino).

30 *esperauel* (as here and in *Comedia de Rubena*), or *esparavel.* Cf. Damião de Goes, *Chron. de D. Manuel* (1617), f. 25 v.: *a modo de sobreceo d'esparavel.*

32 Cf. the *vilão's* complaints of God in the *Romagem de Aggravados.*

35 *nega = senão.*

51 As in Browning's *A Grammarian's Funeral* they are advancing as they converse: 'thither our path lies.'

103 *Nega se meu embeleco = se não me engano.* This line occurs in the *Templo de Apolo.* The *Auto da Festa* text has *nego se meu embaleco.*

113 *mancebelhões.* Cf. Correa, *Lendas*, IV, 426: *Folgara de ser mais mancebelhão.*

127 The corresponding *a*-lines might be:

> Dous açores que eu amava
> Aqui andam nesta casa.

172 *argem* for *prata.* Similarly in Spanish there is the old form *argen* for *argento* (= *plata*). Cf. the proverb *Quien tiene argen tiene todo bien.*

190 *somana* for *semana.* So *romendo* for *remendo* and v. infra: *perem* for *porem.*

225 *gingrar.* Nuno Pereira in the *Cancioneiro Geral* (1910 ed., vol. I, p. 305) has *o gingrar de meu caseiro.* Cf. Enzina, *Auto del Repelon*: *Hora déjalos gingrar* (*Teatro*, 1893, p. 241).

241 *sois.* Cf. *Barca do Purgatorio*: *sem sois motrete de pão*; *Farsa dos Fisicos*: *não vos quer sois olhar.*

290–1 =*odi et amo.*

322 As a rule Vicente's shepherds are natural enough but we may be permitted to doubt whether any shepherdess of the Serra da Estrella would have spoken of 'ending like Queen Dido.' She had probably been reading Lucas Fernández, *Farsas* (1867), p. 56.

328 A, B, C, D and E unaccountably print *querê-lo* (through the bad attraction of *malo*) although *querer* is needed to rhyme with *quer.*

367 *pintisirgo*=*pintasilgo.*

410 *grauisca.* Vicente appears to have coined the word from *grave* and *arisca.*

427 Fronteira, a village of nearly 3000 inh. in the district of Portalegre. Monsarraz is of about the same size, in the district of Evora.

435 *tinhosa cada mea hora.* Cf. Jorge Ferreira de Vasconcellos, *Aulegrafia*, f. 89: *he hũa tinhosa que ontem guardava patas em Barquerena.*

440 *cartaxo.* Cf. *Aulegrafia*, f. 10: *figo bafureiro em unhas de cartaixo.*

443 A pleasant sketch of the presumptuous peasant, then become a common type in Portugal. Felipa considers that to marry a shepherd would be beneath her and her heart leaps up when she beholds a courtier in velvet slippers.

462 The hermit was of course a part of the stock-in-trade of mediaeval plays. He appears in Vicente as early as 1503 (*Auto dos Reis Magos*). The most interesting alteration in the heavily censored (1586) edition of the *Serra da Estrella* is not the excision of over a hundred lines about the evil-minded hermit but the substitution in l. 100 of *un rey* for *Dios.* Regalist Vicente would never have allowed himself to say that 'a king sometimes acts awry.'

530 For *amigo* we should probably read *marido* to rhyme with *atrevido.*

564 *moxama*=salted tun (Sp. *mojama* or *almojama*).

566 Cf. J. Ferreira de Vasconcellos, *Aulegrafia* (1619), f. 84: *sejais bem casada com a filha do juiz.*

608 Sea, Cea or Ceia, a pleasant little town of some 3000 inh. in the heart of the Serra. (Sea, Sintra, etc. is the 16th cent. spelling, now restored.)

616 Gouvea or Gouveia in the same district and about the same size as Sea. The three other Gouveas in Portugal are smaller villages.

621 Manteigas, a small picturesque town immediately below the highest part of the Serra and nearly 2500 ft above sea-level.

623 Covilham, a larger town (15000 inh.), still known for its cloth factories.

652 Sardoal has about 5000 inh. For its ancient reputation for dancing cf. *O Juiz da Beira*:

> Eu bailei em Santarem,
> Sendo os Iffantes pequenos,
> E bailei no Sardoal.

666 This *cossante* needs for its completion a fourth verse. This was so obvious that it was omitted in the writing of the play.

684 *Esse he outro carrascal*, a rural form of the phrase *une autre paire de manches.* The contrast is between the rustic *cossante* and the more 'cultivated' or Court *cantigas* that follow (*Ja não quer* and *Não me firais*).

711 The *chacota, chacotasinha* was a peasant's dance accompanied by a simple song the structure of which answered to the movements of the dance. Here, however, it is danced to the sound of the organ and the words of a Court song in which, nevertheless, the repetition of the rustic dance-*cossantes* is preserved.

724 Cf. *Farsa de Ines Pereira*: *Eu vos trago um bom marido...diz que em camisa vos quer* (='sans dot').

LIST OF PROVERBS IN GIL VICENTE'S WORKS

BIBLIOGRAPHY OF GIL VICENTE*

(1) *Catalogo dos Autores* ap. *Diccionario da Lingua Portugueza* (1793), p. cxxviii–ix.

(2) F. BOUTERWEK. *Geschichte der portugiesischen Poesie* (1805), p. 85–115. Eng. tr. (1823), p. 85–111.

(3) F. M. T. DE ARAGÃO MORATO. *Memoria sobre o theatro portuguez* (1817), p. 46–58.

(4) J. ADAMSON. *Memoirs of...Camoens* (1820), vol. I, p. 295–7.

(5) J. F. DENIS. *Résumé* (1826), p. 152–64.

(6) J. C. L. SIMONDE DE SISMONDI. *De la littérature du midi de l'Europe* (1829), vol. IV, p. 449–57.

(7) J. V. BARRETO FEIO and J. GOMES MONTEIRO. *Ensaio sobre a vida e obras de G. V.* (*Obras*, ed. 1834, vol. I, p. x–xli; 1852 ed. vol. I, p. x–l).

(8) A. HERCULANO. *Origens do theatro moderno. Theatro portugues até aos fins do seculo XVI.* (*Opusculos*, vol. IX, p. 75–84. Reprinted from *O Panorama*, 1837.)

(9) H. HALLAM. *Introduction to the Literature of Europe* (Paris, 1839), vol. I, p. 205–6, 344.

(10) J. H. DA CUNHA RIVARA. *Epitaphios antigos* in *O Panorama*, vol. IV (1844), p. 275–6.

(11) E. QUILLINAN. *The Autos of G.V.* in *The Quarterly Review*, vol. LXXIX (1845), p. 168–202.

(12) LUDWIG CLARUS [pseud. i.e. Wilhelm Volk]. *Darstellung der spanischen Literatur im Mittelalter* (1846), vol. II, p. 344–56.

(13) C. M. RAPP. *Die Farças des G.V.* in H. G. Prutz, *Historisches Taschenbuch*, 1846.

(14) A. F. VON SCHACK. *Geschichte der dramatischen Literatur und Kunst in Spanien* (1845–6), vol. I, p. 160–80.

(15) J. M. DA COSTA E SILVA. *Ensaio*, vol. I (1850), p. 241–95.

(16) F. WOLF in Ersch und Grueber, *Allgemeine Enzyklopädie* (1858), p. 324–54.

(17) BARRERA Y LEIRADO. *Catálogo* (1860), p. 474–6.

(18) E. A. VIDAL in *Gazeta de Portugal*. 26 July, 10 Sept. 1865.

(19) F. SOTEIRO DOS REIS. *Curso*, vol. I (1866), p. 123–52.

(20) M. PINHEIRO CHAGAS. *Novos Ensaios Criticos* (1867), p. 84–93.

(21) TH. BRAGA. *Vida de G.V. e sua eschola.* Porto, 1870.

(22) J. DE VASCONCELLOS. *Os Musicos Portuguezes* (1870), vol. I, p. 117–20.

(23) SALVÁ. *Catálogo*, vol. I (1872), p. 554–5.

(24) TH. BRAGA. *G.V., poeta lyrico* in Th. Braga, *Bernardim Ribeiro e os bucolistas* (1872), p. 233–64.

(25) TH. BRAGA. *G.V. e a Custodia de Belem* [two unsigned articles in *Artes e Letras*, ann. 2 (1873), p. 4–6, 18–20].

(26) TH. BRAGA. *Manual da hist. da litt. port.* (1875), p. 229–42.

(27) J. M. DE ANDRADE FERREIRA. *Curso* (1875), p. 331–50.

(28) C. CASTELLO BRANCO. *G.V. Embargos á phantasia do Snr Theophilo Braga* in *Historia e Sentimentalismo*, 2nd ed. (1880), vol. II, p. ix–xi, 1–25.

(29) J. I. BRITO REBELLO. *A Custodia do Convento dos Jeronymos* in *O Occidente* (1880), p. 145–203.

(30) TH. BRAGA. *G.V. Ourives e Poeta* in *O Positivismo*, vol. II (1880), p. 348–76; vol. III, p. 129–39; repr. in *Questões de litt. e arte port.* (1881), p. 190–225.

(31) *Diccionario Universal Portuguez Illustrado*, vol. I (1882), p. 1884–1904, s.v. *Auto*.

(32) G. TICKNOR. *History of Spanish Literature*, 5th ed. (1882), vol. I, p. 297–306.

* For a more detailed account of some of the works here recorded see C. Michaëlis de Vasconcellos, *Notas Vicentinas I* (1912).

(33) P. Ducarme. *Les 'Autos' de G.V.* in *Le Muséon*, vol. v (1885), p. 369–74, 649–56; vol. vi, p. 120–30, 155–62.

(34) A. Loiseau. *Hist. de la Litt. Port.* (1886), p. 119–36.

(35) A. da Cunha. *Os Autos de G.V.* in *Revista Intellectual Contemporanea*, anno 1, No. 3 (1886), p. 21–24.

(36) Gallardo. *Ensayo*, tom. iv (1889), col. 1565–8.

(37) A. Jeanroy. *Les Origines de la poésie lyrique en France* (1889), p. 330–4.

(38) J. de Sousa Monteiro. *A Dansa Macabra* (*Nota preliminar a tres autos de G.V.*) in *Revista de Portugal*, vol. i (1889), p. 233–50.

(39) Visconde de Ouguella. *G.V.* Lisboa, 1890.

(40) A. Schaeffer. *Geschichte des Spanischen Nationaldramas* (1890), vol. i, p. 26–33.

(41) D. Garcia Peres. *Catálogo Razonado* (1890), p. 564–8.

(42) J. Leite de Vasconcellos. *Nota sobre a linguagem de G.V.* in *Revista Lusitana* (1891), p. 340–2.

(43) W. Storck. *Aus Portugal und Brasilien* (1892). Notes, p. 258–62.

(44) C. Michaëlis de Vasconcellos. *Grundriss der rom. Phil.* (1894), Bd. 2, Abtg. 2, p. 280–7.

(45) Visconde Sanches de Baena. *G.V.* Marinha Grande, 1894 [Review by C. Michaëlis de Vasconcellos in *Litteraturblatt für germanische und romanische Philologie*, Bd. xvii (1896), p. 87–97].

(46) Visconde Julio de Castilho. *Mocidade de G.V.* (*O Poeta*). Lisboa, 1896.

(47) D. João da Camara. *Natal e G.V.* in *O Occidente*, vol. xix (1896), p. 282–5.

(48) J. I. Brito Rebello. *G.V.* in *Revista de Educação e Ensino*, anno 12 (1897), p. 241–58, 308–15, 394–406.

(49) E. Prestage. *The Portuguese Drama in the Sixteenth Century: G.V.* in *The Manchester Quarterly*, vol. xvi (July 1897).

(50) M. Menéndez y Pelayo in *Antología de poetas líricos*, tom. vii (1898), p. clxiii–ccxxv

(51) Th. Braga. *G.V. e as origens do theatro nacional.* Porto, 1898.

(52) Th. Braga. *Eschola de G.V.* Porto, 1898.

(53) Visconde J. de Castilho and A. Braamcamp Freire. *Indices do Cancioneiro de Resende e das Obras de G.V.* Lisboa, 1900. Repr. in G.V. *Obras*, vol. iii (1914).

(54) J. da Annunciação [† 1847]. *G.V.* in *Revista Lusitana*, vol. vi (1900), p. 59–63.

(55) G. A. de Vasconcellos Abreu. *Contos, Apologos e Fabulas da India: influencia indirecta no Auto de Mofina Mendez de G.V.* Lisboa, 1902.

(56) A. R. Gonçalvez Viana. *Lusismos no castellano de G.V.* in *Revista do Conservatorio Real de Lisboa* (1902). Repr. in *Palestras Filolójicas* (1910), p. 243–67.

(57) J. I. Brito Rebello. *G.V.* in *O Occidente*, vol. xxv (1902), p. 122–3.

(58) Damasceno Nunes. *G.V. e o theatro nacional* in *O Occidente*, vol. xxv, p. 127–8.

(59) Th. Braga. *G.V. e o nacionalismo* in *Revista de Guimarães*, vol. xix (1902), p. 53–5.

(60) C. Malheiro Dias. *G.V. Algumas determinantes do seu genio litterario* in *Revista de Guimarães*, vol. xix, p. 57–66.

(61) A. F. Barata. *G.V. e Evora.* Evora, 1902.

(62) J. Leite de Vasconcellos. *G.V. e a linguagem popular.* Lisboa, 1902.

(63) G. de Abreu. *G.V. A independencia do seu espiritu* in *Revista de Guimarães*, vol. xix, p. 84–96.

(64) *G.V. e a fundação do theatro portuguez* [three articles in *O Diario de Noticias*, June 7, 8, 9, 1902].

(65) A. Hermano. *G.V.* in *Revista de Guimarães*, vol. xix, p. 71–83.

(66) J. I. Brito Rebello. *Ementas Historicas. II. G.V.* Lisboa, 1902.

(67) W. E. A. Axon. *G.V. and Lafontaine.* London and Dorking, 1903.

(68) F. M. de Sousa Viterbo. *G.V. Dois traços para a sua biographia* in *Archivo Historico Portuguez*, anno 1 (1903), p. 219–28.

(69) J. Ribeiro. *G.V.* in *Paginas de Esthetica* (1905), p. 77–83.

(70) CONDE DE SABUGOSA. *Auto da Festa (Explicação previa*, p. 7–94). Lisboa, 1906.

(71) CONDE DE SABUGOSA. *Um auto de G.V. Processo de Vasco Abul* in *Embrechados* (1907), p. 65–80.

(72) A. L. STIEFEL. *Zu G.V.* in *Archiv für das Studium der neueren Sprachen*, vol. CXIX (1907), p. 192–5.

(73) SILEX [i.e. A. Braamcamp Freire]. *G.V., Poeta-ourives* in *O Jornal do Commercio*, Feb. 5–9, 14, 19, 1907.

(74) J. MENDES DOS REMEDIOS in *Obras de G.V.*, vol. I (1907), *Prefacio*, p. v–lix.

(75) C. MICHAËLIS DE VASCONCELLOS. *Estudos sobre o romanceiro peninsular* (1907–9), p. 318–20.

(76) J. J. NUNES. *As cantigas parallelisticas de G.V.* in *Revista Lusitana*, vol. XII (1909), p. 241–67.

(77) M. A. VAZ DE CARVALHO in *No meu cantinho* (1909).

(78) J. DE SOUSA MONTEIRO. *Estudo sobre o 'Auto Pastoril Castelhano' de G.V.* in *Boletim da Segunda Classe da Ac. das Sciencias de Lisboa*, vol. II (1910), p. 235–41.

(79) J. LEITE DE VASCONCELLOS in *Lições de Philologia Portuguesa* (1911), p. 355–60.

(80) O. DE PRATT. *O Auto da Festa de G.V.* in *Revista Lusitana* (1911), p. 238–46.

(81) *Sobre um verso de G.V.* in *Diario de Noticias* (1912); Repr. in *Revista Lusitana* (1912), p. 268–89.

(82) A. BRAAMCAMP FREIRE. *G.V.* in *Diario de Noticias*, Dec. 16, 1912.

(83) J. I. BRITO REBELLO. *G.V.* Lisboa, 1912.

(84) C. MICHAËLIS DE VASCONCELLOS. *Notas Vicentinas I* in *Revista da Universidade de Coimbra*, vol. I (1912), p. 205–93.

(85) J. M. DE QUEIROZ VELLOSO. *G.V. e a sua obra.* Lisboa, 1914.

(86) A. LOPES VIEIRA. *A Campanha Vicentina.* Lisboa, 1914.

(87) F. DE ALMEIDA. *A Reforma protestante e as irreverencias de G.V.* in *Lusitana*, anno 1 (1914), p. 207–13; Repr. in *Historia da Igreja em Portugal*, vol. III, pt 2 (1917), p. 119–226.

(88) A. BRAAMCAMP FREIRE. *G.V. poeta-ourives. (Novas notas.)* Coimbra, 1914.

(89) TH. BRAGA. *G.V. e a creação do theatro nacional* in *Hist. da Litt. Port. II. Renascença* (1914), p. 36–102.

(90) C. MICHAËLIS DE VASCONCELLOS. *Notas sobre a canção perdida Este es calbi orabi* in *Revista Lusitana* (1915), p. 1–15.

(91) J. CEJADOR Y FRAUCA. *Hist. de la lengua y lit. castellana* (1915), vol. I, p. 457–60.

(92) F. DE FIGUEIREDO. *Caracteristicas da litt. portuguesa* (1915), p. 27–30. Eng. tr. (1916), p. 18–22.

(93) O. DE PRATT. *Sobre um verso de G.V.* Lisboa, 1915.

(94) A. LOPES VIEIRA. *Autos de G.V.* (1916), *Prefacio*, p. 9–30.

(95) J. I. BRITO REBELLO. *A proposito de G.V.* in *Boletim da Segunda Classe da Ac. das Sciencias de Lisboa*, vol. X (1916), p. 315–8.

(96) W. S. HENDRIX. *The 'Auto da Barca do Inferno of G.V.' and the Spanish 'Tragicomedia Alegórica del Parayso y del Infierno'* in *Modern Philology*, vol. XIII (1916), p. 173–84.

(97) A. BRAAMCAMP FREIRE. *G.V., trovador, mestre da balança* in *Revista de Historia*, Nos. 21, 22, 24, 25, 26 (1917–8).

(98) A. COELHO DE MAGALHÃES. *Tentativas pedagógicas. II. A obra vicentina no ensino secundario* in *A Águia*, Nos. 67–8 (1917), p. 5–16.

(99) A. A. MARQUES. *G.V. e as suas obras.* Portalegre, 1917.

(100) F. DE FIGUEIREDO. *Hist. da Litt. Classica* (1917), p. 61–108.

(101) C. MICHAËLIS DE VASCONCELLOS. *Notas Vicentinas II* in *Rev. da Univ. de Coimbra*, vol. VI (1918), p. 263–303.

(102) C. MICHAËLIS DE VASCONCELLOS. *Notas Vicentinas III, ib.* vol. VII (1919), p. 35–51.

CHRONOLOGICAL TABLE OF GIL VICENTE'S LIFE

G.V.'s Life	Order of G.V.'s Plays	Contemporary Events
c.1465? Birth of G.V.		c.1465 Death of François Villon.
		1466 Death of Donatello.
		1467 Birth of Desiderius Erasmus.
		1469 Death of Jorge Manrique.
		— Birth of Niccolò Machiavelli.
		1469? Birth of Juan del Enzina.
		1470 Birth of Pietro Bembo.
		— Birth of Garcia de Resende.
		1471 Birth of Albrecht Dürer.
		1474 Birth of Lodovico Ariosto.
		1475 Birth of Michael Angelo.
		1477 Birth of Titian.
		1478 Birth of Baldassare Castiglione († 1526).
		— Birth of Gian Giorgio Trissino.
		— Birth of Sir Thomas More.
[1484-6 Snr Braamcamp Freire assigns G.V.'s first marriage to one of these years]		1481 Accession of João II.
		1482 Birth of Bernardim Ribeiro.
[1486-8 Acc. to Snr Braamcamp Freire, birth of G.V.'s eldest son]		1483 Birth of Raffael.
		— Birth of Martin Luther.
		— Birth of Francesco Guicciardini.
		— Beheadal of Duke of Braganza.
		1484 King João II stabs to death the Duke of Viseu.
		1485 [or later] Birth of Sá de Miranda.
		1486 Birth of Andrea del Sarto.
		— Death of Andrea Verrocchio.
		1487 Cape of Good Hope rounded by Bartholomeu Dias.
1490? G.V. comes to Court at Evora?		1489 Birth of Thomas Cranmer.
c.1490? G.V.'s first marriage [to Branca Bezerra]?		1490 Marriage of Prince Afonso and Isabel, d. of the Catholic Kings.
		— Birth of Vittoria Colonna.
		1491 Death of Prince Afonso at Santarem.
		— Birth of S. Ignacio de Loyola.

G.V.'s Life	Order of G.V.'s Plays		Contemporary Events
			Contemporary Events
G.V.'s Life	*Order of G.V.'s Plays*		
		1491	Christopher Columbus sails for America. First Portuguese book printed in Portugal.
		—	Conquest of Granada.
		1492	
		1493	Columbus arrives at Lisbon (6 March) after discovering America. Birth of André de Resende.
c.1492? Birth of G.V.'s eldest son, Gaspar?		1493 or 4	Birth of Nicolaus Clenardus.
		1494	Death of Angelo Poliziano.
		1494 or 5	Birth of François Rabelais.
		1495	(25 Oct.) Accession of King Manuel.
		1496?	Birth of Clément Marot († 1544).
		1497	(July) Vasco da Gama leaves Lisbon. Forced conversion of Jews in Portugal.
		—	Birth of Hans Holbein.
		—	Birth of Philip Melancthon.
		1498	Girolamo Savonarola burnt at Florence.
		1499	(Sept.) Return of Gama from India.
		1500	Pedro Alvarez Cabral discovers Brazil.
		—	Death of Sandro Botticelli.
		—	Birth of Benvenuto Cellini.
		—	Birth of Emperor Charles V.
		—	Birth of Dom João de Castro.
	1502 (Lisbon, 7 or 8 June) *Auto da Visitaçam* (1).	1502	(6 June) Birth of João III.
	— (Lisbon, Christmas) *Auto Pastoril Castelhano* (2).		
1503–6 G.V. fashions the celebrated Belem monstrance with the first tribute of gold from India.	1503 (Lisbon, 6 Jan.) *Auto dos Reis Magos* (3).	1503	Birth of Garci Lasso de la Vega.
		—	Birth of Sir Thomas Wyatt.
		—	Famine and plague in Portugal.
		—	The cousins Albuquerque and Duarte Pacheco Pereira sail for India.
		—	(24 Oct.) Birth of Infanta (afterwards Empress) Isabel.
	1504 (Lisbon) *Auto de S. Martinho* (4).	1504	Heroic campaign of D. Pacheco Pereira in India.
		—	(31 Dec.) Birth of Inf. Beatriz.
1505? Birth of G.V.'s second son, Belchior.		1505	Riots against Jews at Evora.

	Historical events	Gil Vicente's plays	Gil Vicente's life
1505	(end July) Arrival at Lisbon of 15 ships laden with spices. Solemn procession in honour of D. Pacheco.		
1506	(Low Sunday, *Pascoela*) Massacre of Jews at Lisbon.		1506 G.V. preaches a sermon in verse on the birth of Prince Luis (3 March).
—	Birth of S. Francis Xavier.		
—	Birth of Inf. Luis († 1555).		
—	(30 Sept.) Death of D. Beatriz (King Manuel's mother).		
1507	(5 June) Birth of Inf. Fernando.		
1508	The King raises interdict placed on Lisbon after massacre of Jews.	1508 (Dec.) or 1509 (Jan.) (Lisbon) *Quem tem farelos?* (5).	
—	News brought to the King at Evora of the siege of Arzila.		
1509	(Jan.) D. Pacheco defeats the French pirate Mondragon.	1509 (Almada, Holy Week?) *Auto da India* (6).	1509? G.V. writes some verses for a poetical contest at Almada, printed in the *Canc. de Resende* (1516).
—	(23 Ap.) Birth of Inf. Afonso.		1509 (15 Feb.) G.V. is appointed *Vedor* (overseer) of all works in gold and silver in the Convent of Thomar, the Hospital of All Saints, Lisbon, and the Convent of Belem.
—	Birth of Jean Calvin.		
—	Afonso de Albuquerque Governor of India.		
1510	Death of Dom Francisco de Almeida, first Viceroy of India.	1510 (Almeirim, Christmas) *Auto da Fé* (7).	
—	Albuquerque attacks Calicut and takes Goa.		
1510?	Birth of Lope de Rueda.		
1511	Albuquerque takes Malaca.	1511 (Lisbon, Carnival?) *Auto das Fadas* (8).	
—	Henry VIII of England sends King Manuel, his brother-in-law, the Order of the Garter.		
1512	(31 Jan.) Birth of Cardinal-King Henrique († 1580).	1512 (Lisbon, early in the year) *Farsa dos Físicos* (9).	1512 (21 Dec.) G.V. is elected one of the Twenty-four by the Lisbon Guild of Goldsmiths.
1513	James, Duke of Braganza, sets sail from Lisbon with a splendidly-equipped fleet of 450 vessels to capture Azamor.	1513 (Lisbon, Holy Week?) *O Velho da Horta* (10).	1513 (4 Feb.) G.V. is appointed *Mestre da Balança*.
—	Albuquerque in the Red Sea and at Aden.	— (Lisbon, August) *Exhortação da Guerra* (11).	— (17 Oct.) G.V. is elected by the Twenty-four to be one of their four representatives on the Lisbon Town Council.
		1513? (Lisbon, Christmas) *Auto da Sibila Cassandra* (12).	

G.V.'s Life	Order of G.V.'s Plays	Contemporary Events
		1513 Leo X, son of Lorenzo de' Medici, becomes Pope.
1514 (1512–14?) G.V. loses his first wife, Branca Bezerra.	1514 (Lisbon) *Comedia do Viuvo* (13).	1514 Portuguese Embassy to Pope Leo X with magnificent presents from the East. Garcia de Resende and the rest of the Mission reach Italy end of Jan. 1514.
1515 (21 Sept.) G.V. receives a grant of 20 milreis for the dowry of his sister Felipa Borges.	1515? (Lisbon, 2nd half of year) *Auto da Fama* (14). [Snr Braamcamp Freire assigns the *Auto da Festa* to this year 1515.]	1515 (Dec.) Death of Albuquerque in India. — (7 Sept.) Birth of Inf. Duarte. — Birth of Santa Teresa at Avila.
	1516? (Lisbon, Christmas) *Auto dos Quatro Tempos* (15).	1516 (9 Sept.) Birth of Inf. Antonio. — Discovery of Mexico. — Garcia de Resende's *Cancioneiro Geral* published. — Death of Giovanni Bellini.
1517 (6 Aug.) G.V. resigns the post of *Mestre da Balança* in favour of Diogo Rodriguez. 1517? G.V. marries Melicia Rodriguez.	1517 (Lisbon) *Auto da Barca do Inferno* (16).	1517 Luther starts the Reformation. (Feb.) King Manuel organises a fight between a rhinoceros and an elephant in an enclosed space in front of Lisbon's *Casa da Contrataçam da India*.
		(7 March) Death of Queen Maria. 1517 or 18 Birth of Francisco de Hollanda.
	1518? (Lisbon, Holy Week) *Auto da Alma* (17).	
	1518 (Lisbon, Christmas) *Auto da Barca do Purgatorio* (18). [General Brito Rebello, Dr Theophilo Braga and Senhor Braamcamp Freire assign the verses to the Conde de Vimioso to this year 1518.]	1518 (23 Nov.) Queen Lianor (King Manuel's third wife) arrives in Portugal. — Birth of Tintoretto.
c.1519? Birth of G.V.'s eldest daughter, Paula.	1519 (Lisbon, Holy Week) *Auto da Barca da Gloria* (19).	1519 King Charles of Spain elected Emperor (Charles V). — Death of Leonardo da Vinci. — Death of John Colet.
1520 G.V. makes arrangements for the royal entry into Lisbon. 1520? Birth of G.V.'s son Luis.		1520 (18 Feb.) Birth of Inf. Carlos at Evora († Lisbon, 15 Ap. 1521). — Death of Raffael.

Date	Life and Works	G.V. receipts	Date	Contemporary events
			1520	Death of John Skelton.
			—	Fernão de Magalhães discovers the 'Straits of Magellan.'
1521	(Lisbon, Holy Week?) *Comedia de Rubena* (20).		1521	(Jan.) King and Queen's entry into Lisbon.
—	(Lisbon, 4 Aug.) *Cortes de Jupiter* (21).		—	(8 June) Birth of Inf. Maria († 1577). Solemn reception in Lisbon of Embassy from Venice.
			—	Departure of Inf. Beatriz to wed the Duke of Savoy.
			—	(13 Dec.) Death of King Manuel.
			—	(Dec.) Proclamation of João III.
			—	Death of Magalhães.
1522	*Pranto de Maria Parda.*		1522	Famine in Portugal.
1523	(Thomar, July–Sept.) *Farsa de Ines Pereira* (22).	1523 G.V. receives the sum of six milreis.	1523	Clement VII becomes Pope.
—	(Evora, Christmas) *Auto Pastoril Portuguez* (23).			
1524	(Evora, 2nd half of year) *Fragoa de Amor* (24).	1524 G.V. receives two pensions (12 and 8 milreis).	1524	Birth of Pierre Ronsard.
			—	Birth of Luis de Camões.
			—	Death of Dom Vasco da Gama.
1525?	(Evora, Holy Week) *Farsa das Ciganas* (25).	1525 G.V. receives a pension of three bushels of wheat.	1525	Plague and famine at Lisbon. François I taken prisoner at battle of Pavia.
—	(Lisbon?) *Dom Duardos* (26).		—	(17 Nov.) Death of Queen Lianor (widow of João II).
—	(Almeirim, Oct.–Nov.?) *O Juiz da Beira* (27).		—	Birth of Joachim du Bellay.
—	(Evora, Christmas) *Auto da Festa* (28).			
—	*Trovas ao Conde de Vimioso.*			
1526	(Lisbon, Jan.) *Templo de Apolo* (29).		1526	Marriage of Emperor Charles V and Isabel, d. of King Manuel.
1526–8	(Almeirim) *Sumario da Historia de Deos* (30).		—	Sá de Miranda returns from Italy.
—	(Almeirim) *Dialogo sobre a Ressurreiçam* (31).		—	Boscán tackles the hendecasyllable.
1527	(Lisbon) *Nao de Amores* (32).		1527	Birth of Inf. Maria.
—	(Coimbra) *Divisa da Cidade de Coimbra* (33).		—	Birth of Fray Luis de León.
—	(Coimbra) *Farsa dos Almocreves* (34).		—	Birth of Philip II of Spain.
—	(Coimbra) *Tragicomedia da Serra da Estrella* (35).		—	Sack of Rome.
			—	Death of Machiavelli.

G.V.'s Life		Order of G.V.'s Plays		Contemporary Events	
1528	G.V. receives a further pension of 12 milreis.	1527	*Trovas a Dom João III.*	1528	Death of Dürer.
		1528	(Lisbon, Christmas) *Auto da Feira* (36).	—	Birth of Antonio Ferreira.
		1529	(Lisbon, April) *Triunfo do Inverno* (37).	1529	Birth of Inf. Isabel.
				1529?	Death of Juan del Enzina.
		1529–30	(Lisbon, Christmas? Between Sept. 1529 and Feb. 19, 1530) *O Clerigo da Beira* (38).		
c.1530?	Birth of G.V.'s daughter Valeria Borges.	c.1530	*Trovas a Felipe Guilhen.*	1530	(15 Feb.) Birth of Inf. Beatriz.
1531	(Jan.) G.V. preaches a sermon to the monks at Santarem on occasion of the earthquake.	1531	*Jubileu de Amores* acted at Brussels.	1531	Birth of Inf. Manuel.
				—	(Jan.) Great earthquake at Lisbon and other towns.
				—	First Bull for establishment of Inquisition in Portugal.
				1531?	Death of Bartolomé de Torres Naharro.
		1532	(Lisbon) *Auto da Lusitania* (39).		
		1533	(Evora) *Romagem de Aggravados* (40).	1533	Birth of Michel de Montaigne.
		—	(Evora) *Amadis de Gaula* (41).	—	Clenardus comes to Portugal from Salamanca.
		1534	(Oudivellas) *Auto da Cananea* (42).	1533?	Death of Duarte Pacheco.
		—	(Evora, Christmas) *Auto da Mofina Mendes* (43).	1534	Birth of Fernando de Herrera, *el Divino.*
1535	G.V. receives 8 milreis as dress allowance (*vestiaria*).	1535	[The Conde de Sabugosa assigns the *Auto da Festa* to this year.]	1535	Sir Thomas More executed.
1536?	Death of G.V. at Evora.	1536	(Evora) *Floresta de Enganos* (44).	1536	Death of Erasmus.
				—	Death of Garci Lasso de la Vega.
				—	Death of Garcia de Resende.
				—	Introduction of Inquisition into Portugal.

INDEX OF PERSONS AND PLACES

For EU product safety concerns, contact us at Calle de José Abascal, 56–1°,
28003 Madrid, Spain or eugpsr@cambridge.org.